M000110740

For the Love of a Horse

(right and below, right) YOUNG JASON MUNCY airing out her horse on the OX in central New Mexico. Photos by Gene Peach.

(above and right) A LOVELY YOUNG LADY from Truth or Consequences and mount meditate on Percha Creek. Photos by Jan Haley.

For the Love
of a Horse

Max Evans

University of New Mexico Press

Albuquerque

CBLACK
PASO POR AQUI!
5-3-2011

13   12   11   10   09   08   07   1   2   3   4   5   6   7

Library of Congress Cataloging-in-Publication Data
Evans, Max, 1924–
For the love of a horse / Max Evans.
     p. cm.

ISBN 978-0-8263-4274-4 (alk. paper)
1. Horses—Fiction.   I. Title.

PS3555.V23F67 2007
813'.54—dc22

                              2006038716

A special dedication of Thank You's

To Pat, again. Quite simply—for everything.

In Memoriam
To two amigos who left us a little early.
Fond and respectful thoughts of multi-talented producer/writer/director, David Peckinpah, who almost fulfilled the dream of his uncle, the late, great film maker, Sam Peckinpah, of shooting our little book, *My Pardner*. Blessings.

A tilt of the amber to Charles (Charley) M. Ford, with whom we shared much laughter over many bent dreams. An optimum optimist who will be forever appreciated.

And,
A nod of respect and a warm chuckle to our Hillsboro, New Mexico, friends, including that all around generous-hearted ranch woman, Sue Bason.

Prospector, miner, pictograph photographer, and *bon vivant*, Embree (Sonny) Hale.

Photographer, writer, and joyous companion, Jan Haley.

OL' MAX EVANS
Albuquerque, NM

Contents

Introduction

A Very Brief Presentation of True Horse Stories,
by the Author

WHEN I finished rereading my true, published horse stories, I realized I didn't have enough first rate ones for the type of collection I had in mind. I wanted a wide range of adventures from another time, with different horses, of different breeds, and a sense of history of those special days. But I also wanted them to be exciting and revelatory for the reader.

There was only one way to get this. I would have to go back to my own childhood—at the tender age of four—and tell about my very first horse. I dreaded it, at first, since from that same early age, I've had great difficulty remembering names of people, places, or anything that calls for such a handle. To my pleasurable surprise events came back to me as if I were watching a favorite, old classic movie. This almost total recall not only stunned me, but propelled my brain cells into the next horse adventures. But what a thrill to find them also indelible in my memory.

In my search through the already published horse stories, I was amazed to discover my award-winning racehorse story, "Showdown at Hollywood Park," was a short sequel to the famed "Seabiscuit" story.

Also I had two more, over 90 percent true, stories that I slightly fictionalized to make them eligible to be published as fiction. "My Pardner" was one of these. It came from a personal adventure. It was once published alone as a hardback book by Houghton-Mifflin.

My father had taken me (I was about ten years old) and a one-eyed cowboy named Boggs down to Jal, from Humble City, both in far southeastern New Mexico, to start trailing a bunch of half-starved horses to Guymon, Oklahoma, for an auction. Houghton-Mifflin's editor suggested I change Jal, New Mexico, to Starvation, Texas, to broaden our market. I did, and later regretted it. It didn't make much sense since Boggs and I would leave New Mexico after three days and zigzag all across West Texas to Guymon, Oklahoma. Nevertheless, this horse drive, with the inventive Boggs, helped me my entire life to become a survivor.

Sam Peckinpah, who is now being ranked among the immortal film directors such as Fellini, Bergman, and Martin Scorsese, loved "My Pardner." He optioned it many times over. He also owned the option rights to my novel *The Hi-Lo Country*. We traded these two properties back and forth several times. He loved and wanted "My Pardner." I traded him "My Pardner" for *The Hi-Lo Country* so I could get a Martin Scorsese, Stephen Frears' film made. It would star Woody Harrelson, Billy Crudup, Penelope Cruz, Patricia Arquette, and Sam Elliott.

This book brought about the very last conversation I ever had with Peckinpah—two weeks before his untimely death. He was on his way to Acapulco to meet his ex-wife, Mexican actress Begonia Palacios, and their little daughter, Lupita. He was very excited about the trip and pressed for time, but promised that on his return he would sign all film rights for "My Pardner" back to me. But . . . he died, and it never happened.

The other story, slightly fictionalized, was "The Mare." Its incidents had been witnessed by so many people still living that I felt guilty publishing it—in multiple anthologies—as fiction. However, I won't hesitate to say that the names of most of the main characters are exact and they still live where I first placed them.

I'm deeply pleased that I waited until now to distill the essence of what horses can mean in service, in companionship, as partners, and above all the love that emanates from them, if you are open enough or lucky enough to let it touch the adventurous part of your soul.

ALBUQUERQUE, NM, 2005

PART I

CHAPTER ONE

An Equine Montage

THE HORSE (and the mule—which is half horse) has given more to humankind than all the rocket scientists, presidents (all forms), dictators and financial geniuses with all their billions of dollars combined. The horse's hold on humankind, joining in all the human glories and foibles, could actually fill many great libraries.

A small number of examples are:

Alexander the Great used his cavalry in brilliant support of his infantry to conquer all the known world, as did Genghis Khan and his Mongols. Napoleon came very close to dominating Europe until he overextended himself in the army-swallowing vastness of the Russian winter. Even then, the horses saved his great army from total annihilation by supplying meat from their own exhausted bodies for human survival food. Think of it.

When the Spanish explorers Oñate and Cortez brought horses into the West, they never dreamed that the Apaches, the Comanches, and others would adopt, adapt, worship, and use the horse against them in some of the most brilliantly maneuvered battles ever fought. It would take the brave buffalo soldier cavalry, along with a gringo infantry far outnumbering the Indians, to finally bring the Apache and Comanche horse experts to a sort-of bloody peace.

All the hundreds of men on horseback who rode—with thirty-shot pistols blazing—through the dime novels and the Owen-Wister-spawned

"B Western" movies, are unrivaled in a fifty-or-so-year reign as the epitome of the entertainment world. These are the American versions of the knights of the Round Table with everyone mounted on valiant steeds as they rescued fair maidens and saved the poor and downtrodden from greedy, gunslinging powers. These entertainment wonders never would have existed without the horse.

From the chariot races of the *Ben Hur* era, to the fashion show at the Kentucky Derby, or the American quarter horse two-million-dollar finals at Ruidoso Downs in New Mexico, the horse attracts *class*. The cutting horse addicts are more numerous and the sport is as expensive as polo.

And for entertainment, there are the plumed and prancing circus horses that delight all ages, or the polo ponies, or the almost pure white Austrian bred Lipizzan horses who dance and do acrobatics beyond imagination as they perform, all over the world, for the most sophisticated and appreciative audiences.

Contrast these with the hardworking cow horse. A working cowboy will tell of the wonders, the life-saving risks, his cow horse has given him while chasing cantankerous bovines past rib-crushing rocks on mountainsides or hide-ripping brush in the canyons and flats. Even a horse that has bucked him off and nearly killed him, over and over, will still be spoken of with admiration, and his stories will be endless.

I must say that I appreciate the almost mystical colors of British painter, J. M. H. Turner. I also love the convoluted and rippling landscapes Van Gogh did in Arles, France, and the "sky" period of Maynard Dixon's West have always sent my spirit soaring with the red-tailed hawks. However, as beautiful and stirring as the best of these artists' paintings are, they almost blanch in comparison to a young woman, her hair blowing as freely as the mane of the horse she is mounted on, racing across a rodeo arena or a dressage training course, or in a great, open pasture. This vision was, is, and always will be, created by the greatest of gods. There is such joy between the horse and the female rider, such affinity, and a mutual understanding beyond words. Only the greatest of classical musical composers could capture the rhapsodic kinship here.

It comes to mind that our state capital of Santa Fe, as everyone knows—or should—is suffused with actual and movie history, and is always listed as one of the top art destinations in the nation per capita.

It also ranks near the top as a horse-lover's paradise. One finds riders and trainers of pleasure, show, jumping, and mustangs everywhere. To observe a rider finely tuned to his mount coursing the foothills of Santa Fe is a perfect painting itself.

But this book is not a history of horses. This book is supposed to be a memoir of those horses who touched me—and a few of my friends—on a very personal level, beginning with my first horse, Cricket, and beyond. There will be all kinds of horses and a variety of attitudes of mine from age four to about forty, and even past.

In this montage, before the main stories and horses, I wish to mention a few—who for varied reasons I was associated with for only a short time, but nevertheless impacted my memory—even though I didn't write specific stories about them.

On Glorieta Mesa south of Santa Fe, I went to work on a cow ranch about three months before my twelfth birthday. Almost everyone—in this time and place—was so poor that it was a common practice for ranchers to loan themselves and/or their hired hands out to help each other—especially with big jobs like branding and roundups, and even fence building. It made survival possible.

I was on my way over to Pete Coleman's place to help him gather a few head of wild steers. I saw this horse standing at a gate entrance into Pete's horse pasture. He was a raw-boned gelding—brown with a crooked lined, blaze face. He had that long-ago-used-up look about him—sunken holes above his eyes, loose lower lip, and old brands all over him. (None of which I recognized.) I opened the gate and let him into Pete's pasture. He followed me right up to the rock ranch house at Haney Springs where I saw Pete working a colt in the round corral.

As I rode up we exchanged, "howdys," then he asked, "Where'd you get that?" pointing through the gate slabs at my new acquaintance.

I explained.

Pete grew curious. He came out of the corral, walked around the unconcerned animal and studied its brands. He said, "The only one I recognize is the Lazy F E and that's way over into Arizona. Well, I guess we'll just put him over in a stall and feed him. We'll see if he'll do as a night horse."

It went unsaid for awhile about how in heck that horse got over at least a thousand pasture fences to arrive way up here on lonesome, hardscrabble Glorieta Mesa. The grass sure wasn't greener. No answer came, but the fact remained that this old worn-out horse had belonged to a lot of different people and outfits. I decided to call him PDQ. Pretty Damn Quick was meant to be a satire, of course, for the laid-back animal.

Bill McDonald and his son, Little Joe, came over before daylight, and three days later we had worked the piñon/cedar covered mesa and canyons to the east and penned six of the eight wild steers. Bill headed on back to the McDonald ranch over by the tiny Spanish village of Cow Springs, leaving his son to help finish the job.

Pete gave Little Joe and me a day off so we could go over to play and take a much needed bath in the headwaters (Meadow Springs) of the San Cristobal Creek that splits that famous ranch, the San Cristobal, south of Lamy and Santa Fe. There was one little catch to our small holiday—Pete suggested I ride old PDQ.

We were riding along telling one another yarns and big dreams when we came upon a little bunch of mother Herefords and their calves.

I said to Little Joe, as I took down my catch rope, "Pete said I should try old PDQ out, didn't he?"

"Yeah," he answered, and his eyes got big, "But not on *his* calves."

Now, that really was against all the rules on a ranch. To run even one priceless pound of beef off an animal unnecessarily was an unforgivable sin, and the remote possibility of crippling one was criminal. A man, and especially a boy, could get himself fired for that.

Forbidden or not, I couldn't resist.

I took after a calf. Old PDQ built to him with surprising speed. I got just the right distance from him and threw the whirling loop. I caught the calf deep around the brisket and he really whacked the end of the rope as old PDQ set up like a well-trained, rodeo roping horse.

I was just looking around—hoping Little Joe had seen my performance of perfection—when PDQ went cloud hunting. I was a natural-born, "fairly" good roper, but I hadn't learned yet what a poor bronc rider I was always gonna be. However, I believe it was the third or fourth jump when I was bucked into a flock of flying birds. They flew on and I dropped like a ton of whatever. I didn't know if anything was broken, and in that moment of horror and excitement, I didn't care. I sat up, then staggered upright, watching PDQ still bucking and dragging that calf through the pasture.

Little Joe rode after them. He grabbed the bridle and PDQ stopped like he had been brain shot. I held what breath was left in me until the calf got up and I could see he wasn't crippled. Little Joe turned the calf loose and led PDQ back to me.

"Here's your rodeo ropin' horse," he said, flatly.

"No," I said, "here's my rodeo bucking horse."

Of course, we agreed there would be no mention of the cruddy old animal's various and unbelievable talents . . . or mine either for that matter.

Three days later, Pete, Little Joe, and myself were still trying to gather the last two steers. We split up to cover more ground.

I found some fresh tracks, and had been following them for miles when I hit an opening and there he grazed. The wind was in my favor. I decided to try to rope him. Then the race began.

At my own stupid insistence, I was riding PDQ, and he was running like a greyhound with his ears laid back. A little bunch of piñon trees was heading at us fast. I threw the big old prayerful loop and durned if that big old steer didn't stick his head in it. As surprised as I was, I put a choke hold on that saddle horn. PDQ fooled me again. He set up and jerked that steer down even though I felt the back end of the saddle lift my butt about a foot upwards. I was surprised the flank cinch had held.

The steer hit the ground so hard he was stunned. Jerking the piggin' string free where it was tied on the saddle, I bailed off and ran to him. I was actually dumb enough to try to tie that steer's feet, but he raised up, throwing me aside like a dried leaf off his back. While I regained my footing and got back in the saddle, PDQ kept the slack out, working that rope like a pro.

The steer started fighting the rope. He ran around a tree several times, each time shortening the rope and semi-securing himself for me. I dismounted after removing the hondo loop from the saddle horn. With a great struggle and making a mess out of the catch rope, I finally, somehow, got him tied by the horns between two trees, so he wouldn't choke to death. That miracle is one piece of childhood foolishness that is still a blur to me, but the rest of it is as clear as bottled water.

I remounted PDQ and proudly rode off yelling and hunting for Pete and Little Joe to tell them about the miracle that just happened between myself and a rusty-looking old horse.

PDQ was turned out in a pasture with the rest of the *usin'* horses and we kept a different one for a wrangling horse. The next, and last, time I wrangled the horses before heading back to my home outfit—

Ed Young's Rafter EY—I couldn't find PDQ among the horse herd. Pete and I rode the entire horse pasture twice. No fence was down, no gate was open, no horse tracks were outside them. Thinking the worst, we even futilely looked for bear or mountain lion tracks. None. He was gone as if he had sprouted wings and flown away.

That night at supper, Pete's Boston-raised and educated wife, Nancy, brought up the great mystery of PDQ's escape. She said he had to be part deer to jump a barbed wire fence without touching it; or maybe rustlers had rustled him. Nah. We knew that hadn't happened. Maybe he just turned into a coyote and crawled under the fence. Nah. Or . . . maybe he turned into a ghost . . . they don't leave tracks. Well . . .

Several more scenarios passed between us before we let the subject die. Many rivers have flooded and dried up, and I still wonder about old PDQ every now and then. He was a mystery—one I'm blessed to have known. I always hoped I'd meet another one like him, but it never happened.

• • •

When I was still a teenager, I acquired a small, well-watered, (with springs) ranch in northeastern New Mexico. It was located fourteen miles east of the village of Des Moines—which I would later call "Hi-Lo" in many of my writings and a major film.

The first livestock I acquired was a five-year-old bay mare, Molly, from a Grenville neighbor. Molly was broke-out, but these people didn't know much about horse training, so she didn't know much either, but I liked her anyway and set about putting a finish on her.

In those poor and struggling days, coyote hides each brought from five to fifteen dollars—a ton of money at the time. I found three running hounds to pursue the valuable coyote hides, and soon would team up with my all-time hunting partner, uncle Tom Cresswell of a little stock farm between my ranch and Des Moines. He had an old dun gelding he used for horse and hound hunting.

Since most of these hunting stories have been printed in various other publications, we'll get to the real chase with Molly.

I must admit that I was having more trouble putting a rein, a stop, and instilling "rope and cow sense" in this horse than ever before. However difficult she was in those departments, she was just as expert and anxious to do right in another. She literally loved and lived to run after the dogs as they ran down one of the smartest creatures ever born. She must have had the ancient genes of some great general's best war horse for she had a true blood lust. She liked to be in on the kill. Molly craved to watch the dogs' fangs still a freshly caught coyote.

Whenever I turned the dogs loose after a coyote, Molly would tear through brush as if it were Christmas wrapping paper. She would take me around and over jumbles of rocks that would have slowed a mountain lion to a careful creep and make an eagle fly carefully sideways. Downhill and uphill were all the same to her. She just went full cavalry charge all the time, all the way. It is amazing that I ever survived to write my own name much less a million or so words.

Old Tom and his dun horse were far older than Molly and I. I had been living a rather reckless life since first memory; even so, Molly's rampaging runs were putting the years on me so fast I was going to be gray headed and smooth mouthed before I was twenty-one. Then my youth was spared—temporarily.

Silhouetted on a hill across a rock strewn valley, I had seen, and figured Molly had as well, the dogs catch a coyote. I had my Model 62 twenty-two rifle out of its homemade scabbard because we had jumped four coyotes in a pack and I thought I might get a shot at one. Now that was daydreaming, right in the middle of a midday sunray bent by the Hi-Lo country's wind, because Molly never would have slowed down enough for me to take a shot.

Before we could cross the rocky draw and get to the kill on the hill above, Molly flung us down that incline as if she had fallen or jumped off the White Cliffs of Dover. Determined. Then . . . that old, over-used, little understood word—FATE—just jumped up and whacked us.

Molly hit an unseen rock in the grass and over and over she went. At her first flop, she propelled me out into space a distance, even then, I was too modest to mention. I broke my fall with my precious rifle butt so emphatically that it was nothing but lost splinters in the grass.

The ground had knocked me so goofy that I found myself standing, pulling the dogs from the coyote so they wouldn't ruin its valuable hide. I still held a piece of slightly bent steel that once had been a food-providing instrument of mercy for the coyotes. Then I saw Molly coming up the hill, straining mightily through the pain of a smashed shoulder, too late for the kill.

Tom and his dun horse were just now topping the opposite hill.

MOUNTED ON his
first horse Brownie,
after moving to Taos.
Author's collection.

I tried to explain what he had missed, but I was unclear and it was a month before he understood the rapid occurrences.

We hung the coyote on Tom's saddle. I told him to take the dogs on to his house and I would lead Molly home, if we could make it. I had a dislocated shoulder and smashed right hand myself. It was dark when I penned her. I rubbed some horse liniment on her shoulder and on myself. I mostly healed up, Molly didn't. I retired her to pasture and she never quit limping, but if a horse has memories and dreams she was full of wild ones.

It was a short, sweet, and almost deadly time with Molly, but as I write this I feel both my smashed hand and the same exhilaration that Molly and I felt racing after the hounds of the Hi-Lo country. There is a little place saved in a corner of my heart where she'll never stop running healthy and free.

I left the heart of the Hi-Lo country, and went to Taos. I bought some sub-irrigated land and a house and moved there amongst the founders and old masters of the famed art colony. I also acquired my first Taos horse, Brownie. He was as plain as his name—just brown all over. (see photo above) There was nothing outstanding about him. However, for the thirty dollars I paid Horse Thief Shorty for him, he turned out to be quite a buy. Brownie was a good, solid cow horse, with good rein, fair stop, and some cow sense.

I tried to make a roping horse out of him as well, over the protests of my new wife, Pat. She was right. Brownie would lay his ears back and run as hard as he could to give me a loop at a calf, but it was mid-arena before I could whip it on one, and by the time I bailed off, ran to the calf, threw, and tied him, about the best time I could hope for was sixteen or eighteen seconds. Once in awhile—in those days of long scores—that would get a roper in the money, but not often enough though to show a profit.

Just the same Brownie was pretty darn good at everything, outstanding at none, but a loyal friend all the way. A partner. As I look back now, I rank him mighty high for that priceless underrated loyalty. I even feel sorry I didn't see how all around fine he was at the time.

Ah, *beginnings* and the forgetting of the same is the greatest of all human failings. My first Taos horse had given us more than we knew. I had forgotten that Brownie's companionship prize was when I would ride him for pure pleasure. We would move across the great sagebrush desert on top of the west mesa where the Taos Pueblo Indians held their annual, ancient horseback rabbit hunt. It was the sacred rite painted by some of the Taos art founders. I had also forgotten those times when Brownie and I were all alone out there with a 360-degree circle of the grandest, high-desert view on earth. Behind the pueblo, the sacred Taos Mountain loomed—as if it were the king of all earthly

BROWNIE at work. Photo by Pat Evans.

mountains—surrounded on each side by a great arc of timber covered, mighty blue bulges that half encircled Taos to the north and east. The circle was completed by the seemingly endless expanse of sagebrush covered desert on the south and west, across the Rio Grande Gorge— on and on and on. It was a time of peace and of absorbing the beauty of the visible high desert and all those wonders of the spirit unfortunately invisible to most. It was a special gift to share this majesty with Brownie. I must never forget about it again.

• • •

There were other fine horses during this period. I traded one of my original oil paintings for Clabber—also brownish, but nearer to a bay. He had been trained as a roping horse, and worked perfectly in the arena, but he, too, was a little slow for the faster times being developed by ropers. But . . . he had the best riding gait. I never was able to exactly define it—a cross between a running walk and a foxtrot is as close as I can come. Pat loved this horse as well, and since she had spent several summers at her grandparents ranch in east central New Mexico, was a fine rider.

The Ramming family moved to Taos from back East to retire. They fell in love with Clabber. They kept trying to buy him for their teen-age son and a daughter who, they felt, needed a horse to tie them to the earth. I took a liking to their son, John, and finally they caught me with my pockets empty of cash and my heart full of friendship. I sold Clabber to them, but we still had Brownie. Pat and I never regretted it because we would see Clabber often with different members of the family riding, loving, and caring for him. He was destined to be theirs and because of their good care, he lived an extra long life—until his early twenties.

At that time, gambling was wide-open, but illegal, in northern New Mexico and our neighbor, Curly Murray, who lived just up the road from us on the slope of the mesa, had recently taken charge of Long John Dunn's gambling operations. Now, nobody messed with Curly. Curly was tough. He had a widespread reputation as being that and also as being one of the most respected horse traders around. He was renowned as a judge of good horses and although tough, he had a reputation of being fair. He bought and sold horses for the Taos Indians and many of the other pueblos in several adjoining states.

Back in the 1930s the Bureau of Indian Affairs had bought a pure-bred Morgan stallion, along with some quality mares, to upgrade the quality of the Taos Pueblo horse population. Theirs was still a horse world in those days.

Anyway, Curly knew I wanted to get Pat a special riding horse and when he told me about one at the pueblo I went out there. I gave the four-year-old stallion a look and a try out. I took him out in the pasture where the tribe would soon graze buffalo and aired him out. I was amazed and thrilled at the smoothness of his gait. I know it must be a cliché, but he floated when he walked. Just a suggestion from my knees or the reins and he turned so smoothly it seemed his joints were greased. Everything was almost too good, but he was just that special. I bought him for seventy-five dollars—a goodly sum in the early fifties—but one heck of a bargain just the same.

The horse's Indian name was Yuso. He was a rich, deep red bay. His heavy black mane gleamed with bluish highlights and his black hooves and legs blended into his body like he had been painted with a master's brush. He was benevolent royalty. He knew it. Pat knew it, and both of them were made for each other. When I gave Pat her horse, it was as if they had known one another for . . . well, forever.

To this day it was one of the scenes of great beauty ever registered in my brain. Pat had great copper-brown hair, and whether it was loose or in a pony-tail, to see her riding Yuso with the sun bringing out the red glints from both of them was a thing of awe. The way they silently communicated, the perfect rhythm they had together, was what the word "beauty" had been invented for.

She loved Yuso deeply, as he did her. I loved to watch them together. Old Brownie and I would ride with them occasionally, out-classed, but proud to be along.

I have never, now or ever before, had such an animal incident to write about. My uncle Slim Evans, had leased some land and was training horses awhile before he acquired—with the help of his brother, Lloyd—a cow ranch on the second mesa west of Taos. Everyone in several states knew Slim as a cowboy, and top-notch, cowboy horse breaker (the p.c. world calls them horse trainers, horse whisperers, etc.) with few peers. So, when he asked to borrow Yuso for some kind of work, Pat graciously lent him her love.

A few days later, Slim drove his old pickup out to our place. He didn't even knock, but came right on into the kitchen where Pat and I were having coffee. He paced the floor, clearing his throat and his lean six-foot-three body shrunk about a foot as he told us that Yuso had drowned in the creek that split his leased land. There had been a flash flood there, but we were so stunned that I don't want to remember the implausible reason why.

Pat was beyond any feeling. I wanted to blow Slim's head off, but his own suffering defused that very natural thought. Slim got over this senseless loss. Pat never did. She would go on to like other horses and feed them, pet them, ride them, go to brandings and rodeos with me, but she never called another horse her own.

We were kids, really, but this was an ancient hurt. Somehow, in

RENO, the Arabian pleasure horse, in Max's Taos pasture. Author's collection.

some way, in some now unknown world Pat and Yuso will enjoy moving out across a sunlit land together again with their hair sparkling like rubies. I know it.

Then there was Reno, a white Arabian. I traded an old slick-backed Chevy to an ex-cowboy-turned-car-salesman, Marion Minor, for him. (See photo above) Lord, he was a great riding horse. I could ride him all the way across the desert down to the Rio Grande Gorge and back uphill to our place without him breaking a sweat. He seemed fresher on the return than on the start. I began to understand about those legendary, long-distance, and running war horses the Arabs had always seemed to brag about was, in fact, understated. A true pleasure horse, indeed, both for the ride and simply to look at.

In those days, I survived as a trader of anything including antiques, santos, cars, paintings, anything, and yes, horses. So when I had a chance to sell Reno to a rich Texas oilman as a gift for one of his lady loves, I did it. Two thousand dollars was a smart sum for a horse in those days. The most I ever got. I later missed Reno a million dollars worth, but feeding the family and my artistic soul trumped everything then.

Just the same, Reno's great gift has always been with me—the gift of appreciation for the elegant beauty and durability of the Arabian horse. One of life's great pleasures has been the adventure of the Arabian Nationals, often held in my home town of Albuquerque. The eloquence with which their performances speak to their riders, and audiences, is so unmistakable in its distinguished style and movement it actually elucidates this to all participants. The riders, male and female, feel this refinement. Their own beings emanate these courtly movements and feelings. Here the riders become so attuned, so much a part of the spirit of the horse that *beauty* seems like an inadequate word. Thanks to a car/horse trade and that blessed Arabian, Reno, my outer and inner eyes were opened so I could at least vicariously share this magic gift.

• • •

And then, along came an interim horse for several of us. I traded an ancient retablo of Christ on the cross and a worn ten-dollar bill for a ten-year-old buckskin mare. She was called Sleepy Kay because in the roping box instead of tensing up, muscles aquiver, ears working like a champion roping horse does, she just hung her head down and appeared to be asleep . . . a little unnerving to a tensed-up contestant.

However, in some unexplainable way, she knew when the roper nodded his head for the calf to be released. Instantly she would charge

SLEEPY KAY, a great horse but too slow for roping.

forward, all eleven hundred pounds of her with all she could give. She ran hard and heavy. And her *stop!* I tell you, she could have jerked a moose inside out with her stop.

Even as loyal and determined as she was, she sure made a guy work to get in the money. I really had to be ready to throw—even though she seldom gave me a shot before the middle of the arena. With all her drawbacks, I remember missing only one calf on her, and that was because it turned back just as I threw the loop. So, here's the deal—if I could get a matched roping of say four to ten calves against a faster, better-mounted, but erratic roper, I could win on average, and did so until folks caught on.

The mining business was beginning to take over my life and my art, and Pat's, too. I wasn't writing at all, but did keep on taking notes for what would become my major work decades later—*Bluefeather Fellini.*

My mentor's son, Woody Crumbo the Younger, and his best friend, a Modoc Indian named Sonny Jim, were protégé cowboys of my uncle Slim. So I gave them Sleepy Kay. We were all happy about that.

Slim had plenty of cow horses to tutor them on, but they started learning to rope on Sleepy Kay. She was exactly right for them, gentle and totally trustworthy, powerful but not so fast they couldn't keep up their learning. Eventually, they turned her into a steer jerking horse. She seemed to have been born for it. She was so strong it was almost effortless for them to jerk a steer down, bail off, and tie.

In her own—often, seemingly ponderous—way, the buckskin mare was tutoring the blooming rodeo hands almost as much as Uncle Slim was training them in the surprisingly numbered and varied abilities it takes to be working cowboys.

Later, Woody the Younger went on to become a successful rodeo producer, realtor, and art dealer. Sonny was still riding bulls at age fifty in the PRCA but a bad and permanent shoulder injury made him finally quit. He still enters "doggin'" contests, but mainly, he trains horses.

I think right here it would be fair to say that none of this would have happened without the faith and giving nature of the sleepy-looking mare. To show the power of her influence, all these great accomplishments happened after an incident beyond conjuring.

There were scattered cottonwood, elm, and evergreens along Taos Creek that sang and trilled their way through the Crumbo property southwest of Taos. The place would later become the noted cowboy singer, Michael Martin Murphey's ranch. Whenever the boys wanted a break from their various forms of cowboy training, they would sometimes fish, and sometimes hunt squirrels with a .22 rifle.

Then it happened. Sonny missed a squirrel and the little bullet ricocheted into the soft temple of a grazing Sleepy Kay and killed her. There is no use going into the shock, pain, and great remorse everyone felt. However, the remembrance of her giving partnership most certainly carried the boys, yes, even drove them, on to fulfill their many accomplishments. I myself go fuzzy headed when I try to remember our many close losses in calf roping, but the match roping wins are joyously clear as a spring sunbeam. I know that Sleepy Kay (see photo on page 19) left a lot of lasting goodwill and a deeply felt forever thanks from us all.

● ● ●

Woody, the Elder, and I had gone into the mine-promoting business, with great initial success. Finally, way up into my thirties, I had the money to buy my one and only first-class roping horse, Powderface. I got him from a top professional roper named Hamm of Clovis, New Mexico, who had won a lot of PRCA roping contests on him.

POWDERFACE, the best roping horse Max ever owned. Author's collection.

Powderface was a blaze-faced, strawberry roan, quartered up like a champion cutting horse. He was good. In fact, he was way better than I was.

We hauled him around to semi-local, community rodeos and jack-pot ropings. These were the thing in those days because pros could enter with the ambitious amateurs in these winner-take-all contests. A lot of camaraderie was shared and the winner took home a real chunk of money.

I finally had a top-notch horse but no time to practice, since the mining endeavors were rapidly widening. Just the same, I got in the money more often than not and had a lot of fun doing it.

One morning, Pat and I took off from Taos for a Las Vegas, New Mexico, rodeo, had a flat tire, and got there too late to enter. An amateur action, for sure. So, we drove back north to the Cimarron rodeo that was known in those days as the wildest, working cowboy rodeo anywhere. And it was! Their bucking stock and the roping stock were brought in fresh off the range and they were scared and wild.

Their wild cow milking contest—later copied by the Calgary Stampede and a few others—was a Cimarron original. The cowboys pair up

POWDERFACE with cousin David Evans aboard. Author's collection.

THE UNPREDICTABLE Raggedy Ann working smoothly for a change, with Max at a branding. She double-crossed a lot of champion cowboys, including Junior Vaughn at the San Francisco Cow Palace. Author's collection.

in teams—a roper and a foot-header—on one end of the arena. On the other end is a herd of sure-enough wild cows. The goal is: each team must catch a cow (any cow they can) and somehow get enough milk into a Coke bottle that it could be poured out—even a teaspoonful would qualify.

Cowboys on foot scare the cows out to the middle of the arena. At the signal, everything and everybody heads toward each other—all the cows, all the cowboys. When they all meet, total and outright chaos takes place.

It is the wildest, downright hilarious, most difficult event of the whole rodeo, and the most popular—at least it seems to be the audience's favorite. They scream and holler and encourage their favorite team until the whistle blows announcing that the first three bottles with milk have been delivered to the judges. Sometimes that takes a lot longer than expected.

I had picked as my foot-mugger a guy from Taos, Bob Mead, who worked for the telephone company, but owned a few registered cows. I really wanted to win this crazy event. I held Powderface back while all the rest charged into the wildly milling mess. One cow broke out by herself and Powder built to her. I had her out in the arena all alone. The header was digging his heels deep in the dirt trying to slow her so I could get enough milk in the Coke bottle to pour out. Powder was working the rope, moving as best he could to slow the cow. It worked.

I mounted Powder and rode to the judge in the arena and poured the milk out at least a minute before second place showed up. I was as elated as if I had won the *all around* in Las Vegas, Nevada.

I might as well have been on the rodeo circuit full time, because the copper ore Woody and I were profitably shipping by truck and rail to American Smelting and Refining at El Paso, had dropped from forty-eight cents a pound to twenty-four cents in less than 120 days. We were going broke. The struggle trying to save this part of our world consumed every second of my time.

Powderface was turned out to graze and water. A waste of great horse talent. Then, my cousin, David Evans, from Meadow, Texas, and the Kinsolving ranch at Tatum, New Mexico, came into the picture. He had been a fine professional roper until he tore a knee apart. He wanted to borrow Powderface for a special match roping, but first he'd have to work the fat off of him and get him toughened up. He called him Roanie.

David won a saddle and a couple of rodeo ropings on Roanie as well. Before another match roping, he was practicing and just as he was ready to throw a quick loop, Roanie fell and rolled over dead. David escaped injury to his body, but his soul was somewhat bent. There could be no weeping here. In the little time I got to spend with Roanie/Powderface he had delivered the mail and one of my small but fondest wins. He did the same for David. His aging heart had more will than strength and he was gone, at full speed, without pain, in the middle of what he was born to do. Fulfilled . . . all of us.

These horses so briefly introduced here and so briefly in our lives are there as long as we have enough sense to both love and respect them. Now on to those who were lifetime friends and partners. Please open up and share the pain, the adventure, and the special joy of our equine brothers and sisters.

CHAPTER TWO

Cricket

Little Horse of the Prairies

I DON'T remember when I started riding, playing, and working on Cricket. I was a four-year-old kid when I first got him, and he was a horse a year and a half younger than me, that's all. The little gelding was an odd horse in many ways. For one thing: his ears were the size of a much bigger horse—these gave him acute hearing ability. He was smaller than a quarter horse but built just as powerfully in the hindquarters as any showwinner. This breed was called "Steel Dust" back then. The little bay had "bottom," as the saying goes about a horse that never quits, and delivers under the toughest conditions. Cricket always delivered. This formula applies to people, also. It's the only sure way to know a friend. Cricket didn't realize he was thriving in the era of the Great Depression and Dust Bowl of the thirties. I didn't either. It seemed to have always been this way and I thought it always would be.

The year before the biggest stock market crash in American history, my father, W. B. Evans, had founded a town, Humble City, on the west half of our modest-sized ranch in 1928. It was in the far southeast county (Lea) of New Mexico bordering West Texas. Our ranch land was located between the cow town of Lovington and the oil boom

NINE-YEAR-OLD
Max Evans on his
$10 horse Cricket
and his $4 saddle,
Humble City, NM,
1934. Author's
collection.

town of Hobbs. My father envisioned Hobbs and Lovington growing to meet his town of Humble City. He had laid out a huge townsite, fully expecting his town to be the center of a big city. He mailed circulars all over America. A few far-scattered lots sold, and eight or ten houses were built, but it still looked like what it was—a dried-up cow pasture. There was a small grocery and a filling station. He soon got a two-room schoolhouse built and an authorized post office which was located in the front room of our home. My mother, Hazel, was the postmistress.

The crash of '29—and the far-reaching drought that created the Dust Bowl—put a *whoa* on all growth. Except, of course, myself, Cricket, and Dolly, a bay saddle mare. Dolly was a much lighter, brownish-red color than Cricket, and had a starred face. We kept a fenced-in pasture west of our house for the milk cow and Cricket, but we let Dolly roam the entire townsite—which was initially our ranch—with a mule and various colors and kinds of milk cows belonging to others.

It seems impossible, but nearly everyone became poor overnight, and moreso as the weather and the business world deteriorated. Farmers, ranchers, and even most townsfolk tried to keep a milk cow, a few laying hens, a hog or two, and a vegetable garden to help them survive. So did our family.

But even before things got so tough, Cricket and I had started supplying meat for the Evans' table. I would cinch up my four-dollar saddle, mount, call my two dogs and into the vast prairies we'd head. There were cottontails and jackrabbits to be had. And the approach to catching each was different. The compact cottontail rabbit averaged out being more tender and tasty than the more sinewy long ears. Like a racing quarter horse, the cottontails were good for a short dash of great speed to their home hole. They never grazed farther than they felt safe from this protection. If we jumped a long-eared jackrabbit, the two dogs would race out after the quarry with Cricket and me following in pounding pursuit. If the jackrabbit was young or old, the dogs nearly always caught them. They seldom caught the in-between ones.

The moment of capture was critical. Everything had to be timed to precision. If Cricket and I were too far behind, the dogs would rip the rabbit into approximate halves and start devouring it. We had to be right on top of the chase-and-catch so I could bail off my horse yelling loudly, "No! No! No!" momentarily freezing the dogs' actions until I could retrieve the rabbit, gut it, and hang it safely from my saddle horn. The family's protein allotment was at stake, and it was my responsibility to supply it. It was fun. A lot of fun. It was a great game for all of us—except for the rabbits, of course.

More world-class rodeo ropers came from Lea County than any-where else in the world and I've often wondered if this sort of neces-sary activity of rabbit hunting in those great, arena-flat prairies was one of the reasons for that. It makes sense. When I'd hit the ground running to save the rabbit for the dinner table, Cricket had to come to a stop with his hind legs under his belly. He'd stand waiting and watching, as if tied to the ground, with his ears working back and forth thinking silently about his own thrill at our mutual success—or failure.

The dogs, and Cricket, too, for that matter, never got over racing so near it they could almost touch the cottontail and then have it sud-denly vanish underground while they were in full pursuit. It amazed and disappointed them every time.

Of course, we could have waited until the dogs dug it out, which often took two hours of pawing labor, until I learned how to twist them out with a strand of barbed wire. I would simply uncoil the wire, put a V at the end, bend a handle on the other end, stick it down in the hole ,and start slowly twisting. It didn't take long until I felt when the V was solidly snared in the fur, and I'd simply pull them out. Fresh, un-bruised meat for half-starved people and animals.

Yes, that is right. The dogs got the bones and gristle after we had the meat. They loved it. Unlike chicken bones that break into dangerous sharp slivers in a dog's jaws, rabbit bones are safe and delicious as well as highly nutritious. On those unavoidable times when we'd tear and bruise a rabbit so it was unpleasant to humans, we'd profitably feed part to the dogs and all the rest to the hogs.

My mother had many ways of fixing rabbit. Stewed, baked, broiled, and she could fry and season them so many different ways that I never tired of it. Often she'd make hot biscuits and gravy to go with the little lifesaving creatures.

Later, when I was old enough to go to school, I'd sometimes have delicious fried rabbit to go with the sowbelly stuck between two halves of biscuit as well as peanut butter and jelly in the same manner. I loved it. I loved it all and was totally unaware that these were hard times.

Cricket benefited too. Since Humble City was losing residents instead of gaining them, my dad was on the road in a Model T truck trading anything for anything. He knew how important Cricket was to the survival of all of us, and every chance he got, he would swap for whatever amounts of oats or shelled corn he could get, to help Cricket provide for the entire family.

My father had sold nearly everything to finance his dream of a bustling town. He sold all our riding gear, saddles, bridles, chaps, spurs, and anything that would bring a dime or a dollar. He let me keep my four dollar saddle—bridle thrown in—that my mother had bought me with the pennies she somehow saved. The old leather reins kept breaking until I gave up and just used a piece of rope instead. It must have looked awful to some people but I didn't care. Survival was my game, not vanity.

Nineteen-eighteen was an especially bad year for the Evans family. The great blizzard froze to death every single cow they owned on their West Texas ranch, and their eldest son, Elbert, had been killed in World War I. Grandfather Evans never went back to ranching but became the first elected judge for Hockley County (Texas), for two terms, then was city judge at Ropes, Texas, for the rest of his life. When he'd come to visit us in humble Humble City, New Mexico, he always brought me a present. One day he brought me two half-grown shepherd-mix pups. He had already named them Depression and Proration. The first name was obvious, but the second name came from the government prorating oil production. People were so broke that they cut down on buying everything. This caused a glut of oil. It was selling for only a few cents a barrel. When the government cut pumping time to only a few days a month, oil went up to a dollar a barrel and finally became profitable.

Depression and Proration looked like twins, both dark chocolate with partial white faces. They grew big, strong, and fast. I became so close to them and Cricket that I would have done anything for them, and I mean anything.

The two dogs would often just lie down in the horse pasture and watch Cricket. He would graze right between them. They'd never move. Buddies. Well, after all they were the "chosen" and had permanent jobs taking care of our family.

My best friend was Wayne Simpson. His father had a ranch headquarters, corrals and all, about a mile and three-quarters southwest of town. Wayne really liked Dolly. We'd catch her up, and with me on Cricket, we'd ride the vast empty-appearing pastures, just talking horses, dogs, cows, and girls. Sometimes on our fun rides, Wayne would spot something ahead as a marker, and he and Dolly would challenge me and Cricket to a race. Now, on a real working outfit, this would get your tail fired. However, there was nothing left around there but survival places.

Anyway, we'd line up as even as we could and come to a stop and I'd count out loud, "One, two, three, go." Away we'd rip.

Dolly was a lot bigger than Cricket, and she was fast, but when I leaned over and touched Cricket on the neck and told him, "Now, Cricket. Now," the little bay always responded with an extra bit of heart and passed Dolly. Every time.

Sometimes, when I'd had a good day with the dogs and rabbits, I'd simply ride Cricket way out in a big circle either to the east or west of Humble City just to look at the prairie-so-flat that on a clear day—that was a day when the wind hid out—we could observe the horizon to the vanishing point and actually see the earth bend in the beginning of its great circle. And the cloudless sky—well, it was so big and blue that all I could measure in my little mind was forever and ever, up, down, and around. I'll never forget the wondrous feeling of the two of us being all alone way out there, at great peace and thankfulness for the magic of all that quiet space.

Just a few years later, I would get that same feeling looking at the many-colored mesas and blue-purple mountains of northern New Mexico and other vast spaces of the great Southwest.

At a chosen time during the summer, I'd ride Cricket out to visit Wayne at his ranch headquarters. You know, heckfire, everybody is aware of that old saw about *timing is everything*. Well, I learned that timing was food. I managed to arrive at the Simpsons' place when the sun was straight overhead, signifying the noon hour. I'd dismount and lead Cricket to water at the rock tank next to the Simpsons' windmill. Since it just happened to be on the side of the house where the kitchen was, I'd stand in an obvious place, looking all around, and whistling little tunes. If necessary I would try to get Cricket to drink more water than he wanted. I'd loosen the cinch on the saddle to make him more comfortable. I'd gaze at the sky looking for birds. It worked every time. Finally, Mrs. Simpson would spot me, come to the kitchen screen door and yell out for me to come in and join them for the noon meal. Mrs. Simpson somehow managed to raise frying chickens all summer, and they had at least two or three for lunch almost every day. She could cook those things as delicious as my mom could rabbit. I never tasted anything better in my whole life. Not even later when I'd dine in the Beverly Hills Hotel or the late Russian Tea Room in New York City. Lordy, lordy, that Cricket horse had a happy pardner whether it was chasing after wild rabbits or Mrs. Simpson's fried chicken. I would have loved to share half my fried chicken with him, but he was a vegetarian . . .

Here's the landscape as I recall it. There wasn't much of that life-sustaining element on top of the ground—swimming pools and fishing holes—where we lived, but Humble City did have a fine underground reservoir, and there weren't zillions of people then to deplete it. Windmills cost money—real money that folded or jingled. There were some good-producing windmills on all of the few, far-scattered ranches that were still inhabited. Everybody in Humble City had hand pumps. Even in the school yard. There was a solid reason for this. Although there was still a little money left over from oil and gambling in nearby Hobbs, Humble City town folk were as poor as a homeless person without pockets.

I was acutely aware of the best, biggest, and most available water in tanks. Three or so miles northeast of town, where Wayne and I used to set trot lines for the little catfish, there was a long dirt tank with a windmill at each end. And there was another one a couple of miles west of town made out of rocks. I can't remember these fortunate folks' last name, but I sure remember their daughter's first name. It was Lillian. These wise people actually built changing rooms—one for women on one side of the great tank and one for men on the other. They had diving boards at each end near the windmills that pumped the wonderful pure cool water as long as the wind blew and that was 80 percent of the time. They cleaned the pool by emptying it into a large garden spot of corn, green beans, watermelons, and cantaloupes. There was enough extra water to miraculously have some green grass for their milk cows and a few beef cattle. I always figured they were the richest people in the whole world. Folks would come from all over to pay their dime to swim in the precious water and picnic on the lush grass.

During school year, that beautiful big-eyed, rich little Lillian would stop off at Curtis' store and buy me two or three Milky Way candy bars a week. Lordy, that gorgeous young girl got prettier by the day. She was a princess of the prairies. I just knew she'd be crowned queen of the earth someday. After Cricket and my dogs, little "Milky Way Lillian" was my first womanly love. Many years later I heard that someone made a commercial swimming pool at the northeast tank where our only sparse supply of catfish swam.

My dad had sold all the cattle off the east end of our ranch to help found his city on the west end. Then he moved his widowed sister, Pearl Nettles—from across the line in West Texas—mother of five daughters and a son, the eldest, named P. J. They also had a little bunch of mixed-blood cows, a half-Jersey half-Hereford bull, chickens, and hogs. They were relocated to the house, which was formerly the headquarters, where there was still some old grass left. Even in times of great drought some spots would get rain. About half the rained-on, east pastures were in fair shape. My aunt Pearl didn't want to graze it down to the dirt. She wisely wanted some left for the winter.

As hard as her daughters worked, they didn't care much for cow punching, so it fell to me and Cricket to move a few head at a time around to outlying vacated homesteads. Sometimes we'd find a field of weeds or a little pasture that somehow had missed being grazed bare. Once in a while I could get my cousin Kaye, an eight-year-old, to ride Dolly and help me herd these cockeyed cows like sheep.

Since some of them had milkcow blood in them—Jersey, Guernsey, Holstein, Aunt Pearl milked all of them that bore calves. She separated the cream and made butter to sell in Hobbs along with eggs from the hens. With me chousing them all over, hunting feed, they sure didn't get enough browsing to make any kind of surplus milk.

A man from Lovington and one from Hobbs and my dad had somehow gotten a highway right-of-way approved and fenced between the two towns with Humble City in between. There was a narrow fenced lane about a half-mile from Aunt Pearl's to the highway right-of-way. So I figured out that Cricket and I could actually drive most of her motley herd down the lane along the fenced-in, but as yet, dirt highway. There was quite a bit of forage on each side of the road. It took a full day, leaving the ranch right after sunup and returning in the late afternoon with the cows better off than when we left.

At first, I nearly worked little Cricket to death before I got the cows trained to graze only on one side of the road going in the morning on the left and staying on the other side in the afternoon on the way back. About every third day I'd ride Dolly to work and let Cricket rest and feed on the home pasture. Of course, horses will graze at night if they're hungry enough. Their legs lock so that they can sleep standing up.

Everybody was doing their portion. Aunt Pearl and her covey of girls from four to thirteen in years seemed fairly happy and were healthy—growing and learning. P. J. was off somewhere working, sending her whatever he could spare to help out. Later on, he would be killed in the Battle of the Bulge during World War II.

Aunt Pearl had bright, brown eyes that, I was sure, could see through brick walls. She was small in stature, quick in movements and had the endurance of an Arabian war horse, and could somehow find something to laugh at even in a pen of dumb chickens. No matter how hard her labors, she was always kind with her firmness and I respected and loved her. So it is hard to understand—and especially to admit—how I could commit the sin against her that I did.

There was a family that lived on the corner where her lane ran into the Hobbs-Lovington highway. I can't remember how many boys and girls the couple had. All I remember is only one of the skinny little boys, called Peter, went to school, and sometimes I had to share my lunch with him. He simply didn't have any. He was shy and seemed embarrassed about everything. Sometimes I'd take him by the house and my mother would scrounge up something for him to eat. He gulped whatever she could find without hardly chewing it. That boy was hungry. Peter told me his daddy was in California working on farms trying to save enough to move them to the state-of-all-dreams.

School was out for the summer and I'd been herding these cows right by Peter's house. His little sisters and brothers started coming out to the road and staring at me and Cricket as we worked hard to turn the cows down the right-of-way. They were all skinny right to the bone. I was afraid they were going to starve right before my eyes, and just fall down and blow away.

I don't know if I was asked or volunteered, I can't say, but one day it just started happening. Before returning the cattle to Aunt Pearl's, Cricket and I cut out a few cows that had milk in their bags and drove them around behind Peter's house where there was a barn and corral. I told Peter's mother that they could have a little milk from each one as long as they didn't take it all. They gathered ropes, or whatever they could find, to put around a cow's neck to tie them to the corral fence. Then the poor woman started ordering her kids to get clean buckets and pans—anything to hold milk. She, Peter, and the oldest girl started desperately milking the patient cows.

Well, I was feeling like a benevolent king after a few days because the whole family started perking up and looking like they might live. The mother thanked me and thanked me and said she was saying prayers for me to some saint I'd never heard of and I doubted ever heard of me. Oh, I felt like the Savior himself. I was the Salvation Army and Red Cross all in one. It was a good feeling, all right, but it wasn't gonna last long. This milk was not mine to give away.

I began to hear Aunt Pearl puzzling over the sudden drop in milk production. Half of it went to the calves. From the other half she extracted cream for butter and the "blue John" that was leftover was for her kids, chickens, and hogs. It barely went around as it was. Now, due to my generosity with someone else's property, I was possibly creating another health and welfare problem.

I might forget most names, and couldn't remember how many children the hungry lady on the corner had, but I'm here to tell you, I never forgot the silent looking-over Aunt Pearl gave me when she found out what was happening to the milk production. After the first stunned stare, she looked across her garden plot, up at the windmill wheel turning and clanking in the wind, took an extra-long, deep breath, and then she stared back into my suddenly-gone-blind, brown eyes, and said in a quiet, perfectly controlled voice,

"Maxie, you have to decide if you want to help strangers or your blood kin. It is your decision." She then bent over and started pulling weeds on her way to the garden.

I rode wonderful, faithful, honest little Cricket out into the prairie. My throat was swelled up with something mean. My chest seemed to have a badger in it trying to dig its way out with long, sharp claws, and my eyes were full of muddy water. Cricket circled and took me home.

Well, I recovered to a degree and felt guilty as a baby killer, as I worked poor Cricket half to death hurrying the cows past the corner place. The kids peeked around the house at me now; I couldn't stand to look. Then, one morning I saw a rickety old truck beside the house and the whole family were busy loading it. The father had come for them after all. They were all working their skinny little tails off, joyously, chattering like a flock of week-old chicks. The mama said something to the papa, and he looked at me. He got something out of the seat of the old truck and, waving at me, said something I couldn't quite hear. I stopped Cricket and waited. He came on, this family man, and when he got close he looked Cricket over and said, "That's sure a nice looking little pony."

"He's a horse," I said.

"Yeah, yeah, I reckon he is." Then he handed me an orange he'd brought all the way from California and said, "Rosie told me how you helped. May God bless you, son." And he gave Cricket a pat on the neck and me one on my right leg. He turned back to finish loading the truck and taking his entire family way out West to the land of oranges.

I felt right keen for awhile, and that orange was almost as delicious as little Lillian's Milky Way candy bars. I never did get all the way over my deceit to my precious Aunt Pearl. But I improved, and spent the rest of my life trying to be dead-on loyal to my friends whether they were kin or not.

Aunt Pearl and two neighbors got some rain. The rest of the country dried to dust, and there wasn't enough grass to fill up a dozen grasshoppers. The beef cows left were either dying or so weak they wobbled in a slight breeze. The government put up ten dollars a head and slaughtered around 80 percent of all the beef cattle in 1933. I tried not to think much on how lucky we were, even though I learned later in life how terrible times had been. Things seemed plumb natural to me.

Now the winds came even harder at times. I blamed that on the fact my granddad had given me a brand new dude hat. I immediately put a bend in the brim to make it look as much like a real Western Stetson as I could. It gave me a whole new cowboy feeling as Cricket and I drove that string of cows halfway to Hobbs.

It seems that the same little bunch of clouds that had dropped rain on Aunt Pearl and her near neighbor's place, had crossed the road, and there in the right-of-way for about a mile and a half some grass had actually turned green and grown.

There were three cows in estrus at the same time, and that half-Jersey bull was going crazier than he had been born to be, and that was a bunch. He'd given me two tons of trouble, turning back trying to find an opening in the fence, and I don't know what all. That bull had me out of sorts all day.

The wind just kept getting stronger, and the sun was only a light glow through the dust. I pulled my new hat down real tight and wrapped a handkerchief around my face to keep from strangling on the tiny pieces of the wind-borne earth.

Cricket and I finally got the little herd to the end of the lane and were within about a half-mile or less of what had once been the horse pasture gate to the headquarters. I don't know how Cricket kept those cows moving in that truly blinding storm. He did it mostly on his own. I was having so much trouble keeping my new hat pulled down that I just gave the little horse his head.

That blasted bull kept quitting the herd. Cricket had to cut out with him and drive him back, over and over and over. I hope the wailing wind overcame the sounds of the words I used on that bull. If not, I was sure I knew which direction I'd be headed when the final trumpets blew.

I rode out ahead in a lope to open the home gate. I threw it back all the way to the fence so there'd be no excuse for the bull to turn back. I remounted and sure enough, I just barely returned in time to see the bull heading back for the lane. The cows were no trouble. They followed the wagon-rutted road. They knew there was water, some feed, and the windbreak of the barns to be had.

Cricket was working on that bull, his head down, his nose a couple of yards from the bull's rear, like a champion cutting horse. Even that didn't get the job done. The cockeyed bull would not go through the gate. Not only that, he got mad. Real mad. He whirled, charging us.

Just as Cricket sidestepped him with about a strand of hair to spare, I felt my hat go. I grabbed at my head, but it was too late. I somehow saw in that blur of brown, my hat sailing and bouncing off the earth ten feet high. At the same time, Cricket had whirled after the bull and had him going in a dead run.

It was a moment of decision. Did I rein Cricket after my hat or let him pursue the bull? The bull was heading full speed away from the gate but straight at the horse pasture fence with us after him desperately trying to turn him back. I let my precious hat go on toward Texas, or even possibly Louisiana, and concentrated my thoughts with Cricket's on the bull.

Too late again! That sucker had run right smack into a fence post smashing its middle into splinters and taking out about forty or fifty yards of wire. I was barely able to rein Cricket sideways to keep him from getting badly cut with the barbed wire. We just kept on going, running half-blind trying to see the bull. We couldn't find him in the thick brown hide-lashing storm. I eased Cricket into a walk and felt the thoughtless wind tearing the hair on my hatless head out by the roots.

When we got to the corral, Aunt Pearl and a couple of her girls were just closing the corral gate on the cows as they shoved together at the water trough. There stood the bull. I was shocked numb; Cricket paid no attention. He'd done his job. As soon as the bull saw us, he crowded out some of the cows and took three places at the trough for himself. The calves were bawling in an adjoining pen for their mamas and I wanted to leave for mine, but it would not be understood why, so I held it back.

The wind growled all night and then clouds followed, but it only rained in a few little spots again. But once more, Pearl got nearly a half-inch of the lifesaving wet. A couple of days later, my dad and a couple of the Curtis boys roped and snubbed up the bull and put a ring in his nose. I've heard the old saw about "a horse laugh" a zillion times just like everybody else, but I never could hear Cricket laughing out loud. I'm pretty sure he was chuckling silently all the time because that bull got easier to handle than a baby chick.

I never did find my hat, but I'm sure somebody did who needed it worse than I did. It ended up okay because my dad traded for me a real working wide-brimmed hat that had proven itself for about a decade on the head of one of the Curtis boys. It was sort of greasy and too big, but I folded paper inside the band and felt like I was wearing a crown of pure gold. I could tell Cricket was happy for my new-old acquisition because of the extra zing in his running walk. After all, he was a world champion bull chaser himself.

Because of Cricket—and Dolly—and our creative grazing practices, we had given Aunt Pearl's pasture some rest, and with the blessed spot rains the Great Mystery in the Sky had sent her, she had enough grass to run her cows through the fall and winter without damaging the land. That would free-up Cricket and myself to pursue other activities.

Dad had given Aunt Pearl and her hardworking brood of girls his saddle-and-work mule. The family enlarged their garden to practically field-size, and had worked all summer putting up jars of all sorts of vegetables—enough for the year ahead. The hog they butchered was already hanging in the smokehouse, all salted down. Eating pretty well was further insured by the chickens for meat and eggs, and the milk cows supplying dairy products.

However, other citizens of Humble City hadn't planned as well and the town was slowly losing its citizens. They were starving out and leaving the houses empty. That meant school enrollments were dropping. My mother's post office in our home was losing business, and she didn't seem to be doing so well either. I don't think that was what was mainly on her mind, though. She had been with child for about nine months. Dad took her over to stay with our friends, the Mannings, southwest of Lovington.

The Manning family, with their three boys, had tried to make it at Humble City, believing in my dad's vision, but were forced to move temporarily back to their father-in-law's homestead. So, my mother stayed with them near a doctor until my sister Glenda was born. For whatever reason, she couldn't breast feed Glenda. So Cricket and I were enlisted to drive a milk cow—Aunt Pearl had donated her best milk producer—the nine miles to Lovington to, as my dad so cleverly put it, "save your sister's life."

Cricket and I had made drives back and forth so many times on the right-of-way that I was actually looking forward to this honor. Herding the lone cow wasn't so bad from Aunt Pearl's house down the narrow lane, but the minute we hit the right-of-way and I got the old mixed-blood headed toward our desperate destination, Cricket had already broken a little sweat where his neck joined his shoulders. Driving this one animal was a whole lot harder than driving a herd. She wasn't as big or as mean as the bull, but for the first couple of miles she tried to turn back what seemed to me like a thousand times. Finally she quit trying that and started going from one side of the dirt highway to the other to graze, just as she'd been allowed to do for months with the rest of the herd. Each of the nine miles seemed like a month. We were all three beginning to wear out before we were halfway there.

If I hadn't been "chosen" to ride Cricket half to death chasing one cow, I might have thought that, maybe, she would have been more use being butchered for beef rather than milking—and I would have happily volunteered to do the deed. Driving her was like pushing a long chain up a mountain highway.

The sun moved slowly on over the sky, into a hazy sunset. We were still a piece of hard ground from the little cattle town. Cricket was actually lathering a little at the mouth, and his flanks sweated and were drawn down. For the first time I could remember he quit working his ears. This was another worry. And me? After all the riding I'd done lately I figured this drive would be a song, but my butt was so numb I could no longer feel my four-dollar saddle under me.

It was way after dark when we got there, but my dad greeted us with a big smile, along with giving instructions. Feed and water the cow. He would fill the bucket he was carrying with milk.

As for Cricket and me? Well, I watered both of us at the stock tank, put him in a stall and fed him some shelled corn Mr. Manning had furnished. He, also, threw him a shock of grain hay from a stack. My dad was finished milking. My mom was heating baby bottles, and I got in just in time to see my sister take her first swallow of cow's milk. I told my mom several dozen times how pretty her new baby was and how glad I was that my new sister was saved.

All I wanted then was a little bit to eat and some sleep. I didn't even wait for them to show me where I was to bed down. I just jerked a blanket from one of the boys' cots and wrapped myself in it on the floor. I slept. If I dreamed at all it would have been about a dirt highway stretching all the millions of miles to the planet Mars.

I was still sort of numb the next day. I checked out Cricket and he had made a miraculous recovery. He was grazing in a small adjoining pasture on weeds and dry grass. My dad had to leave on some trades involved with trying to save his town. He was to return in a week. I had fun with the Manning boys playing baseball, marbles, mumblety-peg, and a bunch of games we made up as we went.

Dad returned from his business trip and said that he and I were going back to Humble City, leaving Mom at the Manning's for a couple or three weeks. But Mr. Manning convinced Dad to stay over Saturday for a bunch of jackpot horse races being held only a short distance between them and town. I was really excited when he agreed. I can't explain it exactly, but I wanted to ride Cricket over and show him off.

Later, I admitted, only to myself, that I was secretly hoping I'd somehow get to enter a horse race.

Seemed to me like everyone in the world came to the Lovington races that day. A free event always draws crowds. In the great drought and depression, "free" was a magic word. The sun could actually be seen through the dusty haze, mainly, I think, because the wind was quiet. Well, no wonder—I don't believe it was blowing much over twenty miles an hour.

The track was just raw ground with a graded straightaway about a mile long. Some of the crowd—mainly the ones who were going to enter horses in a race or make bets—were at the starting place. This consisted of more open ground at the end of the graded track. The big crowd was down at the finish. My dad, myself, Cricket, and the Manning boys were at the finish line. The race distances were marked: quarter-mile, half-mile, and mile. They were all full of betting, yelling, and sure enough fun for me.

Then it came time for the oddest horse race I ever saw. A hundred-yard dash. I started breathing hard and walking Cricket back and forth, then slow-lapping him to warm him up.

My dad asked, "What're you doing, Max? You're not in the race."

It took all the courage I had left and more than I would ever need again, but I croaked out through a suddenly drought-stricken throat, "We can win at a hundred, Dad." It was like a fervent prayer. It was answered. Dad looked at us, then he smiled so small and quick you could hardly see it, and said, "Keep him moving and let me talk to the officials."

Lordy, lordy and lordy again. I was continuing my automatic praying that Dad had enough money to get me entered. He came back in a little while and said, "There are nine horses entered, all told." I waited while my heart turned to cold rusty nails. "You and Cricket are one of 'em. I'll be waiting for you at the finish line."

Nine miles to Lovington. Nine horses to heaven. Or . . . well . . .

The officials had quite a bit of trouble getting us all in line so the starter could fire the Colt .45 he used as a starting gun. To the day I change universes I'll wonder why he didn't use a smaller gun with less expensive and less booming bullets.

I was a skinny little kid on a well-muscled, but very small horse. As we crowded into the number seven spot, I felt like we were two midgets. I tried to take comfort in remembering the wins I'd had on

Cricket when Wayne Simpson was riding the much bigger mare, Dolly. I was as scared as I could remember—not only because we were outsized and outclassed, but I couldn't lose Dad's money. The entry fee was probably all he had and this odd race was winner-take-all.

The hammer of the frontier gun had gone down on the shell. It exploded. We were off. No one had told me that racing a hundred yards could take a hundred years or a fraction of a second. Or both. I learned this that day all on my own.

I was ahead of the horse on my right, but the big sorrel gelding had half a length on me to my left. It was a slow-motion blur. I leaned over even closer down Cricket's bobbing neck and said, as before, "Go, go, Cricket, go!" and patted him on the right side of his neck.

It was over. Some of the horses ran on to the end of the track. But Cricket and I stopped and turned around pretty quick. Then I saw my dad, Mr. Manning, and the three boys coming at us, laughing, and saying great things none of which I really heard, but I knew we'd won. People crowded around, all congratulating me and the little bay mule-eared gelding called Cricket. Later Dad handed me three one-dollar bills—the most money I'd ever had in my life. I would have given it all to Cricket, but he didn't have a pocket to carry it in. We were rich.

My dad had scrabbled up five whole dollars for the race entry fee. So he won forty dollars. A cockeyed fortune in those days. As badly as he needed the money for other things, he bought me a model 62 Winchester .22 pump. This was a dream gun. More people survived through hard times supplying hungry bellies with this rifle than any other. Things were moving in several directions now. And up and down as well.

Aunt Pearl's son P. J. had come home for a ten-day visit. He did a lot of work around the place for his mom and also brought her a little money. He had a part-time job in the oil fields somewhere besides Hobbs and was hiring out to different baseball teams as a pitcher at five dollars a game. He was that good, and people started talking about him trying out for the Fort Worth Cats. He never did get to, though, for the biggest of all wars came along and took him away before too long.

Even though Aunt Pearl was doing back-bending work for sixteen hours a day. She still needed a little financial help. She got it from Granddad Evans and her brother Lloyd. Her cows were giving a lot more milk now and the calves were actually growing so she could butcher and sell a few head.

I was really proud of my new gun. I built a scabbard out of an old piece of canvas for the .22 and tied it with binder twine under the saddle skirt at just the right angle. It didn't look like much, but it worked.

In the area surrounding Aunt Pearl's outfit, I could hunt quail and doves as well as rabbits. Where the grass and water grew, so did the wild meat. I soon learned that rabbits weren't very scared of a horse. I could get right up on them. Another thing I caught onto was never to shoot anywhere near a horse's head. It hurts their ears real bad. I'd shoot to the side and Cricket would hardly flinch. Bullets were money—and that was scarce as new hats. I soon learned how to make every shot count by easing the sights onto a critter's head and pulling the trigger softly. This not only killed our food instantly, but it saved damaging edible meat or having a wounded animal to run down.

It took me a while to figure out how to hunt doves with the .22. The main thing was patience. I'd tie Cricket to the offside of a mesquite bush a distance from a spill or dirt water tank. I'd ease up and find a bush to hide behind as close to the waterhole as I could. Then I'd wait. Doves water in larger numbers in the morning and late afternoon. But they also come singly, sometimes in pairs, and water all day. They have very small heads and quick movements when they drink and so I'd carefully study where the head was going to be when they raised it from the water and when they dipped their bill back in again. Then I learned to put my sight right on the water where the head would meet the liquid when they ducked their bills in. Plink. Meat for the table.

The blue quail took even more study. They'll run instead of flushing into the air if you work it just right. Walk at them very slowly toward whatever bushes they are using for cover. Then one will see you, then two, three, and they'll all move out until they have a little wash or cow trail to run in. If you give them the proper amount of time, they will run in single file down a cow path. The trick is to lie down when they are at the right distance and aim. As they run, their heads move to the side about an inch each way. So for just a fraction of a second you have a two-inch target and if you fire in that instant you can often get three or four head shots with one round. Clean meat. The best there is. I was having fun supplying two households with rabbits, doves, and quail. Cricket always waited, giving me a close eyeballing, to see if I was going to have enough bounty to hang from the saddle horn.

I swear, he knew when I'd had a good hunt. His running walk got faster, smoother and, I do believe, prouder.

I thought that my dad and mother had my baby sister and me, Aunt Pearl and her fine daughters all doing fine, but I realized later they must have been dancing barefoot through hellsfire themselves. My mother, who was so gratified to be able to deliver letters and packages to the poor folk of the prairies, was about out of a job. Now, where she'd once taken in nickels it was pennies. Soon the government papers would come that would close her post office forever.

My dad, with the help of Pete Manning, dug the first irrigation well in that country. We raised one crop of watermelons, green beans, and strawberries before we moved to Andrews, Texas. We harvested them and sold them in Hobbs. Dad was the driver and I was the peddler. It was too late to save his town, but I didn't know it. My folks never complained where I could hear them. I was enjoying all these struggles so much I failed to see the signs. I occasionally took my dogs hunting, just for fun now, because I had the rifle for necessary food gathering. I should have sensed that with everything going so good for me that the Great Equalizer would show up.

I was sitting out on the edge of our front porch with Depression asleep at my feet. Proration had wandered off around the emptying town site and was walking along with Dolly as she grazed. Suddenly I looked up and saw the dog after a grown jackrabbit. They were racing about a hundred yards parallel to the front porch. I had a tough time keeping still. I didn't want Depression to wake up and waste his energy so far behind the chase. Even so, my heart started thump-thumping like hands clapping to a church song. Old Proration was gaining. I thought he was going to catch that rabbit. Cricket was grazing at best a half-mile away in the horse pasture and my dad was gone in the old truck.

Then I saw it. A Model T was moving along the road between Curtis' little store heading for the Lovington/Hobbs right-of-way. It was the only thing moving in all that huge country to be seen. Proration stretched closer and closer to the rabbit. I was so sure he was going to catch him, I wondered why the driver of the Model T didn't stop to watch the thrilling action. I jumped up, waking Depression, who also stood up, looking around, trying to find the source of my excitement.

Then . . . *then* a mighty coldness grabbed all my insides and I couldn't let loose my breath. Proration's attention was totally concentrated on the flying meat—as he was born to do. Trained to do. Loved to do. This moment in eternity was his world. His entire life.

I stood right there and watched the rabbit miss the wheels of the car by inches, but my beloved Proration smashed into it at full speed, stretching to grab his prey.

I will never be able to recall exactly what I did. In just a moment, though, I, my mom and Depression were running across the empty lots toward the spot of the collision. The rabbit and the car had both moved on, but there lay Proration with his head turned back from a broken neck and his muzzle a bloody mess.

I yanked his head straight, screaming for him to get up. My mother pulled at me to get me away from the terrible scene. It took some doing. However, when Depression started smelling different parts of his brother in confusion, I started bawling so that I couldn't even see. After a while, my mom told me to wait, and she went to the house and got a pick and shovel. We pulled him off next to a big mesquite and we dug his grave. It helped, a little, but my mother later told me that I bawled for two days and nights. The odds against this terrible happening were just too great for me to handle. Old Depression would all of a sudden just start up howling and I'd start crying again for about a week. Then my dad came home and I had to shape up. I could tell something big was about to happen.

About a week before my dog's impossible wreck, I used a *morral* with grain in it to catch Dolly. I put a bridle on her and was riding her bareback along a Humble City street which was turning to weeds.

There was an oilman from Hobbs who had bought two of the vacated houses. He was driving a new Model A sedan to check on the crew stripping all the lumber to move and rebuild something in Hobbs. He stopped and asked me about Dolly. I told him what a fine horse she was.

I could tell he admired her, and to my surprise he got out of the car asking if he could take a short ride. I slid off and handed him the reins. He knew how to mount a bareback horse, jumping up with his belly over her back first and then swinging his right leg over.

He looked good on her all right and reined her around a bit, pretty pleased.

"How much you take for her, son?"

I told him, "She's not really mine. She's my dad's."

He looked over at the house and saw Dad's truck and said, "I'll drop by in a little and see what your pa has to say."

I remounted and rode over to the Curtis store tying Dolly around back thinking foolishly that if nobody could see her, they'd forget about her—just like a dumb kid to think like that.

I fooled around faking shopping, watching out the window, and visiting with Mr. Curtis.

Sure enough, the oilman went into the P.O. part of our house, then he and Dad visited a little on the porch, shook hands, and the man drove away.

I was scared to death, but I rode Dolly over and told Dad what he already knew.

"That man wants to buy Dolly."

"Yeah, yeah, he does. But I told him not now. He'd have to wait and bid at the Lubbock sale."

"Sale? *Lubbock*?"

"I was going to tell you in the morning, Max, but we might as well face it now. Me and Uncle Pit are putting on a sale over at Lubbock." My dad's Uncle Pit Emery was an auctioneer from Lubbock. A good one. "We've been gathering stuff over there for weeks. Furniture, farm equipment, a few cows, and horses."

"Horses?"

"Well, yes, son, all our horses."

Since we only owned two, that word *horses* meant Cricket, too. I came as close to dying right there as I ever would till it really happened.

"We're gonna lose Humble City," my dad said, looking across its emptiness. "Don't you worry, though. We've got some good, solid plans for the future. Just trust me that I'm doing what's right for all of us."

I heard him. The whole world whirled before my eyes. It wasn't just me. It was our own family, and Aunt Pearl and hers, and a whale of a lot more.

I caught up Cricket, called Depression and rode out across the prairie. I couldn't cry now. Heck, I'd done a lifetime of that over Proration anyway. I thought beyond my dog's death, though, to Aunt Pearl's husband getting killed from a hammer falling off a windmill deck and bashing his brains out right in front of her. I thought many, many things—most of them not good. It must have been even worse for my dad because he was losing a whole town and all the people who had believed in his dream. The worst of all was that his dream was as dead as a dinosaur bone.

By the time I reined Cricket back toward the remains of our town, I'd made up my mind to take whatever happened without a complaint. I rode by the little schoolhouse my dad had built, and I couldn't look straight at it no matter how hard I tried.

My granddad Evans and my uncles Roland and Lloyd, came over, loaded, and hauled all of Aunt Pearl's household belongings—her chickens, hogs, and daughters—away. My dad had traded the little ranch Aunt Pearl now occupied for a stock farm two or three miles north of Brownfield, Texas, toward Lubbock. Then he made a deal with the Curtis cowboys to drive her cows across country to her. She spent the rest of her life there, putting all her girls through school in spite of losing her husband to a hammer and her only son to the bullets of an SS soldier's machine gun.

Well, there we were a few days later at the big sale on a farm northwest of Lubbock. I was amazed at the people who came in various modes of transportation, even on horseback. They were walking about, checking out all the farm equipment, and endless household items—tables, chairs, even a four-poster bed.

Dolly and Cricket stood tied to the back of the truck. I had already brushed them till their red coats shone like new pennies in the sun, and now, I was wandering around looking at stuff, but I wasn't really seeing it.

The sale began and my uncle was fast and expert. Time had vanished from the earth. Well, it was probably still there but I didn't know if it was moving backward or forward. Maybe it was just still— motionless—like a broken clock.

Then I felt my dad's hand on my shoulder.

"It's time."

I saddled Dolly first and reined her around showing her off. I was stunned, as I'm sure my dad and his uncle Pit were when the Hobbs oilman bid her all the way up to seventy-five dollars and bought her. He loaded her in a trailer behind his new Model A and took off in the dust for Hobbs. Well, she'd have a good home for sure. I hid the vacancy left somewhere in my little gut and saddled Cricket for the last time. I'd taken my rifle scabbard off the saddle. At least I'd have that. An empty leftover.

I wanted to gig him and spur him till he was acting silly and everyone would think he'd been eating loco weed. I probably could have used a dose of that myself. But I heard the rhythmic chant of Uncle Pit saying: "Looky, looky, looky, what a horse. Small and gentle enough for the kids, and powerful enough for the best grown-up hands. See that rein. A true cutting horse if there ever was one. Look at that smooth stop. Isn't that something? Run him out a ways, Max, and show these fine folks how you won the nine-horse jackpot race at Lovington, New Mexico."

I kicked him out and for the last time I leaned over and choked out, "Go, Cricket, go!"

He did. He scorched the dry earth drier. I couldn't help it. I had to make my dad proud and Cricket show his heart. There was no other choice.

Then Uncle Pit went into his selling chatter and the bidding went up and up, but I didn't want to hear. So I went deaf, and just circled my partner smoothly before the eyes of the bidders.

My dad took the reins, then, and stopped me and Cricket. I stepped down. My dad said, "You did good, Son. Real good."

I never saw who bought him, and I was glad when he was gone. I could feel the water building behind my eyes, but I kept it there somehow. It seemed like hours, and I reckon it really was before all the money was collected, paid out, divided, and all the things they do with money were finished.

That night, Dad drove us back to Humble City. Then he talked to me like I was grown up, as he explained what our next move was going to be in this insecure world.

He told me that up at Guymon, in the Oklahoma Panhandle, they had a big spot of good rain—enough to plow and plant farms again, and run cattle on the pastureland. During the worst of the Dust Bowl, their plow horses and cow horses had either been sold for a pittance or starved out. So now, they were going to need horses to work that wet land.

He also knew of a ranch down at Jal, in the southernmost corner of New Mexico, south of Hobbs. This big outfit had tried to keep their remuda intact, but the animals were so poor and bony, they were going to be forced to sell them all before they died of starvation.

He continued to explain that an old one-eyed cowboy friend of his named Boggs and I were going to make the horse drive from Jal to Guymon. Since it might take us as long as three months to get them there, we'd have time to "borrow" feed along the way and fatten them up for the big sale.

I had no idea that lonely night in that bouncy, groaning old Model T truck that my dad's idea would work and all our families would somehow make a go of it ever after.

The next morning I got up, milked the cow, gathered the eggs, pumped, and carried all the water my mother would need for the house before breakfast. She fed the baby and cooked us a good breakfast of fried eggs, biscuits, and gravy. She even had a new jar of grape jelly she opened so we could spread it over the butter melting in our hot biscuits.

Dad said, as he got up from the table, "I gotta get goin' and settle up some accounts, and I won't be back till late. I'm gonna go down to that ranch and sew up our horse deal, Max. Here's some change. You might want to buy yourself a bar or two of candy."

"Naw, thanks," I said. "I still got some of my three-dollar winnings left."

When he was gone and mom was busy, I yelled at her I was goin' hunting. I took the lifesaving Model 62 out of the horseback scabbard and went out the back door. I didn't have to call old Depression. He was already waiting for me. We walked to the Curtis store, but they didn't have much left on the shelves. Mr. Curtis was selling down, getting ready to close for good, just like our town. I was sure worried he wouldn't have any Milky Way candy bars left, but he had three. I splurged and bought them all. I surprised the old man by asking for a paper bag. He found one. I thanked him and he thanked me, and we started hoofing it out to little Lillian's swimming hole.

She had a little pinto pony, and I had had Cricket. Once in a while we snuck off riding. We'd ride and talk about our dreams of the future and race across the prairies with her hair blowing in the wind and sun, like tiny strings of polished gold. Lillian had given me a lot—what with the candy and all—but the thing that made me look at a girl on a horse racing the wind was priceless. It still is.

I knocked on the door, figuring I'd have to ask her folks where she was. It was wonderful luck she answered it, saying, "I saw you coming," and stepped out.

We moseyed out along a rock path toward the rock swimming pool; two small people making small talk. Then we sat down and old Depression did too. We all three looked into the beautiful blue water as it sparkled like a tub full of diamonds and pearls in Lillian's great big blue, blue eyes.

I reached in the sack and handed her a Milky Way, and then I took one and we unwrapped them and ate away getting chocolate all over our mouths. We tried to wipe it off with the back of our hands, but it didn't quite work. We sat a spell, getting the last of the luscious taste off our teeth with our tongues. Then I handed her the sack with the third Milky Way in it, and I leaned over and gave her a big chocolate kiss. It was the most delicious thing I'd ever tasted.

I got up. Old Depression and I walked in a wide circle out across the prairies where I had ridden so many wonderful miles on Cricket. I carried the rifle on my shoulder. Depression made out like he was looking and smelling for a rabbit, but I knew he wasn't, any more than I brought the gun to shoot one. I could feel little Lillian standing there watching us grow smaller. I loved her very much, but just like Cricket, I knew I'd never see her again. I didn't look back.

The end.

My Pardner

AFTER twenty-odd years, the image of Boggs is just as clear as the day he came walking toward me with his head leading his body a few inches. His skinny legs were bowed like a bronc rider's, but he wore the bib overalls of a farmer and a dirty old brown hat that flopped all over. Both boots were run over in the same direction, so he leaned a little to the left all the time. His nose was big and flat, and his mouth so wide it turned the corners of his face.

As he moved closer, I could see that there was only one crystal in his thin-rimmed glasses. A funny thing though—he had one eye gone and the crystal was on that side, leaving a single blue eye beaming from the empty gold rim.

He swung the heavy canvas bag from his back to the ground and stuck out a hand saying, "Reckon you're my pardner Dan. Well, it's shore good to meet you. I'm Boggs."

"Howdy, Boggs," I said.

"Why hell's fire, boy, you're purty near a grown man. Your pa didn't tell me that. How old are you, boy?"

"Twelve goin' on thirteen."

"Hell's fire, I was punchin' cows with the top hands when I was your age. By the time I was fifteen I was out in Arizona mining gold."

Suddenly I felt real small. Course I didn't weigh but ninety some-odd pounds. But I'd felt pretty big a while ago when Papa had handed me the map and the three dollars and said, "It's up to you, son. I'm dependin' on you and Boggs gettin' those horses to Guyman, Oklahoma, by ten o'clock July nineteenth." He had gone on to explain that we'd be out on the trail nearly sixty days because every other day he wanted the horses to rest and feed so's they'd get in looking good and ready for the big sale. That was the key thing to remember: balance the moving and the stopping so the horses would pick up weight.

I looked over at the corral and counted five mules and sixteen starved, ragged-looking horses of every color. Well, Papa had more confidence than I did, but I couldn't help swelling up a little when he shook hands and said, "I ain't worried a peck." But then Papa had lots of guts. Here we were on the edge of Humble City, New Mexico, living in a shack that was held up by hope, on land that the drought had singled out to make an example of. Half farm, half grassland, and only half enough of either one.

At heart Papa was more of a trader than a land man. He'd traded for a hotel once in Hobbs, but when the drought came a few years back, everybody left Hobbs except the pensioners, the postmaster, and a few others too broke to go. Then he traded the hotel for a herd of goats, and the goats for some dried-up milk cows, and the cows for a truck, and the truck for a car. Somehow or other I liked the old Ford better than the hotel. Anyway, in between he kept something to eat on the table and Ma made it taste good.

Well, lately Papa had done some more figgering. The drought of the thirties had broken and people were putting a lot more virgin land into wheat and cotton. They'd need lots of horses to plow with. Most folks still hadn't gotten used to the idea that it could be done cheaper and better with a tractor. The way Papa looked at it was this: by July nineteenth all the wheat farmers would have their wheat in and by then the grass would be ready for the stock to finish fattening on. People would feel like buying horses for the next plowing. That is if it rained in early July. The spring rains had already been good. So, Papa had started trading for livestock, and finally come up with this ugly bunch. He and Uncle Jock would head up north about a week before we were due and get the sale handbills out and so on. Uncle Jock was an auctioneer, so it wouldn't take much money to pull it off. If everything worked right, we might be able to pay the mortgage, buy some seed, and put in a crop of our own the next spring.

Boggs said, "Let's git goin,' boy."

My horse was already saddled and I'd thrown the rotten old pack on the gentlest of the mules. I had two blankets, a jacket, a stakerope, and a sack of dried apricots tied on it. That was all. Papa had said we could find *plenty* to eat along the way. He hadn't explained exactly how.

Boggs hung his canvas bag on the pack and fished out an old bridle. Then it dawned on me he didn't have a saddle.

I said, "Ain't you got a saddle?"

He grunted, caught a bay out of the bunch, grabbed his mane and swung up bareback. We turned them out and started across the mesquite-, shinnery-, and grass-covered pastures to Oklahoma.

Boggs rode out front and led the string. They weren't hard to lead, because they were in such poor shape, but riding the drag was something else. They just wanted to stop and eat all the time. I was riding back and forth every minute yelling them on. All the same I felt great again—sorta like a man must feel on his first ocean voyage.

Along about noon I could feel my belly complaining. We rode up to a windmill and watered the horses. After my horse had finished I got down and took a drink. Then I reached in the pack and got a double handful of apricots, and handed some to Boggs. He spit out his chew of tobacco, wiped his mouth, and threw in the whole batch and went to chewing.

When he finished, he said, "Boy, get up on that horse. I want to show you something." It took me kind of by surprise but I crawled up. "Now look here," he said. "Look at your knees. See how they kind of bend when you put 'em in the stirrups. Now look here," he said, walking off. "See them poor old bowed legs of mine? Why you could run a grizzly through there without him even knowin' it. Now ain't that a disgrace?" he said.

"I don't see as it is," I said, having always felt bowed legs to be some sort of badge of honor.

"Well, by jingos!" he said. "You don't see, boy? You don't see? Do you realize that I'm a highly educated man—havin' traveled far and wide and knowin' all about the isns and aints of the world? Young feller, I'll have you know that at one time I was made a bona fide preacher. Yessir, a man of the Lord dwellin' in his own house, spreadin' the true and shinin' light. But what happened?" And he jumped around in his runover boots waving his long arms in the air. "What happened?" he shouted, putting that sky-blue eye on me.

"Here's what happened," he said as he squatted down and pulled off his boots and overalls and waded out into the dirt tank. "Look," he said, "look at them legs. By jingos and hell's fire, boy, how would you like to be baptized by a preacher with a pair of legs like that?"

I burst out laughing, even though I was half scared I'd made him mad.

"There you are," he shouted, running out of the water. "That's another thing that happened . . . peals, barrels, tubs full of laughter burstin' across the land. You see, Dan"—he suddenly lowered his voice and it was like dragging satin over satin—a young boy like you with his bones still growin' and shapin' should never ride a saddle. Otherwise, your legs will get bent like mine. A long trip like this will doom the young sapling. Let me have that saddle, son, and save you this terrible disgrace. Grow up straight and tall like Abe Lincoln. And besides"—he leaned at me with his hand in the air signaling for silence—"besides, when our duty is done I'll buy you the fanciest present this side of the pearly gate."

Well that was fancy enough for me. I just crawled down, unfastened the cinches, and handed him my saddle. He threw it on his bay horse, then went over to the pack and took out a half-gallon crock jug.

"Cider" he said, tossing it over his arm and taking a long pull. "Ain't good for young'uns," he said, corking the jug. "Cures the ear-ache. Always got an earache." He rubbed one ear and put the jug back inside the bag. Then he took out a long plug of tobacco and really bit him off a chew. "Let's git goin'," he said, and we struck out.

About five hours later the horses quit. There wasn't any way to keep them all moving at once. Well, I had an inkling why. My belly was just plain gone. It had lost confidence in ever being fed again and had just shriveled up to nothing.

Boggs rode back and said, "We'll pitch camp right over there." He pointed to a dry lake bed with a heavy growth of mesquite most of the way around its edges. Off to the northeast I could see a clump of trees sitting like a motionless prairie ship in a green-grass sea. I knew there was a ranch house there with beans and bacon and good black coffee, but it would be late the next day before we'd make it. Tonight we'd dine on apricots. Dried.

We unsaddled the horses. I took my rope and staked out one for a night horse. I wasn't worried about the others running off. They were too hungry. Besides, they would be easy to hem up in a fence corner about a quarter of a mile off.

I spread my blanket out and Boggs reached in his canvas bag. He had another pull of ear medicine. He fished around in the bag and came up with a coffeepot and a little Dutch oven. Then he said, "Gather some wood, boy. I'll be back in a minute." He struck out in that rocking chair walk of his, leaning to the west.

I started picking up dead mesquite limbs, watching every now and then to see what Boggs was doing. I could see him twisting some loose wire on the corner post. I didn't know what he was up to, but if a rancher caught him we'd sure be in trouble.

He came back carrying a six-foot strand of barbed wire and said, "Come on, let's git goin'."

I followed. We walked out through the mesquite. All of a sudden he yelled, "After him! After him!"

I saw a cottontail rabbit shoot out between us. I took after him feeling like a damn fool. The fastest man on earth can't catch a rabbit. Well, that cottontail wasn't taking any chances on it. He ran and jumped in a hole. I stopped, breathing hard, but Boggs just ran on past me, right to the rabbit hole. He squatted down, took one end of the wire, and spread the strands about two-thirds of an inch apart. Then he bent about ten inches of the other end out at forty-five degrees. He put the forked end into the hole and started twisting the wire. To my surprise the wire went right on down, and even passed the spot where the hole turned back. Then I could see him feeling his way. His eye was bugged out in concentration. His face was red and sweating. Then he gave another couple of twists and said, "Got 'em, boy. Now the secret is, not to bring 'em up too fast or you'll pull the hide out and they're gone. If you bring 'em up too slow then they'll get a toehold and the same thing will happen."

He backed up now, and I could see the rabbit.

"Grab 'im!"

I did.

"By jingos, he's a fat one. A regular feast," he said, and he wasn't joking.

We built a nice fire, and Boggs scraped the fat off the rabbit hide, then we cooked him in his own juice. I'm telling you that rabbit woke my stomach up and really put it back to work. We finished it off with a cup or two of black coffee and half a dozen apricots. The world was all of a sudden a mighty fine place.

I leaned back on my elbow and watched the flat rim of the prairie turn to bright orange. High above, some lace clouds got so red, for a minute I thought they would just drop down and burn a man up. Then the cool violets and purples moved in and took over. Bullbats came and dived in the sky in great swift arcs, scooping the flying insects into their throats. The crickets hummed like a Fordson tractor, and away off the coyotes started their singing and talking howl.

Then Boggs said, "Boy, you ever been to Arizona?"

"No."

"Course you ain't. But you will. That's a great country, boy. That desert and all that gold just waitin' to be dug." He went on a little while and I looked at the sky full of stars and my eyes got heavy just trying to see past the first bunch. Then his voice came again, "I'll tell you all about Arizona one of these nights, boy, but right now my ass is too tired."

I could hear the horses grazing nearby, snorting now and then, slowly in contentment. The fire was a small red glow teasing the night good-bye. I slept.

• • •

"Let's git goin', boy."

I sat up in my blankets.

"Here." He handed me a cup of hot coffee, and kicked dirt over the fire.

It was just breaking day. I swallered the scalding stuff and tried to stand up. This took some doing. I was sore and stiff in every joint, but that wasn't what bothered me the most; it was my hind end. The rawboned back of the saddle horse had rubbed my rump like grating cheese. I had to walk with my legs spread apart. It was not a good condition for horseback riding.

The sun got hotter. My setter got rawer. Every little bit I'd slide off and walk, but the insides of my legs were galled so bad I couldn't keep up with the slowest of our horse herd. There, was nothing to do but get on and go.

By eleven o'clock I was hurting so bad, and the sun was so hot, I got somewhat ill-tempered. I was cussing Boggs, not altogether under my breath. "You old liar and conniver. You old nutwut. You old . . ." It eased my pain.

By two that afternoon we pulled up to the trees. There was a water tank about fifty yards long and a windmill pumping at each end. But the ranch house had long been unoccupied. It looked like now it was occasionally used as a temporary camp for cowboys. It was a disappointment. When not thinking about my sore bottom, and when not cussing Boggs, I thought about the beans and bacon, hot gravy and biscuits we'd have had at the rancher's table. I just got down and lay in the shade and listened to my belly growl.

After the horses watered, we turned them all loose in a little horse trap where the grass was coming good.

"Reckon there's any rabbits around here?" I asked Boggs, chewing on an apricot.

"Might be," he said, looking in the tank.

"There ain't no rabbits taking a swim in that tank," I said.

"You're right, boy, but I'm tellin' you there's some catfish in there."

"Catfish?" I said, bolting up out of the shade.

"Yessirree Bob."

Then I settled back down. "Well, we ain't got no way to catch 'em. Guess we better get to lookin' for a rabbit."

"Now look here, boy, you're givin' in too easy. We're goin' to have an ample amount of rabbit before this trip is over anyway, so let's try doing a little thinkin'. It's all right to go through life just plain feelin', that's fine, but when your old gut is cryin' 'hungry' to your soul, it's time to think. You hear? Think!"

Well, we walked around the yard. If you could call his bowlegged and my wide-spraddled motions walking. We went into the ranch house: nothing but an empty table, cupboard, and four chairs. Out in a shed, we found some tools, old and rusty, a can of axle grease, and a stack of empty feed sacks tied in a bundle.

Boggs said, "Look here, the great gods above done smiled down on us poor sinners. By jingos, boy, we're in for a treat." He gathered up the sacks and out we went.

After untying and splitting the sacks, he spread them out on the ground and began sewing them together in one big sheet. Then he tied some rocks along the bottom, put sticks on each end for handles, and we had us a dandy good seine.

Boggs went back in the shed for a minute. "Here, boy," he said, handing me a can of axle grease.

"What's that for?"

"Rub it on your hind end."

I just stood there holding it in my hand.

"Well, go on," he said, "we ain't got much time."

I rubbed it on. It was sticky and left me a little embarrassed when I walked, but it did ease the pain.

"Pick you out a couple of them sacks to ride on tomorrow."

I did.

"Now, come on, boy. We're wastin' time." Boggs told me to go to the deep end and start throwing rocks into the tank and yelling. He said this would booger the fish into the shallow water so we'd have a chance at them.

About middle ways down, we shucked our clothes and waded in. I sure was glad I had applied the axle grease in the right place. That water would have really finished chapping me. I pretty nearly choked to keep from laughing at Boggs' bowlegs until he got them under water. The seine was spread and he told me to keep the bottom just a little ahead of the top so the fish couldn't get underneath.

"Now, boy, move in steady to the corner and when I yell, come out with the bottom first and hold tight. Then give a big heave out on the bank."

We moved along.

"Haawwww!"

Up we heaved. Sure enough there were seven or eight nice cats, three perch, and a goldfish. I didn't heave quite enough and two of mine fell back, but the next trip through we got another good catch and Boggs said, "Hell, that's all we can eat, so let's go swimming." He put the fish in a wet gunnysack and we took a cooling swim.

When we crawled out the sun felt good for a change. Just when I thought I was going to faint from hunger and the extra exercise, Boggs said, "Boy, get out there and get a bunch of wood."

I went after it. When I got back with the first load he had dug a hole about a foot deep and a yard long. He built a fire in this hole and I kept packing wood for it. After the fish were cleaned and wrapped in some pieces of brown paper sacks we'd found in the shed, he mixed up a batch of mud and rolled them in it. When all the wood had burned down to glowing coals, he buried the fish in them.

We waited and we waited.

"Don't you think they're done, Boggs?" I asked, feeling the saliva run into my mouth.

"Not yet."

"Lord, I'm starving. Looks like to me those coals have done gone out."

"Not yet."

Finally, he took one out and broke it over a rock. The baked mud fell away and there it was, the juicy, white meat of the catfish. Everything was soon gone but a pile of bones cleaned as slick as crochet needles.

All the next day we let the horses rest, water, and eat. We did the same. Then on the move again. The wide, green tablecloth of a prairie soon turned to shinnery bushes and sand where the sun was meaner and the earth drier. We ate rabbits and apricots until the apricots were gone, and that left *just* rabbit.

Then we could see the little clumps of trees increasing in the distance, and we knew we were finally on the edge of the farm country.

We checked our map. If we were lucky, we could make it to a Mr. Street's farm before night. He was supposed to be a friend of Papa's. Papa said Mr. Street was a pure farmer and wouldn't have any pasture grass for our horses, but he would have plenty of cane bundles to give us. It was here I was to buy two hundred pounds of oats out of the three dollars and start graining our herd.

As I followed the old white horse into Mr. Street's road, I finally figured out why he was behind the others all the time—one ankle was twisted just enough to make him slower. He was a stayer though. I was getting to feel friendly toward him and wouldn't have liked any of the other horses back with me.

I went up to the front of Street's house, leaving Boggs out in the road with the horses where they grazed along the bar ditch. It was a neat, white house with a paling fence around it, and a few elm trees scattered about the place. I could see a big barn, several corrals, and feed stacks. Down below the house was a shack for the Negro hired hands. Mr. Street was rich. I could sure tell that.

I tied my horse at the yard gate, went up to the door, and knocked. It didn't feel as if anyone was home. I couldn't hear a sound. Then I knocked again and waited. Just as I raised my hand, the door opened.

"What'd you want?"

I looked up and up and sideways and all around. That door was full of woman. I felt like I was standing at the bottom of a mountain.

"Well, what'd you want?"

"Is Mr. Street in?"

"What'd you want?"

"My papa . . ."

"Your papa? What about your papa. Come on, boy, speak your piece."

"Well, uh, my papa is a friend of Mr. Street's."

"Who *is* your papa?"

"Ellis Thorpe."

"You know any Ellis Thorpe, Nate?" she said back over her shoulder.

"Yeah, used to," he said. "Ain't seen him in years."

I never saw such a woman—little bitty ankles with massive muscular legs above to hold up the rolls and rolls of blubber that ran right up under her ears and spread over her cheekbones so it made her eyes look little and mean. Sure enough they were.

"Well, what *do* you want?" she asked again.

"Papa said you might put us up and feed our horses for a day."

She went in and talked to Nate in low tones. Then she filled the door again.

"Nate says times have been hard what with overcoming the drought and all, but he says you can bunk down at the shack with the help and you can have all the bundles you want at a nickel apiece.

"I, uh . . ."

She started to shut the door.

"Just a minute," I said, and pulled out the three dollars. "I guess we'll take two bundles apiece for the horses. How much'll that be?"

"How many head you got?"

"Sixteen horses and five mules."

"Forty-two bundles at five cents." She counted on her little short fingers . . . "Two dollars and ten . . . er . . . twenty cents."

I handed her the three and she brought me eighty cents change. She slammed the door.

I felt sick. There went the grain money. I'd already started letting Papa down.

We took the horses to the corrals and started pitching them the bundles. Then Nate came out and counted them. He was a little man with a quick, jerking motion to everything he did. When he was satisfied we hadn't cheated him he said, "Tell your pa hello for me," and walked off.

Over on the other side of the corral stood four big, fat Percheron work horses. They made ours look like runts, and I began to wonder if Papa had a good idea or not.

It was almost night when we walked down to the workers' shack. Three little Negro kids grinned at us from the steps. Boggs spoke to them and a man came to the open door.

"Howdy. What can I do for ya?" he asked.

"Well, Mr. Street said we could bunk with you tonight."

"Sho, sho, come in," he said. "I'm Jake."

He introduced us to his wife, Telly. She was almost as big as Mrs. Street, but somehow in a different way. There was something warm about the place.

Boggs sent me to get our blankets and his cider jug off the pack saddle. Telly set out three cups and they all had a drink.

"Sho fine," said Jake.

"Better'n fine," Telly said.

"Best cider in Texas," said Boggs, winking at them, and they all busted out laughing.

Then Telly fixed us a big stack of hot cakes, and set a pitcher of black, homemade molasses on the table. I smeared a big dip of churn butter between about six of them and let the molasses melt all over. I forked three strips of sowbelly onto my plate and really took me on a bait of home cooking. Then two tin cups of steaming coffee finished it off.

A while after the eating was over the three grownups went back to that cider jug.

Every little bit Boggs would say to Jake, "Ain't you got a bad earache, Jake?"

"Sho nuff, Mr. Boggs, I do. I ain't never knowed a ear to hurt like this'n."

Telly said, "Well, you ain't sufferin' a-tall. Both my ears done about to fall off."

The only earache I'd ever had hurt like seventy-five. I never could figger out how these people were getting such a kick out of pain. I spread my blankets on the floor and lay down to get away from all this grownup foolishness.

It was soon dawn again, and it was Boggs again.

"Let's git goin', boy. Leave the eighty cents on the table for Jake."

I was too sleepy to argue.

We moved the horses out fast. Then I said, "Boggs, where's the pack mule? We forgot the pack mule."

"Shhhh," he said. "Shut up and come on."

In a little while, maybe three quarters of a mile from Street's, I saw the pack mule tied to a fence. On each side of the pack saddle hung a hundred-pound sack of oats.

"Where'd you get 'em?" I asked bristling up.

"From Street."

"That's stealin'!"

"No, it ain't, son. I've done him a real favor."

"How's that?" I said smartly.

"Why, boy, you ain't thinkin' again. This way him and your pa will remain friends."

I studied on it all day, but I was a full-grown man before I figured it out.

"Well, anyway that's too much for that mule to carry," I said.

"That shows how little you've been around the world, boy. That mule is plumb *underloaded*. When I was mining out in Arizona we packed four hundred pounds of ore out of the mountains. *Mountains,* you hear. This mule is at least a hundred pounds underloaded."

"Oh," I said, and we moved out with me staring that old white horse square in the rump.

•   •   •

After awhile we stopped at a little grassy spot along the road and poured out some oats. Those old horses were really surprised.

"You know something, boy?" Boggs said, filtering a handful of dirt. "This here's sand land. Watermelon land. They come on early in this soil. Fact is, just about this time of June."

He raised his head, kind of sniffing the air as if he could smell them. Then he got up and ambled off through a corn patch that was up just past knee-high. I sat and watched the horses eat the oats thinking what a damn fool Boggs was for figuring he could just walk off across a strange country and come up with a watermelon. I'd stolen watermelons myself, and I knew better than that.

The ponies finished their oats and started picking around at the grass and weeds in the lane. I began to get uneasy. Maybe somebody had picked Boggs up for trespassing. Then I heard singing. I listened hard. It was coming through the corn. I heard loud and clear, "When the saints . . . Oh, when the saints go marching off. Oh, when the saints . . ." closer and closer till I could see the long stringy figure of Boggs, and the watermelon he had under each arm.

"Had a little trouble finding two ripe ones. Most of 'em's still green."

I didn't say a word.

He took out his long-bladed barlow and stuck her in a melon. It went *riiiiiip* as it split wide apart like a morning rose opening up.

I knew it was a ripe one. He cut the heart out with his knife and handed it to me. I took it in both hands and buried my head plumb to my nose in it. Good. Wet. Sweet. Whooooee.

I ate every bit of that watermelon except the seeds and rind and my belly stuck out like I'd swallered a football. Boggs didn't waste much of his either. It was a mighty fine lunch.

When we stood up to mount our horses, I said, "Boggs, sure enough how'd you know them watermelons was over there?"

"Look right there in them weeds under the fence."

All I could see was a bunch of flies buzzing around. I walked over. Sure enough there was a half-ripe watermelon that somebody had busted open the day before.

"I just figgered nobody could carry one any further than that without seein' if it was ripe. Knew they had to be close by."

"Oh."

We got our horses and rode. We soon came to the main highway to Brownfield, Texas. According to Papa's map, we'd be riding along this bar ditch for a long spell now. It was late afternoon, and that watermelon belly had disappeared and the usual holler place was making itself known.

We looked around and finally found an old fallen-down homestead out in a cotton patch. It was vacant, and there were a lot of weeds and stuff growing around the barns and old corrals for the horses to feed on. But we still had to water them. The windmill was cut off, and if we turned it on in the daylight somebody might see it and maybe have us arrested for trespassing. We had to wait for dark.

Boggs said, "Let's see if we can find a rabbit."

We'd already lowered the rabbit population of West Texas a whole lot, but I was willing to thin it out some more. We rode along the fencerows, all around the old place, but there wasn't a cockeyed rabbit to be found. About half a mile from the homestead, we looked out over a weed-covered fence. There was a farmhouse with chickens, milk cows, chickens, some white ducks in a little pond, chickens, and dogs.

"By jingos, boy, how'd you like to have some roasted chicken tonight?"

"Sure would, Boggs, but we ain't got any money."

"Money? Why only a sinner against mankind would pay money for a chicken."

"What do you mean?" I asked, feeling fingers made out of icicles grabbing my little, skinny heart.

"I mean we'll procure them chickens. Now you know the lady of that house is overworked. She's probably got six kids to look after besides her old man. All them ducks to feed, and the churnin' to do after milkin' those cows. Now it's just too much to ask of her to take care of *that* many chickens and gather *that* many eggs, ain't it?"

I started to say it was stealing, but my belly set up those growling noises again, and I felt my legs trembling from hunger weakness.

"What about the dogs?" I asked.

"No bother a-tall. I'll take care of the dogs while you steal the chickens."

"Me?"

"You."

"Now listen . . ."

"Now you listen close, and I'm going to tell you how to get the job done. Why hell's fire, boy, you're just the right size for such an operation."

I wondered how in the world it could make any difference to a chicken whether I weighed ninety pounds or two hundred.

"Now about them dogs. I'm goin' to go off to the right of the house and howl like a coyote. The dogs will come out barkin' and raisin' cain at me. It'll throw everybody's attention in my direction. Get it?"

I swallered.

"Now the minute you hear me holler and the dogs start barkin', get to that henhouse. Here's the secret of chicken stealin': first, a chicken sleeps pretty sound. About the only thing that will wake 'em is one of their own taking on. *That* you have to avoid. Be as quiet as you can gettin' into the henhouse. When you're used to the dark so you can see a chicken, grab her right by the throat and clamp down hard so's she can't make any noise. Then just stick her head under her wing. A chicken's so dumb, it won't make a sound. Now, as soon as this is done, carry her outside and do 'er round and around in the air," he said, and made a circular motion with his arms held out. "Like this. She'll be so dizzy, it'll take 'er ten minutes to stand up again and that much longer to get her head out from under her wing. You can steal a whole henhouseful in twenty minutes."

"Do we want 'em all?"

"Hell's fire no, boy. Just one apiece."

Darkness came and the lights went on in the farmhouse. Every once in a while the dogs would bark. I think they heard us.

Boggs said, "Let's git goin'."

He circled off to the right of the house and I eased along to the left behind the henhouse. When the dogs started barking, I stopped. They quit for a minute, and I heard that coyote Boggs hollering his head off. I dashed up to the henhouse with my breath coming in quick gasps and cold prickles just breaking out all over. I was scared but at the same time thrilled. I slipped around to the door and fumbled for the latch. The noise pierced the night like a runaway wagon. It was too late to back out now. Besides, I was too durned hungry.

I heard the chickens stir and talk a little as I went in. I stood still just a minute. My heart thumped louder than the chickens. I could make out a dark mass over on the roost. I moved as quietly as I could with my hands outstretched. The dogs were really raising the dickens over on the other side of the house. I wondered if maybe they had Boggs down chewing on him.

Then my hand touched a chicken neck. I squeezed tight and holding her with one hand I stuck her head under her wing with the other. Outside I went. Whirl that chicken I did. I plunked her down and she just sat there like Boggs had said. This gave me confidence. In a half a minute I had another one outside on the ground all dizzy and still. Then I relatched the door. That Boggs had started me thinking tonight. I grabbed up a chicken under each arm, and sailed out of there.

Boggs got back about twenty minutes after I did.

"What took you so long?" I asked, feeling kind of important.

This seemed to rock him back for a minute, then he said, "A funny thing, boy. Just as I raised my head to let out that coyote yell, a sure-enough live one beat me to it. I just hung around a few extra minutes to see what'd happen."

The cooking took place.

The eating took place.

The sleeping with a full belly took place.

And I dreamed.

• • •

We were through Brownfield before sunup, right into the heart of cotton country. It stood up straight and green everywhere. In a few more weeks the hard, round boles would form. Then, in the fall, they would burst open into the white of ripe cotton. The fields would fill with bent-over pickers dragging long canvas bags behind them and their hands snaking cotton from the vine to the sack. Wagons by the hundreds would pull it to the gins, and the gins would hum day and night for a brief spell, cleaning and baling the cotton for shipping and sale all over the world. Now, it was still, and hot, and green.

The people in the autos traveling parallel to us all waved. I guessed it had been a long time since they had seen a remuda of horses on the move. All the horses, except the old gray, were beginning to pick up flesh. Just the same, I couldn't help worrying some. In the first place, if that thieving Boggs got us in jail, our time schedule would be thrown off, and one-half day late would be just the same as a month. I couldn't figger Boggs out. One minute he'd be preaching and the next he was stealing. Sometimes his speech was like a school professor's, and then like an uneducated dunce. On the other hand, I would have starved nearly to death without his help. We were hungry most of the time anyway. Besides worrying about letting Papa down, all I could think about was getting enough in my belly to last a whole day.

We moved on through Meadow, Texas, and then out to the edge of Ropesville. We had a two-day holdup here if we wanted it. There was a patch of heavy grass by the road where a sinkhole had held back some extra moisture from the spring rains. We decided to take a chance on the horses grazing alone on the road while we did a little exploring. This was risky because if someone took a notion to impound our horses, we were done. It'd cost five dollars a head to get them out. That would be impossible to raise in time to make the sale, but Boggs had said, "Our luck's holdin', son. You can't beat luck—even with thinkin'. The odds are that no one'll think but what the owner is keepin' his eye right on 'em. You got to be willin' to take chances. The way to survive this world is knowin' when to duck. That time generally comes when a man has made a mistake while takin' a chance. Now you take my whole durn family. Ma, for instance. She died having me cause she didn't reckon she needed a doctor. Now my brother got killed robbin' a bank. He walked in when two plainclothesmen were making a deposit. He should have watched *everybody* instead of just the guard. That sister of mine jumped in the Rio Grande to save a drowning boy. The boy caught hold of a limb and swam out—she sank. Pa didn't do so bad. I don't reckon you can hold it against a man for gettin' choked on a piece of bear meat. By jingos, boy, you can't hold that against a man, especially since he killed that bear with his own hands wingin' an axe."

"No," I said, "you cain't."

Photo by Gene Peach.

"You're right, boy."

We cut across a pasture looking for a place to hide the horses for a couple of days. The nearest house was about a half mile away, and we had to get out of its sight.

"Looky there!"

"What?" I said.

"A rat's den!"

It was a whopper—three feet high and six or eight feet in width and length—made up of broken mesquite limbs, thorns, bear-grass leaves, and cowchips, with numerous holes woven in and out.

"Rats!" he screamed into the air, throwing his long arms up as if seeking the help of the Almighty. "Rats! Rats! Rats! Oh gracious and powerful Lord give me the strength to wage battle against these vilest of creatures. Pass on to me a small portion of your power so that I may stand strong and brave through the conflict about to come upon us. Lend me some of your skill and eternal magic while I slay the carnal beasts. Guide and protect this innocent young man as he follows forth the bugle's glorious call."

I was getting boogered and looked all around to see what might be fixing to tear us in pieces when he jumped from his horse and handed me the reins.

"Here, boy, this is your duty. Hold the mounts that we may yet escape to wage war another day."

He raced to the large pile of trash and put a match to it. A lazy rope of smoke rose, then burst into flames. Boggs had secured a long, heavy mesquite limb and he had it drawn back in a violent gesture.

"Ah, you four-legged offspring of the devil, I have turned your own fire and brimstone against you. Seek ye now the world of the righteous."

Well, they started seeking it. Rats were fleeing the burning nest in every direction. Boggs was screaming and striking with fury. Dead rats soon covered the ground.

"There, pestilence!" he shouted as he bashed one to a pulp. "Die, evil creature of the deep. Return to your ancestor's wicked bones. Bring the black death into the world will you? Destroyer of man, his food, of his life. Die, rats, die!"

When he could find nothing else to strike at he turned to me breathing heavily, still waving the stick.

"Rats have killed more people than all the wars combined. Did you know that, boy?"

I shook my head "no," trying to quiet the nervous horses.

"Well, they have. They are man's one mortal enemy. They live off man's labor, off his love for other things. They can't survive without man. It's a battle to the great and final death. People shouldn't fight people, they should fight rats. Here, give me my horse."

He dropped his stick on the dying fire and mounted.

"We better get out of here," I said. "That smoke will draw some attention."

"Just the opposite, if it's gone unnoticed till now, we'll be safe in pasturing our horses here. Let's git goin'."

I was in such bad shape after the last few minutes of action that I just rode obediently along and helped gather our horses. It was almost night, and that same old weakness of all day without food was upon me. It never seemed to bother Boggs, or at least it didn't show. He rammed a plug of tobacco in his mouth and chewed on it awhile. He seemed to be studying hard.

Turning to me all of a sudden, he spoke. "Boy, I'm takin' you out for a steak dinner."

"We ain't got any money."

"That's right, boy."

"Well?"

"Don't ask so many questions. Would you like a steak dinner? It's too late to catch a rabbit."

"Yeees," I said meekly.

Ropesville, Texas, had two tin cotton gins standing huge and sightless like blind elephants. The cotton lint from the ginning last fall still hung in dirty brown wads from the phone and light wires and in the weeds and grass around the town. It was a small place, maybe a thousand or twelve hundred people in and around the town. But it was a big town to me this night.

We tied our horses in a vacant lot off the main street. I was scared plumb silly. I had no idea how Boggs was going to get us a steak dinner without stealing it. And I just couldn't figger any way to steal it without a gun.

We marched right around to the first restaurant we came to, stepped in, and got us a table.

A woman came over smiling like she meant it and said, "Good evening."

"Evenin', ma'am," said Boggs.

"A menu?"

"It's not necessary. My pardner and I desire one of your finest chicken-fried steaks."

There wasn't any use ordering any other kind of steak in the backwoods of West Texas in those days. They all served the one kind.

"Would you kindly put a little dab of mayonnaise on our salad? And pie? What kind of pie you want, boy?"

"Apple?"

"Apple for me, too, ma'am."

"Coffee?"

"Coffee for me and orange soda pop for the young'un."

"All right." And she went away writing.

In a little bit there was a whole table load of stuff. I stuck my fork in the steak and sawed my knife back and forth. I put a great big bite into my mouth. Whoooeee! Was it ever good. Before I hardly got it swallowed, I took a big bite of the mashed potatoes on the plate and another of salad. Then when I got my mouth so full I could hardly chew, I'd wash it down with a big pull of orange pop. Great goin'! For a minute I quit worrying about how we'd pay for it.

The time came to face up to it. Boggs was finished, and so was I. The lady came over and asked if there'd be anything else.

Boggs said, "Another soda pop, coffee, and the check please."

Well, I drank on that soda and watched Boggs. I'd been scared plenty on this trip already, but he was really headed for the deep end now. Every once in a while he'd grab out in the air like he was crazy. Then I saw him put his hand over his coffee cup like he was dropping sugar in it. But the sugar was in a bowl.

All of a sudden he straightened up and said seriously, "Lady. Lady, come here."

The lady walked over smiling. Boggs pointed silently into his coffee cup. She looked. The smile crept off her face.

"I . . . I . . . I'll get you another cup."

"Lady," Boggs said under his breath, "I don't want any more coffee—that ecstasy has been denied me now and probably forever. One of the true pleasures of life will now raise only a ghastly memory to my mind at every thought. I feel I should bring suit against this café." Boggs rose now and so did his voice.

The other customers had stopped eating and the woman ran to a man behind the counter. He looked up, listened, and walked over to our table.

"Please, please," he said. "Just quiet down and leave. I'll take care of the check."

Boggs stood a minute with his gleaming blue eye on the man. "Very well," he said, standing there with his head thrown back, "but you haven't heard the last of this yet. Boy, let's git goin'."

As I walked around the table, I leaned over just a minute and looked in the coffee cup. There were two big, fat flies in there, and only one had drowned.

•   •   •

Boggs woke me up, praying. I'd slept late for once; it was nearly noon. All we had to do this day was feed and water ourselves. It didn't sound like much, but it could turn into quite a chore. Anyway, I heard this voice talking on. I raised up in the blankets and tried to rub my eyes open.

"Lord, now listen to me close. We're goin' to be in the land of plows and man-planted things for over eighty miles now. It's goin' to get harder and harder to live off the land. We made a promise, me and Dan, to deliver these fine horses on time and in good shape. We got to keep that promise one way or the other, Lord. All I ask of you is to help me think. And listen, Lord, if I mess up, which being one of those so-called human bein's I'm liable to do, I want you to know I ain't blamin' it on you. Amen, Lord." Then looking over his shoulder at me he said, "Mornin', boy. It's a great day. Care for a cup of coffee?"

"Uh-huh." I looked at it to see if there were any flies in it.

Then he said, "When you finish, let's go to town."

I swallered. We went.

We were riding along the highway when he spotted a big piece of cardboard leaning against a fence. He got down and cut out a couple of eight-inch squares. Then, with a stubby pencil he wrote on one: I'M DEAF AND DUMB. This one he hung around my neck. On the other he wrote: I'M BLIND. This one was his. I didn't need any explanations this time to figure out what we were fixing to pull.

He took off his glasses and put on a pair of dark ones he had in his canvas bag. He put his floppy old hat in the bib of his overalls, pulled his yellow hair down over his forehead, and rubbed some dust on his right eyelid. When he closed it, it looked sunken like his blind one.

We tied our horses in the same alley and started down the street carrying a large tomato can he got from the bar ditch.

"Now, boy, if anybody tries to talk to you just shake your head and make Indian sign language."

"I don't know any Indian sign language."

"They ain't nobody goin' to know the difference. Here, boy, hold my hand. Cain't you see I'm blind?"

I took his hand and walked into the lobby of the town's only hotel. I held the tomato can out in front. An old lady put down the newspaper she was reading, reached in her purse and dropped fifteen cents in the can. She rubbed me on the head saying, "What a pity."

I blinked my eyes real hard for her.

The man at the desk gave me a dime, and on our way out a man and his wife stopped and watched us. The man fetched a nickel out of his pocket, but his wife glared and gouged him in the ribs with her elbow. He came up with fifty cents this time.

The drugstore was next. We left there with nearly two dollars. Boggs dragged his feet along, not only looking blind, but acting like it. The grocery store was good for eighty-five cents. Then a garage for forty. A little girl with a nickel in her hand kept following us around from place to place, running out in front once in a while to stare at us. All of a sudden she ran up and dropped the nickel in the can and gave me a kiss. If my knees had been trembling before, they were going in circles now. Boy, I sure wished I had time to get to know a girl who would give up a bar of candy and a kiss for a dumb boy—and a stranger at that.

We made it on down to a red brick building at the end of the street. There was a bank and a dry-goods store. The bank was closed but the dry-goods was worth ninety-five cents. By the time we'd covered the entire north side of the street, we had fourteen dollars and sixty-three cents. We went into the alley to count it.

"By jingos, we're rich," I said. "I ain't *never* seen so much money."

Boggs smiled clean around his face. "I used to make this much in a day when I was panning gold in Arizona."

"How come you left?"

"The gold was gone."

"*All* gone?"

"Hell's fire, no, boy, not all of it, just all of it in this one spot. I'm goin' back some day. Besides, I decided to try to find my gold already coined in the form of buried treasure. So I left Arizona and went treasure huntin' up at Taos, New Mexico. You ever been up there, boy? Course you ain't. I keep forgettin' you ain't been out of West Texas. Well, Taos is one of them adobe towns full of Mexicans, Indians, gringos, and nutty artists. A feller had sold me this treasure map and told me to look up a *bruja*. You know what that is? Course you don't. Well, it's sort of fortuneteller and witch combined."

He gave that tomato can full of money a good rattle and went on, "Well, I found her. Yessir, by jingos, I found her all right, and she said the map was true and the treasure was buried there, but a lady had built a house over it. So we went to this lady and she said she could tell by the map her bedroom was right smack over the treasure, and if we'd split we could tear up the floor and dig it up. Well, I tore up the floor. The bruja said, 'Dig there,' and I dug. I had dirt piled all over the place. Pretty soon the bruja said, 'The devils are at work and they have caused us to dig in the wrong place.' Well, sir, she grabbed a poker hanging by the fireplace and rammed it about three inches into the dry, hard ground and said, 'There! There it is!' Hell's fire, I stood right there and pulled on that poker, trying to get it out of the way so I could dig. And the harder I pulled, the deeper in the ground it went. When it went out of sight, I naturally couldn't hold on any longer. Now, I ain't the kind of feller to scare easy, but I broke into a run, and I ain't been back to that insane town since! Ain't hunted much treasure either."

"What about the floor?" I asked.

"I never did write to find out."

He would have gone on for two hours telling me yarns, but I suddenly remembered how hungry I was so I said, "Let's go over to the café and buy us a big dinner. I'm starvin'."

"Now there you go, not thinkin' again. We just can't go in there like this. If they catch us faking this blind act, to jail we go. Come here," he said, and ducked my head under a water faucet and washed me off. Then he pulled out a dirty comb and slicked my hair back. "Take off your shirt and turn it wrong side out. Now," he said, "you can go over to the store and get us some grub. Hell's fire, you look just like the mayor's son. I don't hardly know you myself."

He handed me a list and I walked over to the store. I got cheese and crackers, a loaf of bread, and four cans of sardines for tonight. Then I got us another big bag of those dried apricots and a slab of cured bacon. We could take these along with us and they wouldn't spoil. Besides, we had lots of money left. I went all the way and bought Boggs two new plugs of tobacco and me a Hershey bar.

We rode out to our camp that night with Boggs singing "When the Saints Go Marching Off," just chewing and spitting between notes.

• • •

The next day we just loafed around and watched the horses graze. It was the first time we'd been sure of eating for over one day at a time.

Boggs said, "Boy, you ain't wrote a line to your mother since we've been gone."

"She don't expect me to."

"That's right, boy, she don't. But that ain't keepin' her from hopin'. Now is it?"

"I reckon not," I said, getting scared again.

Boggs tore a piece of brown sack up and handed it to me along with a stub of pencil.

"I ain't never wrote a letter home," I said.

"Might as well start now," he said. "It ain't much work and it'll do your ma a lot of good. It'll even make *you* feel better. You can drop it in the mail when we ride through Ropesville."

Well, I was out of arguments with this man Boggs, so I wrote my first letter home.

Dear Ma,

I'm sending this letter just to you cause I expect Pa is gone off somewhere on a deal. He generally is. How is old Blue and her pups. I sure hope we can keep the brindle one. He's going to make a real keen rabbit dog. I can tell because the roof of his mouth is black. That there is a sure sign.

Did the old red hen hatch her chicks yet? I hope she saves all of them so we'll have fried chicken this August.

Me and Boggs are making it just fine. Ever time he talks it's about something different. He kind of puzzles me.

Is the cow giving lots of milk? I bet her calf is fat. Are you going to try and can everything in the garden like you did last year? Don't work too hard on the garden or the canning either.

This man Boggs is a funny feller. Sometimes I think he's the smartest man in the world and sometimes I think he's the dumbest. Are you getting any sewing done? Don't worry about patching my overalls for school. I just plain know we're going to get into Oklahoma with all these horses and make us rich. The horses are looking better.

Love,

Your son Dan

There was no question now, the horses were putting on good solid meat. I could tell by looking, and I could tell by my sore hind end.

Ropesville had been good to us. We fed regular—regular for us, and the horses had done the same. Besides, we had some money in Boggs' pocket and some sowbelly and pork and beans in that pack. Things looked better all the time. That's what I was thinking about five miles out of Ropesville when I noticed the old gray horse throw his head back and stop. The horse in front of him had also stopped and was holding up one foot.

"Boggs," I yelled, "come here. Something's wrong with this bay horse."

Boggs reined back and we both dismounted. He picked up the forefoot and examined it. I could see it was a bad cut.

"He stepped on a piece of glass, looks like to me," Boggs said.

I walked back a few steps and sure enough there was a broken bottle.

"What do we do?" I asked, fearing what he'd tell me.

"There ain't a thing to do, boy. With the best of care this horse is going to be lame for a month or more. The frog is cut deep. We'll just have to leave him. I'll go up here to this farm and see what we can work out."

He was gone maybe ten minutes before he returned with a man. They both looked at the foot again.

Boggs said, "He's yours if you'll doctor him."

"I'll give it a try," the man said, looking worried.

"Now listen," Boggs said, "soon as you ease him up to the barn, throw some diluted kerosene on it. It might burn him a little but it'll take a lot of soreness out quick. Then make a poultice out of wagon grease and churn butter. The grease will keep the flies from getting to it and the butter will take out the fever."

"I'll give it a try," the man said again.

I wanted to say that my hind end could still use some of that butter, but I felt too bad about the horse. Now we were falling short on delivering the goods and we had a long way to go yet.

"Let's git goin', boy."

I rode along now feeling blue and upset. After a while I thought I might as well try to cheer myself up, so I started trying to guess what the fanciest present this side of the pearly gates would be. Maybe Boggs would get me a new hat. Or even better, a new pair of boots. I'd never had a new pair of boots—just old brogan shoes. It was a disgrace. Why, I'd be thirteen my next birthday. And that birthday was tomorrow, according to the calendar in the Ropesville café.

All of a sudden Boggs rode back. "Look there, boy, there's Lubbock."

"I was there once," I said, blowing up a mite. But I was really too little to remember. The tall buildings stuck up out of the plains so's you could see them for miles around. "Man that must be a big town."

"Naw, it ain't nothin', boy. You should see Denver, or San Francisco, or Mexico City."

"You been all them places?"

"Hell's fire, yes, and a lot more besides."

I still wasn't going to give up on Lubbock.

"How many people you reckon lives there?"

"Oh, maybe twenty-five thousand."

I whistled.

"See that building? The tallest one?"

"Yeah"

"Well, that's a hotel. I still got a suitcase in there. One time I was driftin' through here and went broke as a pullet bone. I figgered and figgered how to get out of that hotel without paying."

"You was thinkin'," I volunteered.

"By jingos, you're right, I sure was. Well I took a shirt and put all my other clothes, all my shaving equipment, and some crooked dice I happened to have with me, in this shirt. Then I tied it up in a bundle so's it would look like a bundle of dirty laundry. As I stepped out into the hall, one end of that shirt came open and dice and razors and all sorts of stuff fell right out on the floor. A porter and two maids just stood there—and stared while I gathered it all up and tied it back tight. That was where they let the hotel down. Before they could get to a service elevator to squeal on me, I was already down three flights of stairs and asking the desk man where the nearest laundry was. Well now, once ole Boggs got outside I was gone. That little Ford car just purred me right out of town."

"Ain't that cheatin', Boggs?"

"Why, Lord, no. What's the matter with you, boy? That's what you call tradin'. I left them a sure-enough good, empty two-dollar suitcase for a week's rent and feed."

The closer we got to Lubbock, the more my eyes bugged. It sure was a whopper. We skirted around the east side of town next to the Texas Tech campus. Boggs pulled up.

"Here's a nice little pasture to hole up in. I've got to get on into town and do a little shoppin'. You'll have to stay here with the horses, boy. Part of my shoppin' you wouldn't understand anyway."

Well, just as we were unloading the pack mule, we heard a truck coming. There were two men in it, and one of them said, "What the hell you think you're doin' turnin' a whole herd of horses in my pasture? I've a notion to impound 'em."

Well, my little, skinny heart was tearing my ribs out. That was all we needed to fail Papa completely.

"Why, my good sir," said Boggs, "let it be my pleasure to inform you kind gentlemen that we have merely paused a fleeting moment in our travels to relieve for an instant the burden of this fine pack mule. I am a preacher of the gospel. Myself and my young apprentice are heading north—our eventual destiny to be deepest Alaska. There we intend to bring about a revival of the Eskimos that will shake the northern world. Our horses we shall trade for reindeer upon our arrival. There are some things a reindeer can do that are beyond the capabilities of the American horse. Suffice it to say that with another moment's kind indulgence we shall wend our way over the great horizon to far distant shores."

One of the men just stared puzzled, the other one said, "Well, I don't know about that."

"And what, my beloved fellow inhabitant of this celestial globe, can I inform you of?"

"Jist git out, that's all, jist git out." They drove away mumbling under their breaths.

"Well, we shall skirt on around town, my boy. There's a canyon full of grass to the north of town. Yellow House Canyon by name. We shall perhaps find a better sanctuary there."

I was wishing he would shut up that silly talk, and quit practicing on me. Hell's fire, I was ole Dan.

It took us another hour to skirt town, and sure enough there was a nice little canyon with lots of grass. We pulled up and pitched camp.

Boggs said, "Now get a good rest. There's plenty of grub for a change. I'll see you after a while." He rode off on a black, leading the pack mule. I had me a nice meal. Worried awhile about losing the horse and finally fell to sleep.

It was getting somewhere close to ten o'clock the next morning when I heard a heck of a yell. I looked up and there came Boggs down the other side of the canyon. He kept yelling and singing. And that mule was having a hard time keeping up with him. There was stuff hanging all over the pack.

"Happy Birthday, Dear Dan'l, Happy Birthday to You." He was really singing it out and swaying in the saddle till I was certain he'd fall off. He jumped off his horse and shook me by the hand so hard I thought he was going to unsocket my arm. He lifted the jug from the pack and said, "Here's to you, Dan'l, and a happy birthday it's goin' to be. I got no more earaches, Dan'l. Whooooopeee! Happy birthday to you!" He ran over to the pack and grabbed a secondhand No. 3 washtub. "Gather the wood, boy."

I knew better than to do anything else. But since the mesquite was thin here, I had a devil of a time keeping him supplied.

He dumped a ten-pound sack of flour in the tub. A five-pound sack of sugar followed. Then he threw in a can of baking powder, and I don't know what else. He wouldn't let me stay to watch. Said it was going to be a surprise. I watched for a minute from off a ways. He ran down to a little muddy spring with a rusty bucket and got some water. Then he stirred it all up with a mesquite limb.

Well, when I got back with my next load of wood, the fire was blazing under this tub, and he said, "Here's your surprise, boy. It's a chocolate cake. Now what boy on this earth ever had a chocolate birthday cake like that?"

I had to admit that I doubted if there had ever been such an event take place before. Well, I kept carrying the wood. And he threw it on the fire and stirred. After a while, the cake started rising. He kept shushing me to walk quiet.

"Hawww, boy, watch your step, you'll make this cake drop."

Well, I figger that nine hundred buffaloes could have stampeded right past and that cake would not have dropped. In fact it rose up in the air about eighteen inches above the rim of that tub and just ran out in all directions. Boggs had taken his earache medicine and bedded down.

For a while I thought I needed his help when it looked as if the cake would fill the canyon, but when it finally cooled and I took a bite I was real glad he was asleep. I choked for thirty minutes. After I got finished choking, I hauled most of it off and fed it to the magpies. I didn't want to hurt his feelings. I should have had some consideration though for the magpies, but in those days I was just a growing boy.

• • •

We worked our way north of Lubbock through country spotted with cotton fields, sorghum—thick and heavy leafed—and here and there the brown stubble rectangle of an oat patch already cut and stored. On past Plainview we got into some grassland again, and that's where something happened.

THE PRAIRIE. Author's collection.

We were moving out of a small draw through some cutbanks when the old, gray horse pulled out of line reaching for a special clump of grass. I reined over to the edge of the sharply sloping cutbank and yelled "Haaarr" at him. Just as I did, my horse bolted to the side and I went down hard against the ground. I was sort of off balance laying on the slope of the cutbank. I reached up to get hold of a thick clump of grass to raise myself, when I heard the rattle. The snake lay coiled on a level patch. That's what had boogered my horse.

We looked each other right in the eye. I strained my left arm where I held the grass clump. The snake struck out right at my head, but he was short an inch or two. Now, I *was* in a fix. I could tell the grass roots would give way if I put any more weight on them. If they did, I'd slide right on top of the snake.

His little black eyes looked at me over his darting tongue, and suddenly they seemed as big as light bulbs. And that forked tongue popping in and out was nothing to make me happier. I could feel the sweat all over, and a ringing in my head. For a minute I nearly fainted. Then, for some reason, I thought of Papa and how he was depending on me. If I panicked and got snake-bit, the whole thing would be blown up. Everybody's hopes would be done in. But I didn't know what to do. If Boggs just knew, but of course, he couldn't. He couldn't see me. I'd just have to hold on as long as I could, and maybe the snake would go away. It wasn't advancing, but it wasn't backing up either. It just lay there coiled, its head in striking position, shaking those rattlers a hundred miles a minute. I kept feeling like I was sliding right into those fangs. I couldn't move, but just the same I pressured my belly into the dirt hoping to hold.

Then I heard the voice coming, easy and sure. "Don't move, Dan boy. Boy, you hear me, don't you? Well, keep still now. Just a little longer, boy."

I didn't even twitch an eyeball. I saw him crawl into my range of vision. He had a stick held out in front of him and he was kind of humming the same note over and over and twisting the end of the stick in a slow circle. Closer, closer, hum, hum. The stick circled near the snake's arched neck. Nothing but the tongue and the rattles moved now. Then the head shot out, and Boggs scooped the snake onto the end of the stick and hurled him way down to the bottom of the draw.

I was paralyzed another moment. Then I leaped up screaming, "Kill him! Kill him, Boggs!"

Boggs sat down beside me, and said, "Now, just calm down, boy. You're fine and the snake's fine."

"Ain't you goin' to kill him?"

"Lord a Mercy, no, I ain't goin' to kill him. Why, that poor old snakes in the same war we are."

"War?"

"Sure enough, boy, he's fightin' those pack rats harder'n we are."

I forgot all about the loss of the horse, and when I found out that Amarillo was a bigger town than Lubbock, even forgot about the rattlesnake for awhile.

I did wish I could go uptown and see all the sights, but Boggs said that would come for me soon enough; besides, we had to stay on the march and take care of our horses now.

• • •

Between the towns of Amarillo and Dumas, Texas, runs the Canadian River. We drove our horses along the highway until we spotted the long, narrow cement bridge crossing it.

Boggs threw up his hand and stopped the horses. He rode back to talk to me.

"I don't believe we better try to take the horses across the bridge. We're goin' to block too much traffic. And besides, we've got to have a permit, as well as the highway patrol to watch both ends. It's too late to get either now. We only have one choice, boy; that's bend the horses back to a gate and ride east down the river till we find a crossing."

This we proceeded to do.

I could see the storm sweeping toward us from the west and north. It must have been over a hundred miles in width. We had to cross the Canadian before it hit. This river is nothing to play with. It is full of quicksand and bogholes, and when it rains heavily to the west a front of water drops down out of New Mexico and West Texas with great force and speed.

Most of the time, though, the Canadian is a quiet river. Many places in its bed are as wide as the Mississippi, but during dry spells only a few small, red, muddy streams trickle through its bottom. Cottonwoods break the treeless plain along its banks, and cattle come to water from it for hundreds of miles up and down the river. Wild turkey, quail, coyotes, antelopes, and many other kinds of wild game love the Canadian. But to man, it is always treacherous.

For ten or twelve miles on each side are the sand hills—thousands upon thousands of tiny, rough, ever-changing hills of sand—spotted with sage, shinnery, mesquite, and yucca. The yucca was green now, and the pods were soon to open their beautiful, milk-white blooms.

We rode hard, pushing the horses through and around over the sand. The old gray could only be moved so fast, so that I was constantly having to yell and crowd the poor thing. But he did his best for me.

There was no sun as the huge cloud blanket moved on toward us and shadowed the land. The lightning was cracking so fast now that the thunder was a continuous roar, never letting up but varying its sound like rolling waves. Even without the sun it was hot—sure enough hot. The horses were lathered white. And my almost healed-over hind end was sweated to the back of my mount. The Canadian looked fifty miles wide to me but was actually only about three-eighths where Boggs finally chose to cross.

I crowded the old gray down into the clay and sand of the bottom. There were tracks where a cowboy had crossed here. The forefront of the storm clouds was moving up over us now. I kept glancing up the river, fearing that wall of water I knew had to be moving upon us from the west. The wind was intense and the horses' manes and tails blew out almost parallel with the ground. We struck a few shallow bog-holes where our mounts went through to the hard clay underneath.

Way up the river bottom I could see the rain reaching out into the banks, and I knew a head of water was racing right along with the storm. I saw a small tornado drop down out of the sky for the ground and then return like a hand reaching out of a shawl to pick up something. Several writhing snakes of cloud broke loose in torment. I could hear the roar of the rain above the thunder now and its chorus—the river.

I almost panicked and left the old, gray horse. More than anything I wanted to get out of the river bottom and up to the banks above the cottonwoods. Even if there was a tornado there. And there *was* one just beyond. I could see the inverted funnel ripping at the earth. Black. Mad.

Now we were on a huge sandbar that carried all the way to the bank. There was no turning back. There was no detour. Underneath the slight crust of its top was quicksand. Deep and deadly. The sand shook and quivered like Jello. The bank was nearer now.

The old gray stumbled and the extra force against the ground broke the crust. He went in up to his belly. I rode up beside him and pulled at his mane. My horse was sweated and excited and almost jumped out from under me. For a moment I thought the quicksand would get him. The more I pulled, the more the old gray fought, the deeper he sank. I was crying and begging the old horse now. And it wasn't just because it meant another loss to Papa, but it was a loss to me. He was my friend, this old horse.

And then I heard Boggs. He was riding back across the bar. "Git, boy! Look!"

I saw the terrible churning wall of dirty, red water racing at us. He slapped me hard up the side of my head and said, "Ride!"

I rode on by the old gray, and I saw his nostrils almost tearing his face. His eyes rolled back as he sunk to his withers. In his eyes there was an acceptance along with the terror.

We rode up on the bank as the rain hit us harder and the edge of the tornado squalled on by. I got one glimpse of the old gray straining to throw his head above the river's blood, and then he was gone.

It rained for two hours, and then the sun came out. We were very cold and very wet. It didn't even bother me. The river would be up all night. We gathered our horses and moved on across the sand hills. I didn't look back.

· · ·

I had a numb feeling as we rode along. We were getting into the last stages of our drive, and we were two horses short. It was just plain awful to let Papa down. I was sick thinking about it. We reached the edge of Dumas, Texas, on a Sunday. We knew that was the day, for the churches were filled with singing and shouting. I watched Boggs up ahead. I could almost see him quiver, he wanted to get in there and go to preaching so bad. He raised his hand and stopped the horses. They milled about and started grazing on somebody's lawn.

He rode back to me. "Boy," he said, "it's takin' all my willpower to stay out of that church. I'd like to go in and talk that reverend into ten minutes with Boggs. There's a lot of sinners in there and they think they're saved, but ten minutes later I'd have 'em lined up and headin' for a baptizin'."

It sounded like he wanted me to say "Go ahead." So I said, "I'll watch the horses, Boggs, if you want to go in."

"That's a magnanimous gesture, boy, but I reckon we've got to do somethin' about replenishin' this herd of horses. We just cain't let your papa down. And besides, your ma is staying back there worrying herself sick about the mortgages and all that. Now the way I got it figgered is this: these little West Texas towns all have baseball teams. Today is bound to be Sunday. There'll be a ball game around here somewhere."

Well, he was right. We found the baseball grounds out on the edge of town in a big opening. We turned our horses loose on the grass and rode over where a man was dragging the field down with a tractor and scraper.

"Yes, sir, there's going to be a ball game," he said, taking a chew of the tobacco Boggs offered him. "Spearman, Texas, will be here in just a little while. They've got a good team, but we've got a better one."

"Is that so?" Boggs said. "What kind of pitchers you got?"

"One good 'un, and one bad 'un."

"Sounds about right."

I was sure puzzled about Boggs' interest in baseball, but since we were going to graze the horses awhile we might as well have a little fun watching a baseball game.

The crowd began to gather early. They came by truck, car, wagon, and horseback. The teams began to warm-up their pitchers, and everybody was getting excited. Seems like this was an old rivalry.

I followed Boggs around till he found the manager of the Spearman team. This man also chewed tobacco, but when Boggs offered him a chew he reared back and looked out over his monstrous cornfed belly and said, "That ain't my brand."

Boggs said, "How much would it be worth to you to win this game?"

"Well in money, not much. I only got five dollars bet on it. But in personal satisfaction, my friend, it would be a strain for a millionaire to pay off."

I could tell the way he talked they were going to get along.

"Did you ever hear of Booger Boggs who played for the East Texas League?" Boggs asked.

"Sure. Everybody's heard of Booger Boggs. Why?"

"That's me."

"Ahhhh," and he started laughing and laughing. "You're jist a farmhand. Maybe a bronc rider, by the looks of them legs."

Boggs was quiet for once. He let the manager finish out his laugh then he said, "Can you catch a ball?"

"Sure. I *am* the Spearman catcher."

"Well, go get your mitt and get me a glove and ball, my dear associate."

While the unbelieving fat man went after the equipment, Boggs started warming up his arm, swinging it around and around.

"Now, son," he said to me, and I knew he was really going to get serious because of the "son" bit, "this old arm ain't in much shape and it'll never be any good after today, but I just want you to know I'm going to give 'er all I got."

"You goin' to pitch?"

"You just wait and see."

He threw a few soft ones at the manager, and then he let one fly that purty near tore the catcher's arm off. I knew he was going to get his chance. He went around and started a few conversations.

"You folks from Dumas don't know when you're beat. I'm goin' to sack you boys out today." As usual, when they looked at Boggs everybody just laughed and laughed. That's what he wanted them to do.

One of the sporting boys said, "If you're goin' to pitch, like to lay a little money on the line. Now, if you ain't just a blowhard, why don't you put your money where your mouth is?"

"Well now, I ain't got no money, my dear compatriots, but I've got something better," and he swept a long arm at our horses grazing off a ways. "I'll bet any four of that fine bunch against any two of yours."

One man got so carried away he said, "I'll bet my good wagon and team with the grain and laying mash that's in it and a box of groceries to boot."

That was the only bet Boggs called. They shook hands and had plenty of witnesses.

The game started. I watched Boggs fan three Dumas men in a row. Then Spearman got a man on base. The next two up for our side struck out and the Dumas catcher threw our man out trying to steal second, then Boggs fanned another and two grounded out to shortstop. And right on into the sixth inning scoreless. Then I could tell Boggs' arm was weakening. A Dumas batter swatted a long, high fly that should have been an easy out in left field. The fielder just plain dropped it. The man scored standing up.

Well, Boggs took off his glasses, pulled out his shirttail, and went to cleaning that lens. He took his time about it. Everybody was wondering what difference it could make if he cleaned a glass that fit over a blind eye. So did I.

The Dumas fans were naturally rawhiding him quite a bit, and the Spearman team was getting uneasy. I watched him closely. He was up to something. I knew that no matter what Boggs was, I'd never see another anywhere like him. Come to think of it, that's a whole bunch to say about any man. He was at *least* three different men and maybe a dozen.

When he got through cleaning his glasses, he slowly put them back on. Then he took off his hat and his glove and held the ball high in the air. And he shouted so that everybody quieted down.

"Lord, up there in the great universe, heed my call. Lord, I'm goin' to ask you to put some devil on this ball. Just let me use him a little. I want a devil curve and a devil drop and a devil fast ball, and I'll guarantee you that the end of the game will belong to you, Lord. What I want is victory. Now I know you heard me, Your Honor, Lord. So it's up to me. And if I don't win this game, bring a bolt of lightning down upon my unworthy head and burn me to a cinder. Amen and thanks."

I looked up in the cloudless sky and thought that even the Lord would have to strain to get lightning out of that blue sky.

He pulled his hat back on tight, picked up the glove and ball, squinted out of that glassless rim, took a big spit of tobacco, and let fly. No matter what happened in this game, it was quite a sight to see him pitch. Those runover high-heeled boots, bib overalls, and that old, floppy hat sure were different, to say just a little.

That ball whistled in there so solid and fast the batter fell down hitting at it. Boggs didn't waste any time now, just wound up once and let fly. The ball broke in a curve, and the batter nearly broke his neck fishing for it. The next one was a drop—breaking sharp and clean. The umpire yelled, "Strike!" and thumbed him out. A great roar went up from the Spearman rooters.

After that, it was a walk-over. Boggs had shot his wad on those three pitches. He was faking his way now. The spirit of the home team was broken. The Spearman players started a seventh-inning rally, and the way they batted I could have been pitching for them and they would have won.

The game wound up nine to one and we had us a team of horses, one of which was a mare with a colt by her side, a wagon, a lot of feed, plus a big box of groceries.

Boggs was carrying his arm at his side. It was obvious he'd never pitch again, not even for fun.

. . .

When we headed out of Dumas the next day, I was sure a happy kid. As soon as Boggs was up ahead where he couldn't see, I just plain let loose and bawled. After that I felt fine.

Now our only problem, if we were lucky, was the time. We were a half day behind. At the same time, we couldn't push the horses too hard or it would gaunt them and the buyers wouldn't pay enough. I drove our wagon with my saddle horse tied behind. We'd taken the pack off the mule and so we all moved out pretty good.

Wheat country sprung up all around now. The plowed fields contrasted to the rich green of the sorghum. There was a zillion miles of sky all around. The farms and ranches looked peaceful and prosperous, but every little bit I could see where the drought still showed its fangs—fences buried beneath drifting sand, fields barren and cut to clay beds. But this new idea of contour plowing, so the land wouldn't wash, was sure enough helping. I didn't like to remember the dust that came and choked and killed and desecrated the land like the earth had suddenly turned to brown sugar. I liked to think about the green, growing things. But I was young and I know I'd never have appreciated the wet years without the dry ones.

Night and day became almost the same. We didn't sleep or stop much, and when we pulled into Stratford, Texas, in the upper Panhandle we were dead tired. We camped about four or five miles from town. It was so thinly populated we could see only one farmhouse close by.

We ate, turned the horses loose to graze, all except the one we left tied to the wagon eating grain, and went to sleep.

As usual Boggs was up before the sun. "Go drive the horses over close while I fix breakfast. That way we'll save a few minutes."

I saddled up and rode out through the mesquite. I was surprised the horses weren't nearby because the grass was good everywhere and they like to stay fairly close to the grain. I tracked them a ways and blamed if they hadn't walked right up to this farmhouse. There they all were in a corral. I felt a hurt come in my belly. A hurt of fear. Those horses durn sure hadn't penned themselves, and we were on somebody's private land. I didn't have long to wait, before I found out whose.

80

He sat on a big plow horse holding a shotgun, and spoke in a mean voice, "Thought you'd be around directly. Well now, boy, where's your pa?"

"At Guymon, Oklahoma."

"Guymon, huh? Well now, ain't that interestin'. What's he doin' off up there?"

"Waitin' for me," I said, swallering and feeling the tears start to burn. I choked them back.

"Who's helpin' you with these?" He motioned the shotgun at the horses. He was a short man but broad and big-bellied. He wore a tiny hat that just barely sat on top of his head, and his mouth hung loose around his fat face. I couldn't see his eyes, just holes in the fat where they were.

"I reckon you know you were trespassin'?"

"Yes, sir."

"Well, cain't you read?"

"Yes, sir."

"Well, then how come you didn't heed my 'posted' sign?"

"Didn't see it."

"Well"—he started nearly every sentence with "well"—"I'll tell you one thing, young man, you'll look the next time you come around my place. You got any money?"

"No, sir."

"Well, now ain't that too bad. I'm just going to have to ride into town, get the marshal, and we'll have to have a sale to justify the damage to my land. Five dollars a head, that's the law. If you cain't pay, I take the horses."

"But we ain't got anything else, no way to live . . ."

He interrupted, "Well, you should've been thinkin' about that when you rode on my place and started destroying my grass.

"Please."

"Too late for that, sonny."

I had to stall for time. I said, "Look, mister, I know you're goin' to take my horses, but first, before we go, could I have a drink of water?"

"Ain't no harm in that," he said. "But hurry it up. I ain't got all day."

I went over to the horse trough and drank just as long as I could. I thought I saw something moving out near our camp.

"Hurry it up, sonny. Get on your horse and let's go."

I walked up to my horse and picked his hind foot up. I glanced under his belly and I could see Boggs snaking along from one yucca clump to another, and it sure looked like he was *eating* yucca blooms. The damn fool was going to get himself shot sneaking up this way. My horse heard him and pitched his ears in that direction.

"Here, sonny, what you doin'? That horse ain't lame. Now get up on there before I give you a load of this here buckshot."

I got up on my horse just as Boggs raised up and broke into a wild, arm-waving, screaming run right for us. The froth was streaming out both sides of his mouth. His one eye gleamed right at us just like a wild man's.

That horse under that man with the shotgun just snorted and jumped right straight up in the air. When his hoofs hit the ground, there wasn't anybody on his back. That feller came down hard and the shotgun blew both barrels. The horses and mules broke out of the corral and ran back toward our camp snorting and blowing to beat seventy-five.

I finally got my horse calmed down, and when I did, I saw Boggs sitting on top of the feller who once had a shotgun. He reached over and tapped him up beside the head with a rock. The man slept. Boggs got some rope from the barn and tied him up.

"Go round up the horses," he said, as he stuffed the man's mouth full of shirttail.

I soon had them cornered, and tempting them with a little oats in a bucket, I made them follow me over to the wagon. By then Boggs was back. We caught our team, hooked them up, and got the hell out of the country as fast as we could.

We rode on now through the day and into the night, and then again. We let the horses have twelve hours on grass and a big bait of grain just before we crossed the state line into the Oklahoma Panhandle. The last lap now.

This strip had once belonged to Texas until around 1850, when they sold it to the United States as part of the territory including New Mexico, Colorado, Wyoming, and Kansas. It had been known as the "strip" and "no man's land" until 1890 when the strip was made a part of the Oklahoma Territory.

It was part of the Great Plains we'd just come across. These vast regions shot northward all the way through the Dakotas, Montana, and into Canada. My hind end felt like we had covered our part of it.

Late in the afternoon of the next day we spotted Guymon. We unrolled the map out of the oilcloth wrapper and studied it.

"The sale is tomorrow at noon," Boggs said. "That means we need these horses in there at ten o'clock like your pappy said. The buyers like to look before the biddin' starts."

"We're late," I said, feeling cold and weak.

"No, sir, we turn up here about a mile and then it's nine more northeast from there. If we ride way in the night, we can make it."

"But the horses'll be gaunted down."

"No, we'll feed them a good bait of grain and give them till eight in the morning to graze. If we find grass where we stop, we'll be all right."

"If we don't?"

"Like I said, son, there's risks in everything. That's where the fun comes in life."

"Let's git goin'," I said.

We pushed the horses on. They didn't like it and kept trying to graze in the bar ditches of the country lanes. We made them move. I left it up to Boggs to lead, hoping hard he was going in the right direction. For a long time we could see the orange light of the farmhouses sprinkled off across the prairie, and once in a while a car light moved in the night. Then all the lights were gone except those of the stars and a half moon. It was enough. I nearly went to sleep several times, but I'd wake up just before falling off the wagon. It seemed like we'd ridden a hundred years to me. My body was still working but my mind had long ago gone numb.

Then there was Boggs. "Take a nap, son. There's plenty of grass for the horses right along the road. I'll stay up and watch 'em."

I crawled in the wagon bed, fully intending to sleep an hour or so and then relieve Boggs. It didn't work like that. The sun was up and warm when he woke me.

"Get up, boy, and let's have another look at the map."

I raised up, fumbling sleepily for it.

"Here it is!" he cried. "Here it is! Look, two dry lake beds, then take the first turn to the left for one mile. Look—" He pointed up ahead and there were two dry lake beds. A tingling came over me. Boggs handed me a cup of coffee and said, "Just a minute and I'll fix you some bacon."

"Don't want any."

"Let's git goin', Dan boy," he said, grinning all over.

It took us a while to get hooked up and on the move. The colt bounced saucily beside the wagon. The horses were full and although they weren't fat, they had lots of good, solid meat on them. They were strong, tough, and so was I. I was burned brown as a Comanche warrior, and my hind end had turned to iron.

Papa saw us coming and headed down to meet us in his old Ford. He jumped out and said, "Howdy, fellers. Why look at Dan. Boy, you've growed a whole nickel's worth. Have any trouble Boggs?"

"No, sir, not a bit."

I didn't tell Papa any different. Besides, he had such faith in us he didn't count the horses. If he had, he'd have found there was one extra.

The sale went over big for us. Uncle Jock really got his best chant going. When it was all over, Papa had cleared over twenty dollars a head on the horses and nearly thirty on the mules. Ma could rest easy and go ahead and plan her garden for the next spring. Papa gave me three whole dollars to spend just any way I pleased.

Soon as we got home, I went over to Humble City, to drink a few orange sodapops and get my present from Boggs. He didn't show up the first day and he didn't show up for a whole week. I was getting a trifle worried, but figured maybe he'd had to go plumb up to Lubbock to find me the new pair of boots. I'd made up my mind that's what he'd give me for using my saddle.

Well, on the eighth day I ran into him coming out of Johnson's Grocery, and said, "Hi, Boggs."

"Well, howdy yourself, Dan. How've you been?"

"Fine," I said. "Did you get me the present you promised?"

"Just a minute, boy," he said, and walked back in the store. He came out with a nickel pecan bar. I took it. He said again, "Just a minute, boy," and went back in the store.

I figured he must be getting my present wrapped up pretty for me, so I hunkered down on the porch and started eating my candy bar. It sure was thoughtful of Boggs to feed me this candy while I was waiting. I'd eaten about half of it before I noticed the funny taste. I took a close look. That candy bar was full of worms. Live ones.

I got up and went in the store. I walked on toward the back figuring Boggs was behind the meat counter. Then I saw this table that said: ALL CANDY ON THIS TABLE PRICED ONE CENT. There were lots of those wormy pecan bars among them.

He wasn't at the meat counter and I asked, "Mr. Johnson, do you know where Boggs went?"

He said, "No, I don't. He walked out the back door."

Well it finally glimmered in my little brain what had happened. I got mad. Real mad. I got me a board, and I went all over town looking. I was going to knock his head clean off if I found him. It got dark. I waited at the back of the pool hall, looking through a window for him. I waited till it closed. I waited till the whole town closed. I was in such a rage, I nearly died.

I never found Boggs. In fact, I never saw him again. I don't know where he came from and I don't know where he drifted to. But by jingos, I sort of miss him. After all, he *was* my pardner.

CHAPTER FOUR

A Horse To Brag About

Published in Horse Tales Annual, *1972.*

I RECKON just about every human in the world that was raised on a cow ranch, worked as a cowboy, or just plain rode for pleasure knew and loved a horse like Old Snip. In the memory of us all there is one old pony that comes to mind more often than all the others. A horse to do a little braggin' about. That's the kind of horse Old Snip was.

The first time I saw the little stocking-legged, blazed-face, snip-nosed bay, a long-legged bronc stomper named Robert Ian was hanging the steel in his shoulders. It was in a big pole corral at Cow Springs, New Mexico, and the dust was fairly boiling from under Old Snip. He bucked hard, mighty hard, with long, ground-bustin', neck-poppin' jumps, straight ahead till he hit one side of the corral, then he turned and put out all he had till he hit the other side. He bucked straight just like he did everything else in his life. But that was the only time he ever bucked.

Gradually he slowed and then quit altogether. Robert Ian worked him in and out around the corral letting him get used to the weight on his back, the steel in his mouth, the rein on his neck, letting him know that these things wouldn't hurt him if he behaved himself. The little old pony caught on quick and by the fourth saddling, Robert Ian decided he'd turn him over to me. He said, "Here, boy, get your saddle on this here Old Snip. He's gentle as a loggin' horse."

I was just a gawky, freckle-faced kid hanging around the outfit wranglin' horses, patching fences, anything Robert Ian happened to think of that he thought I wouldn't mess up. Mainly I hung around to get a few square meals, listen to the tall yarns cowboys have a habit of spinning and maybe to learn a little something.

"You think he's broke gentle?" I asked, cautiously eyeing the bay.

"Why, boy," he said, "this here horse would do to go to preachin' on."

I saddled up, gathered the reins up tight in my left hand, grabbing the heavy black mane at the same time. I took hold of the saddle horn with my right and stuck my left knee in his shoulder, swung my right leg smoothly over his back, and Old Snip moved out with a nice running walk. Right away I breathed easy again. I've never known a horse to pick up a fast running walk that quick. He was a natural at it. A running walk will carry a cowboy a lot of miles in a day and bring him back without his tonsils shook loose. Sittin' up there on him I felt just as good as an old coat that a feller's worn a long time and hates to throw away. He was already beginning to rein. The least pressure and he turned smooth as new grass, just where you wanted him.

"Now, listen, boy," Robert Ian said when I came back, "I owe Ed Young twenty dollars and I promised him this here horse in payment." My heart turned mighty cold at these words for I thought he was giving the horse to me. "You been wanting to go over on that San Cristobal outfit and hunt arrowheads, ain't you?"

I said, "Yeah."

"All right, here's your chance. You can leave about daylight in the mornin' and you'll be at the Indian ruins right around ten. I'll make out a bill of sale from me to Ed," he added. "You can stay at the old line camp across from Long Draw tomorrow night and make it in to Ed's the next day."

"Yeah," I said, not liking the sound of that *bill of sale* business.

"Something else," Robert Ian said, "If you keep your mouth shut, listen hard and work like hell you might get a job with the San Cristobal outfit. A regular payin' job."

That last sounded good because all I'd got in the way of pay around there was a dollar Robert Ian gave me when we went to Santa Fe one time. That seemed like a lot of money then but I was a year older now and wanted to put on the dog a little.

Me and Old Snip were out on a piñon-crowded trail heading lickety-split for the San Cristobal ranch when the sun came up. Boy, it was a mighty fine morning. A bunch of deer jumped up out of some oak brush and went tearing up the hill. A coyote crossed our trail and the magpies started screaming. The bluejays flew from tree to tree.

By nine o'clock we crossed the highway between Cline's Corners and Lamy, New Mexico, and were well into the ranch property itself. The highway is fenced now, but then she was wide open. The August sun was warming up fast. I figured it was going to get hotter than blue blazes before noon. Sure enough it did. I didn't care though. Here I was mounted on a little animal that I figured the good Lord had made especially for me and I saw those sky-high, white and red bluffs sticking up like a bunch of cathedrals. I took the worn out catch rope Robert Ian had given me and tied Old Snip to a piñon tree with a knot that wouldn't slip and choke him later on if he got boogered at something. Then I started out across those ruins with my head down and my eyes peeled expecting any second to see a perfect arrowhead.

Some college feller told me years later that these ruins were five or six hundred years old. They were brand spanking new to me that day in August. You could still see the outlines of the sandstone houses built in a big square. Out in the middle was the round kiva—a sort of church for the Indians. Broken pottery with designs painted on them in real bright colors was scattered about everywhere. There were lots of broken arrowheads and pieces of flint all over.

Then I found what I'd been looking for, a great big perfect arrowhead made out of black glassy obsidian. Man! Chills ran all over me and I knew what a prospector must feel like when he pans a big gold nugget for the first time. I got to walking so fast trying to find another one that I probably stepped over several unseen. Boy, I had a pocket just smack full of flint pieces, arrowheads, and bright colored pottery.

Then I saw another one, white and small, a bird point. Just as I bent to pick it up I noticed a shadow spread across the ground around me. It was a cloud. As I straightened up I looked into the sky. There were lots of clouds, black and heavy with water. They hadn't begun to get together yet so I figured I had plenty of time to hunt.

Between the cathedrals and the line camp where I aimed to spend the night was a lot of barren, badly eroded ground and one deep-cut arroyo called Long Draw. Flash floods in the mountains caused these to fill with water and sometimes made crossing impossible. I was so wrapped up in what I was doing, I didn't pay the clouds much attention.

Then she hit—an earbustin' clap of thunder! I raised up quicklike and looked over to where Snip was tied. He was so wide-eyed you could see the white showing. It's not natural for a cow pony to get excited over a little rainstorm brewing. But when Old Snip looked over at me and blasted out with a long loud nicker, I figured it was time to leave. I still swear to this day that that horse was smarter than me and was just giving warning it was high time to drag out of there before it was too late. Sure enough it almost was.

Over to the east in the higher mountains, the clouds were having a family reunion and the more lively members were spitting out forked fire and deep down, rumbling noises. I could see the blue white sheets of rain pour out into the canyons and foothills. The storm was moving on out toward the flats and us, fastlike.

I buckled on my spurs, missing the hole with the buckle tongue a couple of times because I was getting a little excited. I untied Old Snip and mounted up. I leaned over in the saddle and away we went. Snip seemed to understand that the whole idea was to get across all that barren ground before the rain reached us. If it did, we might have to sleep out on this side of the arroyo all night without any shelter. He was really moving now, up and down . . . straining hard with his hindquarters on the upgrade and keeping his forelegs out in front on the downgrade.

We didn't quite make it. About a quarter of a mile out on the eroded flats, the rain caught us. I pulled up and took a look. There wasn't much to see, the rain was so heavy. As we moved out again I could feel the cold wetness already soaked through to the skin and the water running from the brim of my hat like it was coming off a tin roof.

Old Snip was beginning to slip and slide in the slick, muddy clay. We kept going just the same. I was so wet now I didn't feel the coldness so much. We finally made it to Long Draw. I reined down a gradual slope out into the gravel covered bottom. Water was running in little muddy rivers everywhere. Then all of a sudden I could see nothing but water. A solid stream of reddish, muddy churning water! We were in real trouble! The heavy rain up in the mountains was just now reaching this part of Long Draw.

Before I had time to think, the water swirled up around my boot heels. Then it hit, a great big wall of mud, water, piñon sticks, pine needles, and everything else that grows in the mountains. I dropped the reins and grabbed the saddle horn with both hands. My arms felt like they had been stretched out as long as a wagon tongue. I couldn't see and it felt like a whole ocean of water had spilled right on top of us. I knew for sure this was it. I wanted to do some praying but I couldn't get my mind on it for worrying about holding on to that saddle horn.

I began to strangle, and a lot of red, light, and black spaces seemed to jump out of my head. I got a big suck at a bunch of air. It was mighty wet air as far as that goes but there wasn't quite enough water in it to drown a feller. We went splashing under again, up and out, down and under, over and over. After this had gone on for what seemed like about two long years I happened to remember hearing one old cowboy say a horse could swim better if you hung onto his tail instead of the saddle horn. They are only about two yards apart, but getting from that horn to that tail wasn't any simple act.

I had to take the gamble. If I missed I was a gone dog and I knew it. I turned loose and grabbed! One hand caught tail hair! I was washed sideways and every other way. By this time I was sure there was as much water in me as there was out of me. Somehow I hung on and got hold with my other hand. Everything was muddy at this point, including my memory.

A long time later, at least it seemed a long time later, I noticed a horse's hind leg next to my face. I counted one, two, three, four horse's legs. Then I realized I was lying in the mud and Old Snip was standing there with his head down, his sides bellowing in and out, breathing hard. I didn't mind that old sticky mud. No, siree, not one bit. I rightly loved it. I got up and put my arm across that bay pony's neck. I didn't say anything. I didn't have to. I knew he understood.

We stayed all night over at the line camp. Even if we were hungry and a little cold I didn't mind and I hope Old Snip didn't.

The next day about noon I rode up to Ed Young's place and let out a yell. He walked out, or I should say a hat came out with him walking under it, because he wore the biggest hat I ever saw. It was a real, honest-to-goodness old-time cowboy hat.

I said, "Robert Ian sent you this here horse," and I handed him the bill of sale. The best eyes in the world couldn't have made out what that piece of paper said. That old Long Draw mud and water had seen to that. "Reckon you'll have to get him to make you out another one," I said, tickled plumb to death. I figured I still had a chance somehow to come up with the wherewithal to own Old Snip for my very own. I told Ed what had happened, then I said, "Say, Robert Ian said you might be needing a hand."

"I might," he said, looking at me with those gleaming blue eyes across that hawk-looking, humped-up nose. "What can you do, boy?" he asked pointblank.

"Hell," I said, "I can do anything."

Several weeks later I knew that this was not exactly the whole truth. I know now that I stayed on at Ed's in the beginning because I wanted to be with Old Snip, but later on I liked it all the way around. That evening I helped him feed the horses and milk the cows. After supper I got up and helped his wife with the dishes.

This set real good with Mother. All the cowboys in the country called her Mother Young because she was such a top-notch cook, doctor, and anything else a woman had to be to make a good wife and mother thirty miles from town right smack dab in the middle of all outdoors.

Ed had some good horses in his own right. He had broken broncs for the old Waggoner outfit in the early days and a lot of other big outfits, and he wouldn't have anything but good horses around him.

I got to ride and work with them all. There was Old Sut, a coal black twelve-year-old. You could ride him all day and he'd never even break a sweat. Then there was Flax, the golden-maned sorrel—a good range roping horse; Apache, the big hard-bucking paint; Raggedy Ann, the little brown mustang that Ed had roped and broke himself; and Fooler, a blaze-faced chestnut—Ed's favorite. When the cowboys spoke about Fooler they would always say, "That Fooler's quite a horse, yep, he's one hell of a horse."

But none of them compared with Old Snip. As time went on he just got better and better. You could ride him all day without wearing him out because of his fast easy gait. He reined like a regular cutting horse, quick, but smooth and easy. Boy, that stop he had! Those hind legs would slide way up under him with his forelegs shoved out in front and you didn't feel hardly any jar at all. He learned to work a rope. He kept his head looking down the rope all the time and the slack pulled out.

I learned to heel calves on him. Ed and I worked a lot just by ourselves. It sure makes a calf easier to throw and brand if you rope him by the heels. I was getting so I hardly missed a loop when riding Old Snip.

One day Ed said, "We're going down to Eldon Butler's and help him brand about fifty head. He's interested in buying Old Snip. We've got plenty of horses around here and I need the money."

As we worked our way down out of the mountains toward Butler's I felt sort of sick. I cleared my throat and said, "Ed, how much you asking for Old Snip?"

"Aw, around a hundred I reckon the way he's turning out." He added, "Now, I really want you to show off what a heeling horse he is. That'll do more to sell him than anything else."

We cut the calves out from the mother cows and held them in a pole corral. The mothers bawled to beat sixty and stirred up a lot of dust. The branding irons were heating in an open fire. Eldon was getting the black leg vaccine ready and Ed was sharpening his knife getting ready to castrate the bull calves, except one they had picked out for a breeding bull because of his good conformation and markings.

I was thinking, a hundred dollars, at the rate I was getting paid, I would be a hundred years old before I had it saved up. I really didn't feel any extra love in my heart right at that moment for Eldon Butler. He was a fine feller too.

Ed yelled, "We're ready, boy."

I rode out among the calves on Old Snip. He eased in till we had one in the right position, then I dropped a slow loop under one of the big bull calves. Most fellers make the mistake of throwing too fast a loop to be good heelers. You've got to kinda let it float down. Then just as the hind legs move against the loop you pull the slack and you've got him. The big calf began bucking and bellering but I turned Old Snip and dragged it to the fire. Eldon ran up and got hold of his tail and over he went.

Pretty soon you could smell the hair burning where they put the brand to him. Ed castrated, earmarked, and vaccinated him while Eldon held him. I let them have the slack, and the finished product got up shaking his head wondering what in the world had happened to him.

I caught four in a row and felt kind of proud of myself until I noticed Eldon looking at Old Snip with mighty admiring eyes. I don't know what happened after that but it was the worst branding I ever attended. It took me about nine loops to catch every calf and even when I did, it looked like Old Snip and me couldn't keep from getting tangled up in the rope.

It was something or other all the time. I reckon that's the sorriest work we ever did together. I could see the disgusted look on Eldon's face. Ed was downright pale after all the braggin' he'd done about Old Snip. I guess we were all glad to get the job over with.

It was after dark when we unsaddled that night. I told Ed to go on in the house and wash for supper if he wanted to, I'd take care of the horses. I shucked out several ears of corn and forked some hay in the manger. I stood there in the dark awhile and smelled Old Snip. He smelled just like a horse, but not just any old horse.

There always seems to be just a little bit of fun mixed up with all the trouble we have, like the time I sat up on Old Snip and looked at a white faced cow as if she were some sort of varmint. The fall before, we had moved all Ed's cows down out of the mountains to the home pasture for the winter. We didn't move them all at one time, I can tell you that.

Ed had a grazing permit on national forest land and those cows were scattered out in small bunches over about two hundred thousand acres of mountains, hills, canyons, rocks, and timber, but all the rest of his herd put together was easier to round up than this, one old cow. She always took off into the thickest timber or down some rough canyon. She was nothing but trouble, so that's what we named her.

Now there she was out in the bog. There was plenty of grass on the outside but she had to go fall off in it, and now if I didn't drag her out pretty soon she'd sink out of sight. I took the leather loop from the saddle horn and unwound the three wraps from the catch rope. I tied one end of the rope to my saddle horn and built a loop in the other end.

I whirled it a couple or three times and let it go. I had to catch her horns if I was going to be able to let her loose by myself. The loop settled down just where I wanted it and I spurred Old Snip in the opposite direction. Nothing moved. Old Trouble was really bogged down. I began to do some solid cussin' and sweatin'.

After awhile the old fool inched up out of the bog a little bit. "Now, Snip!" I yelled, "Now!" Old Snip threw all his weight against that rope and out she came. She struck dry ground running and hit the end of the rope hard. Old Snip was braced. I felt the back of the saddle raise and pulled the flank cinch tight against Old Snip's belly.

Now, in the first place I should never have tried this by myself. In the second place I should never have got off Old Snip without somebody around, but that's exactly what I did. Old Snip backed fast, moving right and left trying to keep the rope tight. I worked in from the side trying to get to Trouble's head slightly behind her horns. She was slobbering at the mouth, shaking her head, and straining with all she had against the rope. Her main idea was to run one of those sharp horns right square through me.

I finally got to her and gripped down with all my strength on her muzzle with one hand, twisting and holding a horn with the other. She slung me around, but I stayed with her and pretty soon when she made a run forward there was some slack in the rope. I jerked hard and the loop came off her horns. I made a run for Old Snip and Trouble made a run for me. I could feel the breeze across my hind end as she went by.

To this day I've never mounted as fast. Even then I was a mite slow. Trouble turned back and ran her horns under Old Snip's flank. He leaped up and away! I almost fell off. She made a couple more wild passes at us before she turned and trotted. I reckon that was her way of thanking us for saving her life.

Old Snip learned to work in timber. It got so I could tell when and what he smelled even when we couldn't see it. For instance, if it was a coyote or some other varmint out in the brush, he would throw one ear forward and then the other while looking toward the scent. If it happened to be cattle hiding in the brush, his neck would arch and he would pull over toward them. This saved lots of riding and looking in rough country. If it was a bunch of horses, he got a little extra excited and quickened his gait.

One day we got lost. I did, anyway. Suddenly I didn't know exactly where we were. The country looked different than I'd ever seen it. I noticed the fast-moving clouds above. Then everything was solid gray.

The wind came first in big gusts, then the snow. It hit wet, cold, and mean. It was a blowing snow. I turned back down out of the high country; but I didn't really know where we were headed. First, the ground covered over; then the tree limbs began to pick it up. Every once in a while a big shower of snow would fall on us out of the trees when the wind shook it loose. My hands were getting numb in my thin leather gloves, and my nose and ears were beginning to sting. The snow came on thicker and thicker.

I reined Old Snip this way, then that. It just didn't do any good. I had to admit I was completely lost. The blizzard never let up, in fact, it was just getting started. Before long I could just barely see Old Snip's thick black mane out in front of me. He was plowing along with his head low. The snow was drifting. Sometimes we'd go in up over my boot tops.

Finally I let Old Snip have his head. I just sat in the saddle and hoped he didn't fall off a sheer bluff. Soon I didn't feel anything. It wasn't so bad. Then I remembered hearing that was the time of greatest danger. So, I began to move my arms back and forth, back and forth, faster and faster, until I couldn't hold them up any longer. Then there was just a world of cold white, with Old Snip and me right in the middle of it.

I sat a long time wondering why Old Snip didn't keep moving. Maybe he'd frozen stiff standing up! Then there it was—a gate, by doggies. It was the horse pasture gate into Ed Young's Rafter E Y Outfit.

After I fed Old Snip about three times as much as he could eat and stood with my hind end so close to the fireplace it just about scorched, I ate the biggest batch of Mother Young's hot biscuits, sow belly, and pinto beans that a man ever wrapped himself around. That was twice Old Snip had saved my life. I don't know how he found his way down out of that world of frozen white, but he did.

I worked for the Rafter E Y and was loaned out to the San Cristobal outfit for two years and then somebody got the idea I should go off and get some book learnin'. I had to leave Old Snip behind.

Ed sold him after I left to the owners of the Kansas City Stockyards. Of course Ed didn't know him as well as I did or he'd never have done it.

I never did get a bill of sale to Old Snip, but I felt he was mine just the same. He belonged to me then and he does now—wherever he is.

CHAPTER FIVE

Flax

FLAX was as beautiful as a Taos sunset in deep summer, as faithful as your grandmother, as smart as a border collie, and his dark-as-shoe-polish eyes shined with intelligence. Pull the stray hairs from his flaxen tail, curry his blondish mane, brush his light sorrel body with his muscles reflecting rippling lights and shadows as he moved, and he'd shine all over in appreciation. At another time, in another place, decked out with a black leather, silver-studded bridle and saddle to match, he could have been a parade horse that anyone would have been proud to show off.

But Flax was mainly a cow horse, and it was a privilege and a pleasure to work cattle with him. I never could tell how many hands tall a horse is, but I knew Flax was just exactly the right size to handle any job I rode him at—because he always delivered. He kept his eyes on whatever number of cattle we were driving, working his ears all the time. He could tell if a cow was a real bunch-quitter and be on her before she got started. Or he could read the body motions of bluffers and ignore them. He could make the sorriest cowboy look good. He instilled a green kid like me with the confidence of a top hand—even though I had a lot of long trails to ride before that term could be used about me—if ever.

Up there—just south of Santa Fe—on sixty-mile-long, fifty-mile-wide Glorieta Mesa, people were impoverished. The recovery from

96

the great drought and the Depression had hardly gotten a toe hold. Everyone borrowed hands from one another for roundups, brandings, and sometimes, even fixing fences and windmills. Often I was the only hand working for Ed Young on the Rafter EY. Those were the times I liked best, because Ed was one heck of an old-time cowboy and he knew I wanted to learn. I felt honored. No kid before me had ever lasted as a hand with him. I didn't know if I'd make it either, but I was gonna give it a hide stretching try.

The one place I didn't mind being loaned out to was the great San Cristobal ranch—part of Ed's land joined it on the west side. Mr. Gould, the ranch manager, was kind to horses, dogs, and kids and was a real hand. Of course, the San Cristobal had eastern money backing it, and was the only outfit around that could afford its own crew. Part of Mr. Gould's fine fettle came, I'm sure, from drawing good wages, being fed well, and knowing all his hands would be paid every month. I only got paid in the fall after shipping time—at least for the first two years I was on the Rafter EY,

The San Cristobal ran black Angus cattle, the first I'd ever seen. Their eastern fence line was partially along the west edge of Glorieta Mesa where it joined the Rafter EY. There were a few scattered waterholes among the miles of boulders and tall untouched grass in secluded little meadows. The San Cristobal cattle had plenty of range on the flats and it was against their nature to climb uphill—in jumbles of boulders—to graze. So, we did a strange type of "ridin' fence" in those days—nature, you see, will give you help if you let it. We looked for places where the barbed wire was loose and down, but instead of repairing it we'd drive little bunches of cattle along those places. Flax and I would circle around and sort of get in their way, until finally one of them would discover the downed fence and stray off the rocky slopes of the mesa onto San Cristobal's grassland. If we were patient, the other cows would soon follow. Ed called this "borrowing grass."

In order to give me time to do my cowboy job, we had worked it out so I could go to school in Andrews, Texas, just across the New Mexico line, during football season, then back to the EY in the late spring. I was a fair halfback and punter so I was allowed certain privileges. I could take text books and library books from the school to the ranch. I chose Balzac, Tolstoy, Chekhov—and Shakespeare-by-assignment— and stuff like that to continue my education. However, ol' Flax was going to educate me in a different manner the next spring.

Ed had cattle scattered about the mesa in different pastures so we had to have at least three roundups and three brandings. First the cattle had to be gathered and penned.

I was on Flax and Ed rode a black-legged bay—his favorite.

We had already moved ten or fifteen cows and calves into the biggest meadow at Chico Flats where the windmill and corrals were—and where we would hold our first branding. But now we were working the rocky slopes of Glorieta Mesa finishing up a hard gather.

I was tracking a "dry" cow who hadn't calved that year. She charged into a bunch of brush below me and headed back north instead of southwest to Chico Flats. Flax was after her, working his way through the rocks at considerable speed. I could hear the brush popping below, but I couldn't see the critter. I had a fleeting panic shock as I reined Flax hard to the right to head the cow off. He didn't want to go, but I spurred him in my chosen direction anyway. Well, I had just that second returned to cowboy kindergarten . . . me, not Flax.

I had reined him out on some big flat rocks that dropped off at a pretty steep slope. I tried to pull the horse up and he tried to obey, but the slope and the momentum, along with the speed and weight, carried us right over the edge of about an eight or ten-foot drop. Flax's steel horseshoes had to have made sparks on the rocks as he shoved his hind legs under his belly in a desperate attempt to save a bone-busting fall.

Instead of letting the momentum and gravity take us smashing and rolling to our doom, the horse launched us with his powerful hind legs way out into space and we came down on almost level ground, tearing through some small cedar limbs as he struggled mightily to stay upright. He did. A miracle. Even though my tailbone felt like it had been driven right up between my ears, I somehow stayed on. Flax just kept going with me trying to tear the horn out of the saddle because I'd lost a stirrup. Durned if he didn't turn that ol' cow and line her out southwest. He knew, all the time, what we were supposed to do and where we were going.

I had learned—in that ripped apart second—that you rein a horse in the best direction your instantaneous judgment tells you to and then leave it up to the animal to pick his own way through the rocks. There is no other reasonable way. In spite of knowing this, I figured I'd never work in rocks enough to know if I'd make a real hand at it or not. Since then, I've talked to lots of cowboys who were raised in rock country, and every one of them told me "just leave it up to the horse, that's all you can do."

Ed came in on his bay with two more cows and calves. We started bunching them and then the dry cow that had nearly got us in a permanent fix hit the trail down to Chico Flats and the rest followed. It was smooth going, downhill all the way to water now. I wanted real bad to brag about Flax's brilliance to my boss, but I had to pass because I couldn't figure a way to conceal my own ignorance.

At just the right moment I circled around and down to the flats to open the corral gate. We'd been so busy on the rocky slopes that we hadn't noticed the thunder clouds gathering overhead, herded together by some mighty force in the sky not unlike the way we had rounded up the scattered mother cows and calves.

Flax and I made it across the half-mile flat and had taken a flank position. We could hear the cattle coming and Ed yelling them on "Ho cattle, Ho cattle, Hoooo."

They left the trail and hit the flats headed for the water they could smell. The windmill tank was half in the corral and half out, convenient watering for both loose cows and confined ones. They were beginning to spread out a little and most of the mother cows were breaking into a trot, the calves, running and bawling, trying to keep up. Then it hit.

The lightning bolt came down and split a cedar tree into splinters not over a quarter mile to our north. That bolt had shredded the hugging clouds as well, I reckoned, because the rain just dropped like a waterfall and the lightning and its thunder roar came as fast as a World War II artillery barrage and just as loud.

Here was the deal. During the great drought, most of the springs had dried up forcing wild game and cattle to come to this good water from all around. They had tromped the grass, and all other vegetation, except for the scattered cedar trees, into barren ground, and now, as the rain sheathed it like a huge mirror, it really turned slick.

The cows were scattering more as their calves lost track and smell and sight of them. The lightning made a vast glow of the earth every time it flashed and addled the little herd.

Flax and I were working back and forth. He had his head down, spinning with every breakaway cow just like a cutting horse. There was nothing I could do but just give him his head and let him work. I half expected him to lose footing on the glassy world and land right on top of me any flashing second. Sometimes he'd slide sideways several feet, other times he'd almost go down, but by some power of will and skill, we put the last of the cattle in the corral just as I heard Ed yell off to the south. He and his bay were coming out of a gully after a cow.

I reined Flax around and moved back, trying to get the distance exact so we could maneuver to block the corralled cattle at the gate if any decided to break out. At the same time I had to leave an opening for Ed's bunch-quitter. When she heard the calves bawling, instead of trying to turn back, she raced toward the corral gate. I leaned forward and touched Flax lightly with the spurs. He moved at a cautious speed now. When we reached the corral, I bailed off and shut the gate behind the last cow just as Ed rode up.

The sudden thunder cloud had moved on, raising about a half-square mile of hell up on the mesa. Our slickers were still on the back of our saddles, but I felt so proud of our work my chest felt plum puffy and I didn't even notice that I was soaked to the liver.

When I remounted Flax I reached down and patted him on the neck—the side away from Ed. He was standing up in the stirrups making a count. He eased back in the saddle, saying softly, "We got 'em all." I waited for more words, but none came.

We had to head home if we were to make it before dark, but we'd be back tomorrow morning at sunup. It was a mile up to the trail and

FLAX in his retirement pasture at age twenty. Author's collection.

about three more to headquarters. At first the ground was slick, then the mud started drying, and it just got sticky.

Eldon Butler, who had a little outfit that joined the south end of the San Cristobal—just across the Clines Corner/Lamy dirt highway to the west of Chico Flats—would come help us brand the calves. I was thinking how I would love to heel and drag 'em to the branding fire from the back of Flax, but he'd had an Olympian day of performing and no matter how great and tough he was, he'd be stiff and sore as hell by morning. I would have to use a lesser mount. Of course, the way I felt right then, every horse in the world was second place to the golden-maned warrior.

We left the trail when we finally found a wood hauler's wagon road allowing me to ride side-by-side with the boss like I'd been trained to do. My mind drifted back to that mighty leap from the flat rock that Flax had taken, and I suddenly wanted to tell Ed how much I admired Flax's great feat and feet. But, you see, words were for other purposes to these old-time, rough-butted cowboys.

Ed Young spoke one sentence all the way home, suddenly, almost under his breath I heard. "You and ol' Flax did a perty good job today."

That was it, but that was a bunch. Even if ol' Flax might not have understood the words, I knew my bent tailbone was sending him proud messages right through the saddle seat into his valiant heart.

Actually, I was a little uneasy about bragging too much about Flax due to the shock I had suffered the year before when I returned from school to work on the EY. I didn't want a repeat happening.

I had ridden a horse called Old Snip—who was also a "young-learner"—to apply for a job with Ed Young, and was instructed to turn Snip over to Ed in return for a debt from the cowboy/horse-trainer-superb, Robert Ian. Ed let me ride Snip as often as possible because I was putting a good neck rein on him and perfecting the proper hind-legs-stuck-way-under-stop on this horse. We worked great together. We fit. I loved him, and he at least respected me.

One must try to understand the times. The family food and sparse clothing came before all else. In the '30s, those who didn't go on relief survived in any manner they could.

We all shipped cattle to Kansas City, Missouri, in those days, and it seems an authority was scouting for special horses to work in the Kansas City Stockyards. He had seen, and tried, Old Snip and of course, the horse was perfection. Ed had sold him for the almost-unheard-of amount of two hundred dollars. A true fortune for a cow horse in those days.

When Ed told me about selling Snip, all I could say was "Oh."

This horse had saved my life once and probably twice and my fourteen-year-old heart was broken, but I couldn't let on. These people were tough by circumstance and tender by nature. They just took the blows and moved instantly onto something else. I had to be like them. There was no other way, but now, Flax had filled in the hollow spot. A loss had been turned into a gain. Ed let me work with him more than ever. I guess he knew.

The area cowboys liked being loaned to the Rafter EY just as much as I liked going to help out at the San Cristobal. First, Mrs. Young—everyone called her Mother Young—was a truly great cook. Next, Ed had a fine string of top horses, and the bunkhouse had been built adjoining the main house, making them feel welcome and at home.

Two hands from White Lakes ranch and I had just finished about a mile and a half, or more, of fencing, so, they had returned to their home base. I regained my position as "the hired help." That's when Ed assigned me and Flax the second toughest adventure we were to share.

Right after breakfast, Ed lit up a "town cigarette"—the one luxury he allowed himself besides a single big swallow of whiskey at night just before supper—then he spoke at great length, for him.

"Max, go wrangle the horses and saddle Flax. You're going on a trip. Get a *morral* out of the tack room and put a pint of corn in it."

I went to the corral and got the night horse, wrangled the horses, roped and saddled Flax and led him out the corral gate toward the backyard where Ed stood waiting.

"All right now," he said with the authority of General Patton, and he gave me instructions on how to get to a big pasture on the south end of the San Cristobal. He had loaned one of his mules to Mr. Gould to pack some of the Eastern owners into the Pecos wilderness for a camping and trout fishing trip. Ed had told him not to worry about returning it. He would come get him when he needed the animal. That time was now.

Ed had contracted to deliver a couple of hundred cedar fence posts to a well-to-do person in Santa Fe who was going to use them placed side by side for a rustic and long lasting yard fence. He needed the Jack mule to work with his other mule, Mary. They would pull the wagon loads of cedar posts I was going to be assigned to cut. These survival moves of Ed's were an inspiration to me throughout my long life. Right now I was anxious to see what he had planned for Flax and me that was so special.

Ed said, moving to Flax and taking the catch rope and morral from the saddle, "I'm just going to show you this one time."

A morral is a canvas feeding bag you hang over a horse's or mule's head and they eat the grain in the bottom. We used corn that we raised ourselves. Only the San Cristobal could afford the preferred oats. Ed put the "tie hard and fast" honda knot over the saddle horn and formed a roping loop. He held it out in front of him with one hand and with the other he rattled the grains of corn in the center of the loop.

"Listen up. When ol' Jack gets his head close enough to smell that corn and figures he's gonna get a bite, you whip this loop over his head and jerk it tight in the same motion. If you miss you'll never get him, and if you don't bring him home, just ride on to Arizona." He went on out to the corrals without looking back.

I mounted Flax and rode off down the trail to Chico Flats on the way to the big pasture. I can still feel the pressure in my gut all these years later. My belly felt like there were two regiments of scorpions doing battle with swords and axes as sharp as the edge of freshly broken glass. These were unpleasant sensations, but those words, "Just ride on to Arizona" were amplified in repetitive echoes pounding through my brain until I was sure my head was gonna spin right off my body into space.

I got to that fated pasture about midafternoon. It had sounded easy, but this pasture was big—somewhere around ten or fifteen thousand acres. The biggest on the ranch. I had helped gather cattle there, so, I knew how big it was. And now here I was, trying to gather one mule with my life's travel itinerary at stake.

I started looking as far as I could see. However, as good as my eyes were in those youthful days I couldn't see through a single one of the thousands of hills, mesas, and clustered clumps of piñon and cedar. So I started riding in a big circle, checking the ground for sign. I stopped every now and then to search inside the circle. I saw the tracks and spoor of coyotes, deer, bobcats, skunks, rabbits, birds, cows, and calves, but no mule.

About an hour short of sundown, I crossed a little open patch and there were scattered tracks of a whole remuda of horses. It took me awhile, but finally I found the smaller, sharper tracks of the mule Jack, who was also a jack mule, or for the layman, a stud. I felt a bunch better. I had a chance of missing a long, lonely, probably hungry horseback trip to Arizona.

I tried to follow the general trend of their directional grazing. A remuda of loose horses moves in all directions hunting for the best grass, but they were generally en masse heading north.

Suddenly I felt Flax bunch under me and his steps quicken. He sort of danced. When he heard or smelled out-of-sight horses, he threw both ears forward at the same time.

I rode expectantly up to the top of a long rise. There they were. It took me a spell to spot Jack, but he was the first one to raise his head and spot us. Then one after the other, about thirty head of cow horses from newly saddle broken to some that were pretty near worn out, were looking at us in curiosity. It looked like I might get my *one* chance after all.

As I was planning my move, the sun was setting. I failed to enjoy the orange bronzed blazes across the thousands of miles of space as I usually did. I was staring at a mule slowly fading into darkness just like the sunset was doing.

The night came quickly. I shuddered at the suddenly cold air and the full realization that I was going to spend the night here with no food and only a saddle blanket for warmth. It bothered me even more that I hadn't brought any hobbles for Flax so at least he could have grazed and not gone hungry like ol' dumb-butted me. There is no use going on or regretting ignorance. It only multiplies the problems.

I unsaddled Flax and tied him to a tree with a no-slip, no-choking knot. I turned the saddle upside down, got half the folded saddle blanket under me and the other half over my legs and lay back staring at the stars. As dumb as I felt, it shouldn't have been any trouble not to think. After counting past a hundred thousand stars and listening to coyotes howling to one another into the soft distance that seemed as far away as Arizona, I must have slept more than I thought, because when I woke up with the sun, I was raring to go.

First I had to get Flax to water. I could see a windmill about a mile back to the southwest. I hated to backtrack, so for once I broke Flax into an easy lope. We both watered up at the tank and I forgot about being hungry. Flax didn't let on one way or the other. I rode back up on the long rise and the horses were gone.

Of course, they were gone. Horses graze on at night, just like deer browse. There was a little panic but I could see tracks under us and as long as tracks were visible we'd have a chance.

Flax found them with his ears before my eyes spotted them. We, by some unknown instinct, moved slowly back and forth about a hundred yards from the closest horse. It took about thirty minutes. They were mostly grazing and ignoring us as I dismounted and slowly led Flax back and forth to where we'd just ridden. This created a little curiosity, but they soon went back to feeding.

I hooked the honda over the saddle horn, got the loop out and hung the morral over my left shoulder. I led Flax ever so slowly toward them. He kept trying to graze with his bridle on, flipping the bits back to get a bite or two.

Three or four of the horses had become nervous and were watching us with heads high, ready to break away in a run. If they did, all the others would go with them. I stopped about fifty yards from the grazing remuda.

I love Arizona. It is my second or third-favorite state, but at that moment the thought of it turned my blood to hardening cement.

I waited motionless as Flax grazed around me. A year whizzed by. A decade. A century. At the millennium mark, I eased Flax's head up and set my loop with the morral in its center slowly shaking it. One horse heard and looked, then another, and another. Then Jack. Five or six took tentative steps forward. I increased the corn's rattle. Jack was paying attention, but not enough. However, when six or seven horses slowly moved toward me, his interest began to peak. He started following them.

When they neared us, the lead horse stuck his head out, smelling, watching, almost to the morral. I'd have to pull it back very slowly and silently. I had already stopped breathing. Then I'd shake it some more. Six or seven of the horses had gotten so close I might have snared one if that was what I was after. Then Jack inched through the animals in his turn. Everything fused together now, the horses in front, Flax in back. *Jack. Hello dear Jack. Come on, sweet Jack. Just six more inches, beautiful Jack. Three more inches, handsome Jack.* Hungry all the way to Arizona or Mother Young's delicious cooking on the Rafter EY was only a rattle away.

Now!

I made my one move just as the velvet nose of the Jack mule touched the morral, nostrils wide, smelling the luscious corn. The loop went around his neck. I jerked it tight and moved to get hold of Flax's reins. I didn't have to worry about Flax, he had felt me hook the hondo on the saddle horn. He was ready—braced and looking down the rope—when the Jack mule hit the end of it sideways. The mule leapt backward, spun in a circle to run, but the rope straightened and jerked him around facing Flax.

The instant the Jack mule started choking, he eased up and actually took two or three steps toward us to loosen the loop proving that: mules are smarter than most animals. I mounted Flax, took the first breath since the catch and rode up toward Jack, taking coils. When there was about four or five feet of rope left, I made a good half hitch on the saddle horn and rode toward the Rafter EY. It was a great surprise to me that Jack moved out with us as if he had trained all his life for this moment of polite relief.

I couldn't believe how events had turned our way. I'd hooked that prize long-eared fish and was reeling him into the home corral. We were almost halfway up the Chico Flats trail, only an hour and a half from headquarters and some of Mother Young's biscuits and trimmings. I could imagine Ed grinning all over even though I was a day late getting back.

Then we came to a sudden stop. I tapped ol' Flax with the spurs and he dug in for about five or six yards, literally dragging Jack mule who had all four legs stiff as iron pipes. Flax knew a lot more about mules than I did. And he knew there was no way he could ever drag that mule to the top of the mesa. Gravity was all in Jack's favor.

I reined Flax all the way in a circle, a rough one because of the brush beside the hill. The mule sort of turned with us but we hadn't gained an inch. I rode up to him and then spurred Flax, trying to jerk him sideways. It didn't bother Jack at all. In fact, I started believing he was enjoying this. For a fleeting moment I wished I'd left the choking loop as it was instead of making a hackamore loop over his nose. Then I remembered Ed needed Jack healthy to join his gray mule to pull wagon loads of posts.

I dismounted. I left Flax and Jack staring at one another down a short length of rope while I looked around in the brush for a dead but strong pole. Finally I found one. I walked over to Jack, looked him in one eye and said—paraphrasing here—"See the cedar pole, Jack? Well, I'm going to knock your cockeyed eyeballs right out your long ears. You hear me, you . . . ?"

I raised the pole high over one shoulder and then the most unbelievable thing happened. Flax stepped forward head to head with Jack and if I'd have come down with the pole I would have smashed my beloved sorrel. I held the silly pose with the post for a moment, then hurled it off into the brush. I mounted Flax, and Jack followed us home like a calf follows its mama to water. I don't know how horses and mules know the same silent language, but the gorgeous gold-maned cow horse had either threatened or sweet-talked that mule into doing his duty. I prefer to think it was the latter, and to this long since time I still believe it without any doubt whatsoever.

We all three rode up in front of that ranch house and I just couldn't help it. I reared back and let out a yell that would have woken every hibernating bear in the Rocky Mountains if it'd been winter, but it was early summer and the grass was green and growing for the first time in a long spell.

Ed came around the corner from the work shed and Mother Young came out of the house. She was smiling and spoke first. "Well, Max, get 'em watered and in the barn and fed. I've got a big meal just about ready."

We all three moved right past Ed who was studying the condition of the mule. He was soberly puzzled. Heck, I knew Jack was in perfect shape. I had only *threatened* to kill him. When I dismounted at the corral gate and was pulling it open, I took another quick glance back at Ed. He sure didn't want anybody to see it, but he was grinning so wide his ears were practically touching on the back of his head.

The two animals were out in the corral eating hay. Jack finally got those few bites of corn that had lead to his capture. It had taken two days of playing cow-pasture-roulette, but there were winners all around. We had fried chicken with our biscuits and gravy that special night on this rocky earth. Oh yeah, I almost forgot. We had sweet potato pie for dessert. Don't try to tell me anything about heaven, I've done been there.

Ed sure gave me the right advice about one thing to look for whenever I hooked Jack up to the wagon, "Watch that hind foot." Sure enough. Every time he was being hooked up alongside the gray mule, Mary, he lifted a hind foot and would leave the hoof tipped right on the edge just waiting for me to get careless. Then he was gonna kick my brains out. Once in the traces, he worked perfectly, balancing out the pulling ability of the ginny with precision. No doubt about it, some human had unforgettably mistreated him in his youth, and like all mules, they never forget the good or the bad.

I selected and cut posts out of big cedar trees for days before I finally got two hundred straight ones. Ed told me to resharpen the ax, because he'd had word from the Santa Fe buyer it was going to take three hundred posts for his yard fence. When I had cut, trimmed, loaded, hauled to headquarters, and unloaded all three hundred, it formed quite a pile. Ed hauled them to town in a cattle trailer pulled by a little Chevy coupe.

After he returned from delivering the last load, he seemed pretty pepped up. He and Mother Young decided to throw their once-a-year dance and party for the few far-flung people of the mesa. That after-noon about sundown, just before the first ranch folk began to arrive, he told me some good news—he had decided to raise my pay from twenty dollars a month to thirty.

I said, "That's right keen."

If you think that was not enough elation, you are right. But here I was, still a fourteen-year-old kid and I was going to be drawing equal wages to all the other full-grown, working cowboys of the American West. It was a great moment in my life and it's a miracle I could speak at all. The dance was a dandy. I wanted to tell the entire citizenry of Glorieta Mesa that was gathered here about my raise, but I couldn't tell anyone. It would have seemed like bragging. Anyway I owed at least a third of the thirty dollars a month to ol' Flax.

Instead of cowboying, Ed temporarily turned me into a corn farmer. Every outfit—except the San Cristobal—had to raise a patch of corn for horse feed. So, I daily walked twenty—seemed-like-a-hundred—miles behind a two-horse, two-mule harrow. I cultivated, killed weeds, and aerated the soil around the dry land shoots of corn stalks. I was consoled by the fact that ol' Flax would get to enjoy part of the harvest—if it rained, that is.

Well, one thing was for sure—the axing of three hundred cedar posts and the twenty-mile walk in plowed ground had sure as shootin' got me in shape for the football season down southeast at Andrews, Texas.

Each summer Ed Young leased a section of land—640 acres—from an elderly couple, Mr. and Mrs. Curry, eight miles to the north. They had left a starvation farm in Texas and homesteaded the 160 acres which they eventually traded into a section of starvation ranch land. They had been there since somewhere around the turn of the century. They kept the grass idle except for three or four horses owned by their off-to-work sons, Shorty and Francis, so, it was pretty good grazing. Every couple of weeks, Ed would send me over there to make a count on the thirty cows and calves he ran there from July until shipping time in late October.

The vast Glorieta Mesa also held many, many little mesas and canyons on its massive deck. There were a few windmills and only a precious few springs. The elderly Currys had one of the best of the latter located at the foot of a cream-colored sandstone mesa.

The Currys had dug a cavelike house into part of the bluff about thirty feet from their spring. Then they used the rocks they found in the ruins of an ancient Indian hunting camp to build a good sized extension in front of their cave home so they could have a wood cook stove with a chimney. The surrounding mesa was covered heavily with piñon and cedar trees, furnishing them plenty of firewood. The location of their home didn't seem to make much sense, at first glance, because they had to pack all the household water, and water for the chickens, hog, and garden, up a crooked path to their dugout. Seemed unhandy, but it was obviously what they wanted.

This strange little home was insulated by the whole world. They were, themselves, insulated and isolated beyond the reach of most of society. About every two months, one or the other of their sons would show up with their sparse mail, some staples such as pinto beans, flour, salt and pepper, and some canned milk. They had a milk cow or so, at one time, but could no longer handle the feeding, gathering, watering, and care to have their own milk and butter, but as I would learn, the old couple were ultimate survivors.

Mrs. Curry was about five feet and filled out even from her shoulders to her 1890s hemline. Mr. Curry had once been about six feet, but the years of carrying two big buckets of water at a time, up the steep, cutback trail had bent him like wire, so he was probably about five eight now. It was strong wire for sure, and his large knuckled hands looked like they could crush granite. When I shook hands with him, I couldn't help but try to flex my fingers to see if they were still there. One thing, though, that I'll never forget—no matter the shape of their bodies, they both had black eyes that shined right into your heart with good honest feelings.

It took Flax and me from before sunup to twilight to make this trip to the Curry's. This was the only time I'd break him into an easy lope so we'd have time to have a meal and a visit with these gracious people. This total of around a twenty-mile ride was my picture show, my ice cream soda, my Sunday picnic of fried chicken and biscuits and gravy dinner at grandmother's all rolled into one. The wildlife was scarce, but once in a while I'd see a coyote or a deer or a mountain lion track. There were two things I could count on, though: the blue jays and magpies were always flickering from tree to tree and the chipmunks chattered both a greeting and a warning to all the unseen listeners, that you were present.

It was a joy to slow lope across that mile of sparse pasture. Flax made it so easy after the first time. I could watch his ears working and tell when we were near cattle, even in the sometimes timbered hills. That horse had a memory better than an elephant or almost as good as a mule. When I had finished the cattle count, usually by straight-up sun, I'd water him at the Curry spring. Then we'd ease on around to where the mesa flattened and open a gate, riding the hundred yard trail to the front of the Curry's dugout. Their old black dog had already told them I was there.

"Well, I'll be," was Mrs. Curry's greeting every time, and Mr. Curry was just as brief, with "There you are," as if I'd somehow mailed them a message ahead. Maybe I had, without knowing in some wonderful way of the wilderness.

As I dismounted, Mr. Curry always commented on how good both Flax and I looked. He'd walk out with me to his little shed and corral and insist we give Flax a morral of corn. I knew his sons had to deliver this priceless commodity to them, as their little garden would never supply their chickens and the butchering hog, much less a horse. I felt sort of guilty, but I didn't want to hurt their feelings and Flax certainly appreciated it. He had—for two summers now—looked forward to this treat.

It wouldn't be long until Mrs. Curry had the biscuits baking, the great permanent pot of pinto beans warming, and she was stirring up gravy and slicing some sow belly. I swear she would have cheerfully cooked their last bite for company.

Long years back Mr. Curry had helped Ed work on the Rafter EY and he knew Chico Flats, wild horse mesa, the name of every pasture and waterhole, so we had plenty to talk about. In later years, when I thought back on it, I was awed that they never asked me about the outside world . . . things like war, politics, or the price of cattle. We simply visited about the mesa land he knew, but Mrs. Curry always wanted to know about Mother Young's house and if she still painted pictures and raised flowers.

The old black dog stood with head through the open doorway listening and smelling the food, but he never set a paw in the house. Just as soon as the old half-gallon blue-enameled coffee pot boiled, we were ready to eat.

Flax and I had already covered about twelve to fourteen miles, so I was plenty hungry. That feeling was soon cured. We all three had a ceremonial cup of coffee strong enough to dig a water well in solid rock. Then me 'n Flax left. I don't think it was possible to feel more at home than we did in the Curry cave. They were polite enough not to insist we stay longer, even though they may have desired it. I surely loved those two old folks. Their kind made the good part of the world and they are all that holds it together. They also understood how long the eight or nine miles would stretch out that Flax and I still had to cover, returning to the ranch.

To my excited surprise, on the next cattle count, Ed decided to go with me. The Currys would be inundated with visitors this month enough to do them for an entire year.

Ed Young was the only gringo I ever worked with who used the Spanish spade bit. Few riders could handle it without cruelly tearing up and eventually permanently numbing a horse's mouth. It had a spade mouthpiece of the bit that could tear a horse's mouth if used improperly. The cowboy had to use it with great delicacy and knowledge. Ed could do it. I could only marvel.

Every now and then Ed would mention a little bit about working with Ysidro Sandoval, who was now the last of the real vaqueros in this part of the country. I could hear the awe in his voice when he spoke of him. Since Ed was such a knowledgeable and skilled cowboy/cowman himself, I dreamed of someday meeting Ysidro. I'm here to tell you, miracles do happen.

We—Ed on his bay, I was on Flax—were in an open pasture about three miles from the Curry place when we heard these crashing noises on the edge of a long brush and timber-covered hill about a quarter mile from us. We reined up. All four of us were wondering what kind of critters were tearing up the world and making all that racket. I could feel Flax's muscles bunching under me and his ears were working so hard I thought they might tear loose from his head.

Talk about witnessing a happening. First there were ten, maybe more, head of steers that came ripping out of the timber. These were followed by a little dog working, back and forth, nipping at their heels and the whole crashing thing was followed up by a tall man on a tall, dusty-colored horse. We could see they were trying to pen the stampeding cattle at one of the few working windmills and adjoining corrals down in the flats.

We spurred forward to help hold the flank nearest us, but the tall man and the tall horse and the little black-and-white heeling dog penned them before we got there. He had dismounted smoothly, shutting the gate and remounting before we could join him.

We pulled up. Ed spoke a greeting in Spanish and it was returned the same way. Then in English, he said "Ysidro, this is Max Evans. He lives with us."

I was really proud of the 'lives with us' instead of 'he works for us' stuff, but I forgot that as I finally got to meet the last of the greatest of all cowboy lines in our part of the country. I went a little blind, but I can still remember that one and only handshake with 'the greatest' as if I'd been invited to join Babe Ruth in the dugout when he hit his sixtieth home run. The blur cleared up and I regained full control and soaked in everything about this living legend from his black flat-brimmed hat, the silky bandana around his neck, to his leather catch rope. I could tell by the coils that the riata was at least forty feet long.

Ysidro had an elegance in the straight, but relaxed, way he sat the saddle rolling a cigarette while he visited with Ed. The dog lay down in the shade of the corral, but he watched every move and listened to every sound his master made.

Suddenly, Ysidro turned his head to Flax, examining him. And in English better than mine, said, "I remember when Ed Young was first reining that sorrel. He is beautiful. How does he work the rocks and brush, Max?"

It was my turn to talk. I choked and then it poured out, "He's just the best . . . he knows cows better'n me. I just let him do most of the thinkin'."

This seemed to please Ysidro. He lightly touched his own mount on the roots of the mane, smiled broadly under that perfectly chiseled face and said, "A good horse knows when you give him freedom. A great horse knows how to use it." I never have had to paraphrase that last statement. It is indelible. I felt as honored as if Flax had just won the Kentucky Derby.

Ysidro's land had been divided up so many ways among his children that his once large holdings had shrunk to small leases and some original ownership near Cow Springs between the Coleman outfit and Haney Springs.

We said our good-byes to Ysidro and finished making the count. To this day I can visualize Ysidro riding off away from us, straight as a shovel handle but soft in the saddle. The little heeling dog trotted along beside the horse as if he was harnessed in the traces with the tall, slightly burnt sienna sorrel. That team could do more cow work than five good cowboys . . . if it was in rough country. I felt so privileged that Flax sensed his importance and headed out with a running walk as smooth as the first swallow of vanilla ice cream in summer.

When we arrived at the Curry's, Ed told them about seeing Ysidro Sandoval, his horse and his dog. They announced proudly that once or twice a year Mr. Sandoval stopped by and had coffee with them.

Ever since I was four years old, I thought of myself as a grown man and joined in the conversation with the grown-ups like I was one of them, but during that lunch break that day, with Ed and the Currys, I just listened. They were telling stories about the last of the true vaqueros. I didn't want to miss a single word. I knew this was a day, riding Flax beside my cowboy mentor and boss, and meeting the legendary vaquero, I would always remember.

The following week, Flax and I were making a count, looking for sick cattle, and riding a fence line. We had watered at the well near Chico Flats and read sign around the tank. Six mother cows were grazing off about a half mile and four of their calves were lying down, and two of them raced away, playing, bucking, whirling, tails up. Their white faces stood out like big snowballs.

I sat there on ol' Flax with his velvet muzzle in the water taking in long draughts of the cool high-altitude water. I was thirsty myself, but you never dismount a horse while he's drinking. They'll run backward and maybe cause a hell of a wreck. Their ancient genes still make them feel vulnerable to a tiger or a lion creeping up on them while they are watering with their heads down.

We moved up the Chico Flats trail east toward headquarters as we'd done so many times before. A good breeze whispered through the piñon and cedars. I had some hopes for rain. Down on the southeastern plains of New Mexico, a good east wind meant, quite often, that moisture from the Gulf of Mexico was accompanying it. Today, however, this wind would create a different kind of storm.

About a hundred or so yards from the rim of the mesa there was a tiny meadow where I always reined off if I was alone. I looked back west across Chico Flats, the Lamy/Clines Corner highway, the rolling hills, and endless mesas of the San Cristobal. On across a million acres, up into the dark blue Jemez Mountains, I could even see a section of my beloved White Bluff Anasazi ruins. I've since this time seen paintings of some of the world's great landscapes, many by immortal artists, and even brushed a few fair ones myself, but this canvas before my young eyes colored and patterned by The Great Mystery in the Sky is etched into my being forever.

I was in an unexplainable trance, and then I was pulled back to the moment by the unmistakable tensing of Flax's muscles under me. His ears were thrown forward and stayed there. A sure sign, and his flared nostrils revealed he not only heard but smelled horseflesh. There was a salt lick just as one topped out on the trail. The east wind was sending Flax signals and blowing our sound and scent away from whatever was partaking of the salt.

I rode ol' Flax around rocks in the trail the best I could to soften our sounds. Then I saw the backs of some horses through the brush. Wild mustangs.

I eased Flax to a stop. I took my catch rope loose from the tie and slipped the honda knot over the horn. I built a big Mother Hubbard loop and leaned a little forward, signaling Flax to move on up. He did. I could feel the excitement surging through him. He was almost dancing. My heart whammed against my chest like a wild eagle trying to escape a cage.

There it was! A colt from an old mother in the front of five or six others. There was no time to check whether they were stallions or mares for they all spied us at the same time, whirling and racing for the part of Glorieta that was called Wild Horse Mesa. The old mare and what would probably be her last colt were behind. A dream realized.

Flax and I were flat running and riding with all the strength we had and we were slowly gaining. Forty, thirty, twenty feet. Now contrary to many written and filmed tales, I've never heard of a cowboy catching up to and roping a full-grown, healthy mustang. The weight of the saddle and the rider is just too great a disadvantage.

I leaned forward and started whirling the big loop. Flax was stretched out in a dead run. He was giving me all he had when I saw a big opening through some piñons. On the other side the timber really thickened. It had to be now.

Flax moved through the scattered trees expertly. We were within about ten feet. I was ready to rope the bay colt when I had to duck a little for a limb. I had unintentionally let the loop drop as we dodged a tree limb, getting ready to rope the colt. Instantly thereafter I was gazing for a brief moment into the blue, blue domain of birds, billions of planets, and, some say, heaven. Oh, this vision was brief and just before I lost sight of the endless blue, something like a kind of monstrous prehistoric bird flew across my line of sight. Then nothing. Blank. Nada.

The first thing I saw when I came around was a mountain with red monsters moving back and forth on a road. They were coming and going like . . . like . . . ANTS. My vision cleared before my weak mind did and I realized I was full length on the ground, face sideways, staring at a very active anthill. This revelation caused me to move, even though I was amazed I still could. As I sat up, I was certain every bone in my body would snap apart like dry kindling. I struggled over and started analyzing the scene—the happening—the wreck.

Flax was standing, shaking. I knew he had gone down when I spotted the big tree stump with about half my rope around it. The other half draped down to the ground still attached to the saddle. I sat there until I knew most of what happened. Somehow, instead of the wild colt's neck, I had dropped the loop around a stump. We had jerked it out of the ground at the full speed of a thousand-pound horse. It had yanked Flax and me both into the air. What saved us was the fact the stump was old and somewhat rotted, and at the same time, the overly-used catch rope had snapped. That monstrous bird flying over me just before I whammed into the earth, was the stump.

I finally gathered the guts to try standing. I made it. Next I ventured walking. Amazingly I could with little pain. Now that it looked like Flax and I would both live, I walked over to him, rubbed his neck and said, "Forgive me, old pard."

I saw where the torn skin of the earth marked the spot where he, too, had greeted the ground in a maladroit manner. To my continued amazement, the saddle and the front cinch were still intact. In some unfathomable happenstance the flank cinch had broken without disemboweling poor faithful Flax.

I led him over to the stump. He didn't even limp and had quit shaking. I took the half rope from the stump, the other half from the saddle horn, coiled them together and draped them over the horn and swells of the saddle. I wanted some evidence when I would have to try explaining to Ed Young the inexplicable series of events.

Before I reined back toward home, we followed the wild horse tracks all the way to the heavier timber where they disappeared. I stared and stared. I have no idea why. All I saw was trees. Then Flax and I moved toward the Rafter EY to whatever interesting events might await us there. I don't know what made me look back, but I did.

A coyote was following us, about forty paces back. When we stopped, he did. This little show was repeated a dozen times before I got down and opened the horse pasture gate a half mile from home. When I mounted up, the coyote had turned around and was moving away down the trail. Then he stopped and looked back at me. We locked long-distance eyes. I swear I could see a grin on that sucker's face. I felt right then that the canny little critter had observed and enjoyed our recent wreck and was relishing the thoughts of how stiff, sore, and foolish we were going to feel tomorrow. The wind was wrong or I'm sure we could have heard him giggling out loud.

A couple years later, I miraculously acquired a small ranch of my own in northeastern New Mexico; Fought in The Great Ground War and survived; Surrendered to the obsession of becoming an artist which moved me to Taos and many other things.

I was living with my new wife Pat in Taos, New Mexico, when we got the letter inviting us back to the mesa for the once-or-twice-a-year dance and a lot of catch-up-gossip. Those gatherings were famous on the mesa.

We drove over the dirt road and purposely got there right after lunch. We knew the Youngs would be overworked preparing for the *grande baille.*

It was a very welcome sight to enter Ed and Mother Young's living room and see the rock fireplace Ed had built back in the 1920s with his own hands. No matter what the season, he kept two or three piñon logs going. It was the strobe light of its time and the pride of his construction life. In preparation for the party the room was stripped bare except for the fireplace and a couple of benches. These were soon filled by the Young's close friends some of which were: the Witte family, the Macdonalds, the Colemans, the Curry boys, the Sandovals, the Cozarts, the Eldon Butlers, and the Tapias. They arrived in old cars, trucks, wagons and teams, and on horseback. The women all brought food and the men came with a hidden bottle, mostly pints. Also furnished by the guests was the music—usually a fiddle, a banjo, and a guitar or two. They alternated between the waltz, the two-step, and the cowboy stomp, and it went almost non-stop. The kids joined in. Some danced with other kids and some with grownups. Everyone had a great time.

There was an unwritten law of the land—No hats worn indoors, and all thirst quenching was done outside the yard fence. No exceptions ever appeared. The visiting, the dancing, the teenage sparking

FLAX at twenty-two shortly before his death. Author's collection.

went on all night until the roosters truly crowed. No fights. No arguments. Just plain conviviality and pure fun. I would never see it again like this anywhere in the world.

Just about everything was the same except Flax. When Flax had reached eighteen years he could still work a branding and was a good night horse, but Ed decided to retire him while he was in good enough shape to enjoy the long grass and fresh water. He'd long ago paid his way and a whole lot more. He had four precious horse years of total freedom left to make his own choices.

He had given me, an unskilled kid, five human years of his vast earthly and spiritual knowledge. It was priceless. And all I ever had to give back to him was my loving memories. Everlasting.

The end.

PART II

A Few Notes to the Reader

IN PART II of this three-part book I thought the reader might enjoy some photos showing the wide range of work and pleasure the horse bequeaths us.

I personally know—or have known—most of these people, horses, and activities as well as a number of the photographers.

Since I accidentally discovered a few random snapshots of my first horse paintings and ink drawings done at Taos, New Mexico, when I was about twenty-four years old—we decided to print them in the book.

We also concluded we would scatter the live action shots among three of my favorite stories. Some of the people and horses viewed here are famous, others unknown, or possibly infamous. I was amazed and pleased to find them. It is with all best wishes that you horse lovers enjoy them as well.

Sincerely,
MAX EVANS

CHAPTER SIX

Horses and Their People

JOSH BRYANT, actor, voice-over expert, and two adopted wild mustangs. Photo courtesy of Em.

WALON GREEN, author of the screenplay for Sam Peckinpah's *The Wild Bunch*, Oscar-winning director and producer/writer of numerous successful television shows, his wife, Anne, with their prized Icelandic riding horses. Courtesy Walon Green.

WORLD CHAMPION steer roper, Cotton Lee, preparing for a calf run on Old Baldy, claimed by many top ropers to be the greatest roping horse ever. Unheard of at the age of twenty-three, Old Baldy was still putting on championship runs, and for those twenty-three years he put out all he had every time out of the box. Author's collection.

NEW MEXICO GOVERNOR David Cargo, talking with a Mora area farmer while the farmer's horse rests from plowing, circa 1969. Author's collection.

WOLF SCHNEIDER, editor, writer, and literary consultant. Wolf was senior editor of a major West Coast movie magazine, who left her job to move to Santa Fe to take care of her aging mustang, Ryo. Courtesy Wolf Schneider.

RUDY GARCIA and his son, Pat, finishing off two colts at their horse ranch near Des Moines, NM. They breed and train working and pleasure horses for clients all over the country. Author's collection.

TUFFY COOPER, circa 1952, famed roper and teacher on his favorite horse Cortez. On Cortez he won Tucson, Calgary, Pendleton, Salinas, and many others. The Cooper family members of Lea County, NM, have won many world championships and have been inducted into the National Cowboy Hall of Fame in Oklahoma City, and Rodeo Hall of Fame in Colorado Springs. Courtesy Tuffy Cooper.

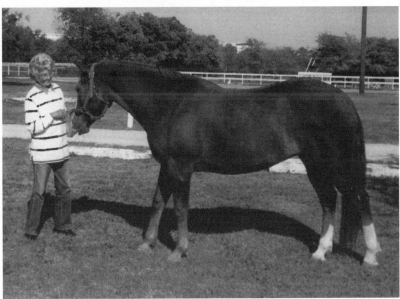

CAROL SONNICHSEN, widow of the late dean of Southwest literature, C. L. (Doc) Sonnichsen with her eighteen-year-old saddle horse, Ginger. Author's collection.

SLIM PICKENS and Max Evans with their stagecoach horses in Sam Peckinpah's film, *The Ballad of Cable Hogue*. Author's collection.

J. P. S. BROWN, well-known Sierra Madre novelist, with his first horse, Pancho, presaging the title of one of his most recent and finest novels, *The World In Pancho's Eye*. Courtesy J. P. S. Brown.

TWO OF the greatest actors of all time, Glenn Ford and Henry Fonda, transporting their nemesis, Old Fooler, and other companions during the filming of *The Rounders*. Author's collection.

JAMES GAMMON, one of the world's great character actors of stage, screen, and television, with his winningest racehorse, Penny, now retired. Courtesy James Gammon.

JOE BERNAL (center), legendary Taos Pueblo medicine man, trading horses with equally legendary horse trader Curly Murray. Author's collection.

MABEL DODGE LUJAN,
Taos doyenne, who enticed
world famous composers,
writers, and painters to
Taos to experience the
great spiritual presence of
the Taos Indians and the
surrounding landscape,
among whom were D. H.
Lawrence, Georgia O'Keeffe,
and Thornton Wilder.
Author's collection.

MAYOR MARTIN CHAVEZ leading the Albuquerque, NM, tri-centennial
parade (2006) mounted on a spirited horse. Chavez's ancestors had entered
the New Mexico territory in the same manner hundreds of years before.
Photo by Gene Peach.

CHAPTER SEVEN

Showdown at Hollywood Park, August 6, 1947

*Winner of the National Cowboy Hall of Fame Wrangler Award
for best magazine article of the year, 1987.*

THE RACE was at Hollywood Park, and it was a classic. In its excitement, color, conniving, and later importance it had to be one of the top-matched quarter horse races of all time. The head-on bet of one hundred thousand dollars by the owners was chicken sprinkling compared to the vast amounts gambled on the side by the country boys for their favorite brush-track quarter horse, Barbara B, and the city slickers for their imported thoroughbred, Fair Truckle.

It all began in Texas. Barbara B's trainer, Lyo Lee, was in Houston waiting to see if the Texas legislature would legalize pari-mutuel betting in the state. The racing crowd was eagerly anticipating success. Lyo was there to have his horses ready before anyone else, but the bill failed to pass, leaving Lyo with twenty-five good horses and not much to do but try to scare up a few match races. That's when the call came from Ray Bell that would start it all.

Ray was a commission buyer, mainly in Europe, for such stables as C. S. Howard, the wealthy San Francisco entrepreneur and owner of Fair Truckle; and Louis B. Mayer, the movie mogul head of MGM

BARBARA B. winning the Rocket Handicap. Author's collection.

Studios. At that time, Mayer was the highest paid corporate officer in America, drawing down over a million a year. He had many stars under contract—Clark Gable, Joan Crawford, Spencer Tracy, and Katharine Hepburn, to name a few. Just four years later the iron fisted Mr. Mayer would see his power begin to erode because of his love for horses and horse racing.

Lyo and Ray Bell were long-time friends, but even if they hadn't been, Mr. Lee would have given him a good listening. This man dealt with wheels . . . the kind that breathe the dust that money is made from.

Ray knew Lyo was looking for some races, so he passed on the comments C. S. Howard had made about his fancy horse, Fair Truckle, after winning a thoroughbred race and leading from wire to wire. "When you go all the way to Ireland to buy a horse you're going to race in the U.S.A., you expect him to be good, and I'd like to see some of those smart-ass quarter horse men try to take him." Fair Truckle was good. He was unbeaten. He'd shown the roots of his tail to all contestants.

After the phone conversation with Ray, Lyo got moving. He called Barbara B's owner, Roy Gill, and told him they had a good chance to get a big win here if they played it right.

Roy Gill's Arizona family had huge cattle feed lots and farms all over. They were *big*. Roy got into racing with Lyo as his trainer, buyer, and all around man, so he could have extra money—lots of it—to play with. He didn't want to draw money from the family empire just to gamble with. He knew this would be heavily resented. He lived the highest life his winnings could buy wherever he was. There were always lots of lovely ladies in his presence, and some of these were escorted by men with much political muscle and moola.

Roy Gill didn't especially care about the art or sport of racing. It was a money machine to him. He expected to win and Lyo Lee delivered for him over 95 percent of the time. Gill wouldn't bet less than ten thousand a race. So, with anything below that Lyo was on his own. Gill took care of all expenses and Lyo received 10 percent of the winnings, including the side bets made by Gill. Since Lyo was one of the best trainers in the world (he finally wound up with over five thousand lifetime wins) and Roy was one of the finest spenders, it was a marriage made in horse heaven. At one time their stable had five of the top ten quarter horses listed in the *Quarter Horse Journal*. Among them were Tonta Gal and the great horse Pelican. When they cemented their partnership, Roy Gill had only one instruction for Lyo, "Win."

Lyo had some advice for Gill as well, "Anytime we find a horse that can outrun you, buy him. This rapidly eliminates the competition."

In further phone conversations with Ray Bell, Lyo learned that C. S. Howard wanted to run Fair Truckle at anything they had, but would bet no less than fifty thousand dollars with ten thousand up front as forfeit money. That put a lot of pressure on Lyo. He wasn't about to recommend to Gill they match the race until he'd done a thorough job of checking.

He went first to the *Racing Year Book*. Fair Truckle had been running at good West Coast tracks: Santa Anita, Golden Gate, and Hollywood Park. These tracks were all clocked with electric timers and the year book gave the exact time at every turn and quarter pole. These tracks all had a running start of twenty to seventy feet from the gate before the timer started. At Hollywood Park that distance was forty-nine feet. Fair Truckle was running the first quarter in 21.3 and 21.4 and had never been behind up to the three quarter pole.

Barbara B had never been timed with a running start. So Lyo got ready and gave her a go with the forty-nine foot advance. Well guess what? Her time would make scavengers and gold watchmakers look wildly around and rub their hands together. Twenty-one flat, it was, and on a lot worse race track than the Irish-bred Fair Truckle had been using. Interest picked up around the Roy Gill and Lyo Lee stables like a banker's loan. Lyo didn't want this information spread around, but he wasn't worried. He said, "I had my help tied up so I could control 'em . . . not exactly a dictator, but close."

Lyo called Ray Bell and told him, "We'll run Fair Truckle in Texas for a hundred thousand." Gill was putting up fifty of this and a few close friends were picking up the other half.

Howard turned this down. He said he would only race at Hollywood Park under their rules and with their officials. He said he didn't want to risk such a valuable horse on rough country tracks. After further consultation with Lyo, Gill agreed to go to California. Then another of the many snags came up. California pari-mutuel racing was only for thoroughbreds, not quarter horses, so the Racing Commission refused to let them race during the meet or any other time. However, the go-between, Ray Bell, went to Louis B. Mayer and some of his rich, politically powerful cohorts, and an agreement was finally reached that the race could be run on Monday, August 6, 1947, the day after the big meet closed.

Gill, Lyo, jockey Tony Licata, Barbara B, and the rest of the crew arrived in California with everyone doing his own special job. Roy's was a little easier than the rest—he was there to gamble and have fun. He was a master at the latter and with Lyo Lee's help, first rate at the former.

Roy Gill had let his sixteen-year-old daughter come to the races with him. She wanted to be in on the thrill of mixing with the Hollywood celebrities and high rollers. She mixed a little too well to suit her father. One of the younger men of the thoroughbred group mesmerized her into falling in love with him. Gill tried, to no avail, to convince her that the young man only wanted inside information about the race. To prove it, Gill offered to bet the suitor five thousand dollars, headup. Surprisingly, he took the bet.

By now word was out all over the quarter horse world about the big race. Phones rang back and forth from the California stables to all points, concerning every little rumor and chip of gossip. The match-race crowd, the bookies, the habitual, and the part-time gamblers were all astir anticipating the day of action with almost a carnal craving. Finally the old, old question about the difference between a quarter horse and a thoroughbred had a chance to be answered. The press was picking up on the vast interest and excitement this race was creating. This put even more charge in the betting batteries.

C. S. Howard resided in San Francisco, so Lyo Lee drew up the contract himself and flew up to deliver it personally. The substance of it was that they'd use the seven and nine gates set exactly on the quarter pole. The post position would be decided in the paddock after the horses were saddled. This way no one would have the time or opportunity to alter the track to his own advantage. On a few rare occasions at match races, when the gate number had been decided in advance, the ground had been dug up soft and deep in front of it and then smoothed over to look untouched.

Howard admitted he was afraid that some of these match race guys would attempt to trick him, so Lyo tried, in front, to make everything as up-and-up as possible. He included everything—the money, the track timer, the officials—that had already been verbally agreed. In spite of all Lyo's care, Howard refused the contract. He insisted the gates be left where they were—forty-nine feet back of an even quarter mile.

This would change the outside bettor's opinion of the race, most agreeing that the longer it was, the better chance Fair Truckle had. Howard and his people figured that Barbara B would slow at the quarter marker whether she was ahead or behind, and be slowing every foot after.

Lyo argued that this gate situation hadn't been mentioned until now and he complained, truthfully, that they would be out a lot of money in time, travel, and wages if the race was called off now. It did no good. Howard was adamant. He was what the town fellers call a "worthy adversary." Howard was a tough and clever man. He was also rich and powerful, having bailed General Motors out of a hole after World War I. He got a large block of stock and a percentage of every GMC car sold in California.

Lyo flew back to see Gill in L.A. feeling like he'd swallowed a bee hive—honey, bees, and all. He convinced Roy that they could beat Fair Truckle anyway, because he already knew that Barbara B could go three-eighths. Lyo had saved back this secret information to put with his other forty-nine-foot ace he had in the hole.

Lyo flew back to San Francisco, and told Howard, "Well, it was tough, but I've finally convinced my people to go along with your terms."

Howard okayed the contract and they each deposited ten thousand dollars with the Racing Commission in L.A. If one defaulted before post time, he lost the money and, of course, there would be no race.

The rest of the money was to be put up on race day. Then after they left the paddock everybody was on his own provided there wasn't an official foul in the actual race. The latter was included in the contract. They would take urine and saliva tests after the race as well. There would be no pari-mutuel betting, but the gates were open free to everyone.

The electricity was bouncing through the air. This race was crucial to advancing the status of the quarter horse, and could be the vital element needed for the legislature to pass the bill accepting the quarter horse into the pari-mutuel race tracks. At this time, the only places they could run under the pari-mutuel system were Tucson and Albuquerque.

It was in Albuquerque, in fact, that Lyo discovered Barbara B. She was entered in a handicap. Tom Snow owned her and they happened to be in the stall next to Lyo. He noticed, when they were shoeing her, that her feet were extra tender. She came in fourth, even with her feet in that condition. Lyo knew that here was a hell of a horse. He bought her for Roy Gill, at the extremely high price for the day of six thousand dollars. Barbara B was out of the stud B'ar Hunter II and a Wagonner ranch mare with rumors abounding that the dam had once sold for thirty dollars. Lyo patiently got her feet in shape and they started winning races.

Cal Kennedy, a horse trainer friend of Lyo's, came to him about a week before the "big 'un" with some information he thought Lyo might enjoy cogitating upon. Lyo knew Cal to be a knowledgeable man who would take every legal advantage to win a race—as who didn't in this world of worried inches.

Kennedy trained a horse named Three Bars. He'd run him three times against Fair Truckle at five-eighths. Each race Fair Truckle had taken him, but also each time Three Bars had been lapped onto him at the quarter mile pole. Now Kennedy was all for his old friend Lyo, but he wanted to make a bunch of money by gobbling up a cinch. He explained that the only way to do this was to run Barbara B and Three Bars. If she couldn't take him, then the Gill and Lee stables better forfeit their ten grand and head for Texas, turning back a few thousand bettors on their way out. A dilemma, indeed, Lyo was under a glorious type of pressure from all angles.

"How much will she have to outrun Three Bars to be a contender against Fair Truckle?" Lyo asked Kennedy.

"A couple of lengths," he replied.

To keep Barbara B company, Lyo had hauled Tonto Gal out in the trailer and stabled her right next to the mare at Hollywood Park. Lyo didn't really want to give away any of his position, but when he made up his mind to go with something, he put all he had into it. He decided to run Tonto Gal with Barbara B and Three Bars.

Very early that morning, a lot of race barn folks saw the three horses heading for the quarter pole in front of the gate and being lined up for the run. People were yelling and looking for stopwatches to time the race. (Just what Lyo didn't want to happen.) Over a hundred of them watched the event.

Lyo decided to run Tonto Gal in case Barbara B got a bad start; he could still make a fair judgment because most of the time the two mares were only a head or neck apart.

Barbara B outran Three Bars by three lengths and Tonto Gal was lapped right on her. So now Lyo had what appeared to be a slick gut cinch . . . but instead of having twenty- or thirty-to-one odds, they were now dropping to even. Most of the track habituates knew Three Bars and a few seconds before had thought of Barbara B as a dog cow pony who Fair Truckle could outrun like breaking sticks. That had all changed. The word flew out like a West Texas sand storm.

The noted sportswriter, Ned Cronin, who did stories for *Pathe News* and many large daily papers, dropped by the barn and asked Lyo, "Has she ever been in a starting gate?" Lyo answered, "Think so—once or twice before we got her, but I'm not sure." "Do you use a stock saddle or a racing saddle on her?" "Oh, whatever's handy." Lyo knew that Cronin was only halfway putting him on, but he liked the reporter and played the game with him. Cronin asked, "Did you ever rope any calves or steers on her?" Lyo grinned and said truthfully, "Naw, I haven't rodeoed in years."

Lyo was having too many visitors around the barn now. Friends and acquaintances—hundreds of them—were beginning to arrive from all over the Southwest. The wealthier of these would be staying at the Coliseum Hotel on Figueroa Street in downtown L.A., because that's where Roy Gill and his "partying" party were headquartered. So were Lyo and his wife, but the last two nights he would stay at the barn with his horse. There were too many things that could happen to an unattended animal when hundreds of thousands of dollars were already laid down, and several million were yet to come. Lyo's pressures increased hourly.

Then another, more deadly form of squeeze play, unexpectedly entered the game. Two finely dressed men came to the barn. One carried a large black leather folding bag. With extreme politeness they asked to speak with Lyo in private. He took them to the tack room.

The man placed the bag down, saying, "You see this? It contains five hundred thousand dollars. Now all we want is a guarantee. Just guarantee us which horse will win the race and this bag and its contents are yours."

Lyo felt like he'd been gored by a Spanish bull; and he heard the gates of heaven swing shut behind him at the same time. After a bit, he convinced the two money men that he'd need the night to think it over. They reluctantly agreed and left.

Now, there was only one way he could guarantee the outcome of the race and that, of course, was to have the jockey hold the mare back. In spite of the race tests with Three Bars, where they were as close to a cinch as they could get, many strange things could happen to cost a man the race. Lyo had been in the game too long and too intensely not to know this.

He would spend a rough night. With a half a million dollars, he could go to a tropical island and be a minor king. He could envision the dancing girls and feel the soft warm sea breezes. Various temptations oscillated before his eyes, and he was truly entranced. On the other hand, he wouldn't be free to roam the country matching races anymore. The excitement of having a horse come from behind in the stretch and pound on to win with good odds would no longer be his. Doubt settled in like a Malibu fog. Then, too, there were all the people he'd dealt with over the years who'd had faith in his talents . . . most of them here at Hollywood Park now betting on his abilities as a trainer. The golden sparkling thoughts of the islands washed caressingly across him again. Indecision. Agony.

The next morning he told the bag men to forgive him, but he just couldn't go along. Surprisingly, they made only one more pitch, then left. Of course, Lyo would feel a chilled ghost over his shoulder until the race was run.

The flag was to fall at 2:25 that afternoon. By eleven o'clock that morning there were over five thousand people at the track to watch the only race for the day. The final number of the gathering was estimated by different writers to be between 7,000 and 25,000. Lyo Lee figured the unpaid attendance at about 20,000. It was a tentless circus. Heavy newspaper coverage had brought a lot of the spectators, but several thousand were there by word-of-mouth. The quarter horse enthusiasts from every southwestern state showed up to back their favorite Barbara B. The West Coast thoroughbred people and the rich, clubby followers of the financial wizard, C. S. Howard (justifiably known as Mr. Seabiscuit), arrived in even greater force. They didn't have as far to come, however.

This was an unofficial meet . . . two horses and one race. The money would either flow from the pockets of the booted, broganed, wrinkled suit crowd to the Brooks Brothers and silk shirt set, or vice versa.

The Fair Truckle followers were almost smug in their betting—and why not? They'd never seen anything ahead of their hero in nine races from wire to wire. The quarter horse boosters were more enthusiastic. One was heard to say that the brown, four-year-old mare could beat that "Eurrrupeein' horse pullin' a plow." Another said, showing considerable confidence, that Barbara B could win by a length and stop twice to graze on the way.

The movement of mouths and tongues was matched by arms and hands reaching in and out of pockets counting money and layin' it down. There was a vast kaleidoscope of color, erratic and pulsating movement, and a chattering symphony of sound made up of laughter, bantering, bragging, and ridicule. It was almost as if two massive brains were in mortal money-crazed conflict: one controlling the Fair Truckle crowd and the other manipulating the Barbara B bunch. It would finally boil down, though, to the more concentrated gray matter of the city-sharpened Mr. Howard and the brush and bramble seasoned Mr. Lee. The fact that Howard had bought the great horse Seabiscuit when he appeared to be no good and with his trainer had turned him into one of the fastest of all stake racers also enhanced this race.

The jockeys and horses are always expected to give their best in every race, but according to a perpetual race track yarn that started that day, Tony Licata could collect all honors for the most dedicated jockey of all. He was having trouble making the 114-pound weight for the race, so it was bandied about that he went out and had all his teeth pulled to lessen the pounds. (He did ride the race without his dentures.) Here was a racehorse man from the hocks to the gums. He was getting eight thousand dollars for the race, win or lose. He'd bet every penny of it.

The even money was changing hands by the barrel, and the only way to get odds was to bet on the length of the win. That's the way it was until the horses entered the paddock. It took two men to hold Fair

Truckle while he was readied, while Barbara B, always the lady, took the money-changing madness around her with such calmness that she looked like a sleepy, dead-headed cow pony. Deception unlimited. Between the paddock and the starting gate the Barbara B clan got odds on hundreds of thousands of dollars at four or five to one. Lyo had held off betting until this moment. Again figuring ahead, he had a friend get down ten thousand for him at three to one.

Billions of tiny bolts of lightning were heating the blood of thousands of people with the oldest passion in the world—contest fever. Unless there was a dead heat, one horse would have to chase the other.

As agreed in the contract, they had to flip a coin for the choice of a post position . . . gates nine and seven. Lyo was anxious to win the toss. Fair Truckle, having always come out of the gate ahead and leading all the way, naturally charged to the rail—the shortest route around the track. So, if he had to cut across from the nine gate instead of the seven, he would have a little bit more ground to cover. Lyo Lee's mother had not raised an unthinking son. He had taken this into consideration. Neither had C. S. Howard's mama birthed a son without the thought process. Where Lyo was hoping to gain maybe a few feet with the gate choice, C. S. had already fudged in a forty-nine-yard head start. Lyo won the coin toss and picked the number seven gate.

Now the horses left the paddock and the thoroughbred crowd became more fired up because Fair Truckle was prancing and dancing, led by a pony horse whose rider was having a little trouble. Barbara B just strolled along with her head down and the reins slack like a worn-out ranch horse.

The track looked fast, but Lyo had tested it carefully and found it cushiony underneath. He told the groom that there'd be no timed records set today, but the money being bet would break all gambling records on a match race.

Because he'd won the seven gate, Lyo loaded the mare first. She stood there calmly. Fair Truckle, on the other hand, was really acting up. When they finally got him in, he hung a hock in the gate. So they had to let him out and walk him around to see if he was all right. Several thousand hearts froze! He didn't limp, so they decided to go ahead and run him. During this little ceremony, Barbara B seemed to be catnapping.

They were off! Barbara B was neither a fast starter nor a slow one. Fair Truckle came out of the gate a good neck in the lead. There was just one thing though as Lyo had said: "Barbara B reached full speed at the third jump and would be running faster at that point than any horse I'd ever seen. She was also hitting a stride of twenty-four and a half feet by then . . . I'd measured it many times. And that's how she won most of her races.

Because of the extra forty-nine feet, the gates were set back in a straightaway chute from the main track. By the time they hit that point, Barbara B had leaped out in front by a little over a length.

The great jockey, Johnny Longden, felt he now had a problem. He sure did! Fair Truckle had never been hit with the whip. Since he was always out front, there had never been a reason for it. Now there was, Longden figured. When he tapped Fair Truckle, he ducked in behind Barbara B and went to the rail. That move increased Barbara B's lead by another length as Lyo had anticipated.

The country crowd went slap dab crazy. The stadium waltzed and the air was shredded into slivers by the roar. Fair Truckle really put out. He pulled up almost neck and neck and held there.

Now it was the thoroughbred's touts turn to shake the earth and create vacuums in the air. The horses were sailing along on even terms, so that now everyone could go mad at once.

Then! Then Tony Licata smacked Barbara B right across her gear box with the whip. Ned Cronin wrote about it in the *Los Angeles Daily News* the next day.

"Somewhere in Barbara B's clouded past there is a jackrabbit among her forebears. There's got to be. How else could she cut loose with a jump that almost took her out of her hide? As that jackrabbit blood bubbled and boiled through her veins, she sprang with a few such prodigious leaps that they carried her under the wire an easy winner by two and a half lengths in the respectable time of 21 and 3/5ths seconds."

Payday at the mines! Wild and good times for the Barbara B's. Lyo Lee, Tony Licata, and the lady with four fast legs had delivered the baby full grown. Most of the winners had traveled hundreds of miles to bet and sweat their all on less than twenty-two seconds. They'd sliced up C. S. Howard's thoroughbred club elites like venison jerky. The Final Score: Country team—several million. City team—zero.

There was great rejoicing in and around the Coliseum Hotel that night. Other areas of Los Angeles rang out with resounding victory yells and toasts before the grass and plow folks headed back home.

Roy Gill patted his daughter's suitor on the back as he collected his five thousand, and said, "Why, you're a fine young feller. You come visit us in Arizona some year, you hear."

Aside from the money, the real significance of the event was that it woke the racing world up to the fact that among all its other multiple and supreme abilities, the quarter horse was also a race horse. The momentum this highly visible, publicized race gave to the entire quarter horse industry is incalculable.

Ned Cronin and a lot of other journalists broke this fact to the world the next day with satirical force. Too few people remember that this race was instrumental in the legislature legalizing quarter horse pari-mutuel racing in the state of California.

Barbara B went on winning races, but she lost one to Miss Princess in Del Rio, Texas, after stepping on a small round rock and falling to one knee with her nose touching the ground. She still got up and made the acknowledged King ranch Best in the World Champion run for it. In 1950, after Miss Princess retired, Lyo ran the seven-year-old Barbara B against the four-year-old mare, Stella Moore, for the generally agreed championship of the world at Sunshine Park, in Oldsmar, Florida. Again the national press, including *Time* magazine, picked up on the story and made several million more people aware of the quarter horse. Barbara B won the 330-yard race by a length and a half in 17.1 seconds.

All this is and should be recognized as a permanent part of quarter horse history. It was a vital part of the action that eventually led to the richest races in the world at Ruidoso Downs, New Mexico, and to the King ranch recently purchasing the two millionth registered quarter horse. Considering the involvement of the West Germans and other countries around the world, in breeding and using of this very special breed, the number of three million or more will someday be announced. Even so, it will shower tubs full of hail in hell before a more momentous and exciting race will come along than the great matched shoot-out at Hollywood Park in August of 1947.

Lyo Lee and Barbara B—they made H-I-S-T-O-R-Y.

CHAPTER EIGHT

The Freak

Published in Southern Horseman, *May, 1985*

FOR AN animal that would eventually be registered and run as both a thoroughbred and a quarter horse, breaking several world's records and called by many "the greatest potential all-around race horse in the world," he was an odd-looking creature. He was awkwardly big, Roman-nosed, and had several white spots and streaks here and there among the overall reddish-brown. He grew long, ragged fetlocks like a Percheron workhorse. Considering how different he was from other running horses it seemed altogether proper for him to get his name in a strange manner, too.

Rancher Marvin Ake, from Datil, New Mexico, had acquired the colt some time back but couldn't find a name that fit him. This particular early morning, Marvin and his wife were sitting at the breakfast table drinking coffee. They were having a struggle holding the then modest sized ranch together. Marvin was daydreaming about better cow prices and more rain when he looked out the kitchen window and spotted something totally out of place.

He cleared his throat and asked his wife, "Do you see what I *think* I see?"

She looked and answered, "If I don't you're in a bunch of trouble. And if I *do* we're both gonna need help."

It just couldn't be, but there on the rim of the round metal stock tank, many hundreds of miles from any ocean, sat a pelican. That's right. In the lonely, isolated, semi-desert ranchlands of Datil, New Mexico, seeing the saltwater bird would be akin to climbing the Alps and finding a steaming pool full of Florida alligators.

Since he couldn't think of anything else to say that made any sense, Marvin told his wife, "That's it."

"That's what?"

"We'll call him Pelican." When his wife looked at him as if she was going to the rack for a gun, he added, "The horse, I mean . . . the new colt. We'll call him Pelican."

And so they did. To add more mystery to the situation, he had had a crippled wing. How did it get there in the first place? They fed it a couple of cans of sardines, but the next day it was dead. A mystic would have said it had come for no other purpose than to lend a name to greatness.

Marvin had once worked as a cowboy for A. D. Woofter, who owned Pelican as a yearling. When Marvin first saw the animal he decided he wanted to own him. He bought the colt for five hundred dollars and brought him back over the massive Magdalena Mountains.

When they first made the deal it was natural that Marvin should ask about the colt's breeding. Woofter hesitantly said he was almost certain he was out of Joe Hancock, Jr. (a great racing quarter horse sire from the famed Wagonner ranch at Vernon, Texas), and a little registered thoroughbred mare named Evelyn's Pride, but when Marvin went to pick up Pelican, Woofter changed his story and said the colt was out of Joe Hancock, Jr., and the mare Covollie. Marvin really

MAX AND LYO LEE, one of the world's great horse trainers, 1984. Author's collection.

didn't believe Woofter knew for sure and, at the time, didn't care, but he challenged him just for the hell of it. Woofter blew up and said he'd just keep the horse. It was too late. Woofter had five hundred dollars in his bank account and Marvin Ake had a horse that would eventually astound, entertain, and confuse the racing world. It's too bad that the horse's ancestry got mixed up in the passage of time, for even today most old-timers still give differing opinions. Probably the only one left who might really know is the great horse trainer Lyo Lee, currently of Acala, Florida.

Marvin bought Pelican in the summer and that fall saddled him up, but didn't ride him. The next spring he broke him out without any real problems. The horse was gentle by nature. Marvin did have a little trouble getting him to rein or stop properly like his other cowponies.

One day he ran onto a bunch of wild burros. He shook his loop down and took after them. Now, it takes a hell of a good cowboy and a better horse to get close enough to one of these creatures to throw a loop. Pelican built to one so fast Marvin didn't have a chance to get set properly. He threw the loop anyway and damned if it didn't fit right around the burro's neck slick as a Navajo necklace. The only trouble now was that Pelican just wanted to keep running right on over the top of the Magdalenas. Marvin was afraid they were going to drag the burro to death before he got Pelican stopped . . . but then everyone knows that a burro's neck is made out of stretchable, unbreakable rubber.

Right there Marvin Ake caught on to the fact that it didn't matter about the horse reining or stopping; Pelican's game was *running,* and how he loved it!

Up to now, Marvin had matched a lot of races with fast cowponies around small rodeos and county fairs, but he'd never taken a horse to a real meet. He thought he just might have a meet horse on hand now.

Pelican had a few other unusual characteristics that showed up early. Besides being gentle, he just plain liked people. He seemed to care more for his human masters than for his own kind. Marvin could walk up to him out in a pasture and catch him anytime. Later, when Marvin started racing him, he was a novelty around the stables and barns because he didn't sleep standing up like all the other horses. He found it more comfortable to lie down flat on his side like a person or a dog. Pelican was peculiar. Marvin said he was strong enough to make a good plowhorse . . . the exact opposite of a great racing animal.

Marvin chewed Beechnut tobacco in those early racing days, and just for a joke he handed a wad to Pelican. Surprisingly, he took it and loved it. From then on, whenever Marvin came near, Pelican would nudge him for a "chaw." The trainer said it wouldn't hurt him and added, "Shoot, everybody knows chewin' tobaccer kills worms."

Perhaps the key thing that altered Pelican's life, and the lives of a lot of sporting folks, was the illusion of his sleepyheadedness. The horse simply had an instinct to conserve energy and never waste the tiniest spark of it. Even as a two-year-old, Pelican never ran around and played like the other horses. As we shall see, this particular attitude, when improperly interpreted, would keep a lot of folks' money from burning a hole in their pockets, and send them back to digging postholes. Those few who knew would drive Cadillacs, eat the biggest, tenderest steaks, dampen their throats with the finest liquids, and occasionally giggle and do joyful little jigs here and there about the earth.

It all really started moving when Lloyd Crockett, a one-armed feller from over in the San Andres Mountains who really knew running horses, recommended Walter Harris of Artesia, New Mexico, as the trainer for Pelican. Marvin had nominated the horse for the Albuquerque Futurity in the upcoming fall meet at the New Mexico State Fair without having ever raced him on a track. Marvin must have been a strong believer in faith.

Since he had no horse trailer, Marvin and his wife loaded Pelican in the back of a wobbly old open topped pickup and headed southeast for Artesia. So did the lovely, wet mountain clouds. Cold sheets of rain pelted the naked horse all the way down there. Pelican was wet, chilled, and shaking. He was drawn down and looked like a Calcutta dog when the trainer first took a look at him. They all thought he'd get pneumonia and die, but he didn't.

Marvin asked Walter Harris if he thought he could get Pelican registered with the Quarter Horse Association.

Walter Harris swallowed, turned half around, tipped his hat back, and finally said, "Tell you what . . . I believe I'd get him filled up real good fore I showed him to the inspector."

Marvin and his wife could tell that Harris didn't like the horse. Since they'd made a long, risky trip, they went ahead and made a deal for Harris to train the horse for a month before a small meet in Alamogordo, New Mexico.

On the long, muddy trip back that night, Mrs. Ake could tell that

Marvin was feeling a little down. She said, "Now don't you worry, honey, we're gonna come out all right. That Pelican is an honest horse."

How right the woman was. The meet came off. Harris still didn't believe in the horse. He hired Frankie Nixon, a fifteen-year-old kid, as the jockey. The three-hundred-yard race was for two-year-olds only.

Tony Morrison showed up with a little bay stud, Joe Mac, that was really good. It was a big gamble for Marvin, considering his financial condition, to enter the untried Pelican against the fast and well-known Joe Mac. He figured he might as well find out right here if the horse could run. It would be less costly in the long run.

There were six horses in the race. At the gun Pelican broke last. Marvin was watching him closely and holding his breath. The horse was so green that he bent way out completely off the dirt track into a cow pasture. Even so, the kid did his best and got him angled back toward the track and the finish line. Pelican's long, ground-ripping strides pulled him on the bay and he finished second, only a head back. Now Marvin knew! He felt like throwing his hat about forty feet in the air and jumping up to grab it before it started down. Marvin's surface stayed as calm as an afternoon nap. Mrs. Ake, a smile almost ripping her face, patted Marvin on the arm, and said with soft control, "Stay inside your hide, honey."

That's what you call "jerking the fuse" or "capping the well."

Marvin was invisibly hilarious when George Foster, a horseman, said dryly, "That's gonna be a good'un."

Marvin greatly respected Foster's horse sense. He said, "George Foster was one of those rare men who could see deep into a horse."

They were both proved far more than right. Needless to say, Pelican's trainer now became an instant admirer.

The next small town meet was at Truth or Consequences, a New Mexico desert town about half the size of its name. It does have grand hot water springs and a large boating and fishing lake called Elephant Butte.

Now the trainer had renamed the horse Red Apple without consulting Marvin. The owner decided to keep quiet about the name until after the present race was run.

It was a 350-yard race. A ten-foot cutbank served as a rail on one side, but was still four or five yards from the track. Pelican had drawn the outside position next to the bank. They had the same jockey up. He was full of confidence after the race at Alamogordo. Marvin

FRIENDS helping
Roy Gill gather up
his winnings thrown
on the ground by a
disgruntled loser.
Author's collection.

PELICAN at the New Mexico State Fair, 10–14–1946, with owner Marvin Ake.
Author's collection.

believed Pelican had a chance to take the race because they had fifty extra yards for distance, and maybe the cutbank would keep him on the track this time. He put down an additional hundred dollars, getting two to one odds. It was a lot of money for the Akes to gamble at the time.

The eight horses finally got lined up and were off. Again Pelican made his natural bad start and was eating the dust of every other horse in the race. Not only that, he arced out, and was running almost up against the cutbank. Marvin was afraid he would drag the kid off and cripple him. The kid felt differently. He fought the horse back onto the track at about the 150-yard marker. Then Pelican straightened up and at two hundred yards swallowed the whole bunch and won by four lengths going away.

Walter Harris said, "Well, I got to admit it . . . I've never seen a horse jump the track and come back like that in my life. That Red Apple is . . ."

Marvin interrupted with, "His name is Pelican."

"Pelican! God uh mighty, that's the damnest, awfulest name I ever heard of for a horse."

Marvin closed the conversation with, "P-E-L-I-C-A-N. That's the way you spell it."

The next move was to the Albuquerque fairgrounds for the futurity. Marvin thought that Harris had Pelican in pretty good shape so about three days before the race he showed him to Ed Heller, the inspector for the American Quarter Horse Association. Heller hailed from Dundee, Texas, and traveled around to big meets looking for possible recruits for the organization. He wielded quite a bit of power and knew it. Marvin proudly held the halter of the shiny, brushed young stallion.

Heller circled Pelican several times expressionless. Marvin waited anxiously. Finally Heller said, "Well, you know, Marvin, that horse has got an odd conformity . . . I . . . just cain't put my finger on it. I think I better watch him for a year or two before we decide for sure."

After all the faith, hard money, and risk that the Akes had put in the horse, Marvin was deeply hurt. Again his wife came with the right words and correct prophecy, "Don't let it bother you, honey. They'll be coming to you before long."

Three days later, after the usual slow start, Pelican won the Albuquerque Futurity by six lengths and was going away again at the line. Heller dropped by the stables and asked Marvin if he could take another look at Pelican in the morning. Marvin, remembering his wife's words, simply nodded "yes."

The next morning Heller only circled the horse once and said, "That's an altogether different looking horse today than he was yesterday. We'll register him."

Marvin said, "You know, Heller, I think we'll turn it down for now. I better talk to the National before we go ahead." The National was a rival quarter horse association.

Marvin took a big chew of Beechnut, gave Pelican a wad of the sweet tobacco, and they enjoyed the masticating together. Heller stared stunned for a moment before he walked silently away. That's what you call "pullin' the string."

Next stop, Tucson, where Marvin entered Pelican in several $500 purse races. At that time Tucson was the only track in the country to run quarter horses in the winter. The first race had a sure-enough fast horse named Jap. The odds were good on Pelican. Marvin put down $200 and got back over $2,500 when Pelican just blew the field away. They won three more races in the same easy manner, and then Marvin entered him in the Arizona Derby, which was a stud race against the best in the field. Pelican took them by three lengths.

Now the famous trainer Lyo Lee had been watching Pelican ever since Albuquerque. He represented a rich Arizona and California rancher and playboy Roy Gill, who loved to gamble on horse races and usually won. According to Benny Binion, owner of the world famous Horseshoe in Las Vegas, Gill was one of the winningest gamblers he had ever known. When a horse backed by Gill, Tonto Gal, beat another gambler's mare named Prissy, the irate loser had lost so often to Gill that he threw his ten thousand dollars in cash out on the ground in a high wind (see photograph on page 148). Gill just laughed as the brush-track crowd helped him gather up his winnings. All but one hundred dollars was recovered and returned.

Coincidently, Marvin Ake and Lyo Lee had worked on some of the same cow ranches in Arizona and New Mexico when they were boys. So when trainer Harris brought Lyo to Pelican's stables it didn't take the two very long to get down to business. Lyo offered Marvin four thousand dollars for Pelican. The cash was a great temptation for Marvin, since the Akes' goal was improving and expanding their ranch holdings. Even though horse racing was only a side activity, the last thing he wanted to do was give up the horse.

Marvin said, "I'll take six." He never dreamed Lee would take him up on it, because six thousand dollars, at that moment, was the highest price ever asked for a quarter horse.

When Lyo Lee joined Roy Gill he told him, "If you see a horse that can beat you, buy him. That way you cut down the competition." Gill had totally agreed, and it sure worked. They had from five to seven of the top ten quarter horses in the world at any given time.

"You just sold him," Lyo said.

Marvin had a sick feeling way down deep, but there was no backing out. From that moment on he would have to enjoy secondhand the wondrous exploits of the horse he'd given so much to. As he handed over the bill of sale he told Lyo, "Just see to it that he gets his little chaw of Beechnut regularly."

Several decades later, after becoming a very successful and knowledgeable rancher, Marvin Ake said, "I believe at four years old Pelican could outrun any horse in the world from three hundred yards and all the distances in between, all the way up to a mile and a quarter—maybe a mile and a half. No other horse I've ever seen or heard of had that many distances. He was the top of his time."

The first thing Lyo Lee did was measure Pelican's stride. It was a phenomenal twenty-seven and one-half feet. He entered him in a race at Rillito Race Track in Tucson in a fast field. Included was the famous thoroughbred Piggin' String, whose owners were trying to turn him into a quarter horse, and doing a fair job of it.

At the latch, Pelican broke slow and awkwardly, rapidly flaring away from the bunch all the way to the outside rail. Even so he straightened up enough to come in a close second to Piggin' String. A week later Lyo Lee matched the same field at 660 yards. In the meantime he'd given Pelican a strong dose of schooling of the gate. This time the second-place Piggin' String was nine lengths behind, and Pelican set his first of many world track records. He ran the three-eighths in 34.1. He was so far ahead of the second-place horse that the photo shows Pelican hitting the finish line and there is nothing but empty track until you get to the far left of the photograph where you can barely see the top of Piggin' String's nose.

Now Lyo Lee was a trainer who would win over five thousand races in his long career, setting records with both quarter horses and thoroughbreds. He was the one to set up the famous race between their quarter horse mare, Barbara B, and C. S. Howard's thoroughbred, Fair Truckle, at Hollywood Park. The one-hundred-thousand-dollar match race made headlines all over the country and first launched the quarter horse into public racing prominence.

With all this first-rate professional background, Lyo soon found himself in a hell of a quandary with Pelican. He was beating everything on all the prominent brush tracks as well as the registered parimutuels. Now the owner, Roy Gill, didn't give a whoop about training horses or matching races. His game was to furnish the money for all this. His fun came in the minimum ten-thousand-dollar bets he loved to make. His order to Lyo Lee was, "I'll take care of all the costs, and your job is to win." And win they did—so much so they were having great difficulty getting a race set. About half the time Pelican was just turned out to pasture while they made the tour with the rest of their string. It was a terrible waste that a horse was so good that he had run himself out of both training, racing, and visiting his varied friends. It was a loss of love from a lot of Pelican's fans as well. They missed his antics around the stables. Besides chewing tobacco, he had a strange game he played with his best buddy, a mixed-breed dog named Guard. The dog would stand, in front of Pelican's stall and permit himself to be picked up by the scruff of the neck over and over. Up, down, up, down. The dog never flinched because Pelican knew just how to do it. They both loved their private game and would sometimes perform it for an hour at a time. "We coulda sold tickets," Lyo said. At night Guard was put on a long stretched wire with a loose ring and a short rope to its collar in front of the Gill stalls. He was free to run back and forth on the wire. Nothing strange ever came around their barn runway. Not ever. Sometimes Guard would lie down and sleep with Pelican, both stretched out in the same position. For a while one of the trainers had a pet raccoon. When he was walking Pelican, the ring-tail would sit up on top holding onto the mane like a tiny jockey. Pelican didn't mind having his unique passenger.

Finally, by giving three to one odds, Roy Gill got his minimum at the famous Del Rio, Texas, brush track. The competition was a fast mare named Peggy. Lyo told Gill that they had to lose one if Pelican was ever going to get even a few more good races. Not racing was getting more and more frustrating for both trainer and owner, not to mention the people-loving Pelican. Neither Lyo nor Gill wanted to lose on purpose, but the mighty horse was getting fatter and older out in the pasture. This really galled them. Racing was their lives, and to see one of the greatest racers of all time just thrown away was more than they could take.

WORLD RECORD race at Rillita Race Track, Tucson, AZ, 4-11-1948.

Lyo told the jockey, "Let's go fishin'." The jockey understood. He tied a piece of fishline from the snaffle of the bit under the horse's lip against his gums. It was out of sight and only took a tiny pressure for the horse to feel it. Peggy won by a half length.

They rematched the race a month later, getting over twenty thousand dollars up, and Pelican buried Peggy by three lengths at four hundred yards.

They went to Silver Park, Silver City, New Mexico, with their string of horses. They took Pelican along as a pony horse. (For the uninitiated, a *pony horse* is the plain animal with the rider sitting on a stock saddle, leading the fancy racehorse to the gate.) Lyo didn't even dream he would get Pelican in a race here, much less make history, but by chance an opening came up for three-year-olds or older and he slipped Pelican in.

Lyo says, "Even so, the only reason they offered to let him in was because they'd seen him ponying horses and didn't figure anyone would enter a horse without proper training. I thought to myself, 'Well, lookee here, I found a bird's nest on the ground.'"

However, it was a three-eighths mile, where Pelican held the world record, so the odds were even. All Roy Gill could do was make side bets and put some heavy money on other horses to place and show.

It was a six-horse field. There was a palomino mare entered named My Question, owned by some Albuquerque people. They were wealthy folks and didn't run her except at their convenience, so little was known about her.

They were OFF. My Question took the lead right away and at about 150 yards Pelican was third by about a length and a half. Lyo wasn't worried at this point because even when Pelican got a slow start he didn't just play catchup. With his twenty-seven-feet-and-over stride he'd just whip on by going away. It was *"adios amigos."* However, Lyo got a sudden case of the shaky wobbles when the mare was still ahead at the four-hundred mark. Pelican, with a little inducement from jockey Tony Licata, made a move here and came head to head with her. But the mare just hung on. Pelican literally inched ahead to win by a neck. It was the only time he'd ever been legitimately crowded, and he set a new world record of 32.4.

Years later, Lyo said, "I've never heard of a horse running that fast before or since. It'll never be broken." In that race, the show (third) horse was Señor Bill, a fast horse that Lyo had trained for

PELICAN at Hollywood Park, Ruidoso, NM, with owner Roy Gill and trainer Lyo Lee, just after sale by Marvin Ake. Author's collection.

another owner. He was over three lengths behind the second place My Question.

One wonders what speed would have been attained that day if Pelican had been in training. Of course we'll never know, but plain judgment would make one think the mare would have pushed him to the one truly unbreakable record in all racing.

This race, sadly, cinched Pelican to become a white elephant in the Roy Gill and Lyo Lee stables. There was no one to race against. Out of frustration, the Gill Stables ran a large ad in the *Quarter Horse Journal* and other periodicals for over six months offering to take on any horse in the world from 300 to 660 or anything in between for $50,000 and up. There were no takers.

There was this majestic animal grazing out in a pasture away from the other horses, alone, as was his strange nature. It got so Lyo couldn't stand to have him around to pony on because he spent all his time trying to think of a way to run him. It was a hopeless, mad feeling. One of the great trainers of all time and probably *the* greatest all-around horse that was ever raced were tied to the ground like two dead trees because of quality. A paradox. A sadness. A shame. A great loss.

In desperation Lyo had a friend write to Ernest Lane, the trainer of Miss Princess. The mare was owned by the King ranch in south Texas, and was reputed to be the fastest quarter horse in the world at the time. She did hold the world's record at 440 yards—three-tenths of a second faster than Pelican had been clocked at that specific distance. You have to consider here that Pelican had only run an exact quarter a few times and had never been crowded at all.

Lyo offered to bet $50,000 split evenly on three distances in one race: 350, 440, and 660 yards. They were still turned down.

He then called the man who had owned and developed Seabiscuit, C. S. Howard. Now, as earlier stated, Lyo and his mare Barbara B and half of western America had won millions when Barbara B blew Howard's unbeaten thoroughbred Fair Truckle off the track at 440 yards.

Lyo said, "Well, Mr. Howard, I've got a horse that would run a distance that would be more to Fair Truckle's liking, 660."

Howard replied, "I took care of all you cowboys last winter, and I don't have anything else I'd like to donate to you right now."

Lyo had missed the Albuquerque meet the last fall. This happenstance got him a race for Pelican. A good gambler and racehorse man named Stan Tanner had won the championship stud race there with his horse Be Seven. Out of the upcoming match race, half by chance, would come some partly accidental knowledge that would change the character and characters of quarter horse racing forever.

Up until the early 1940s, all quarter horse racing champions were mares. Even after that, for years the sport was dominated mostly by ladies such as Miss Princess, Tonto Gal, Barbara B, Miss Bank, and on and on. It was taken for granted in the industry that a stallion could seldom outrun a mare.

The only obstacle Stan Tanner had in Be Seven being recognized as the top quarter horse stallion was Pelican. Just one horse and one race separated him from this distinction. It came about by accident, or design, that Roy Gill and Stan Tanner got boozed up together in a Tucson hotel. As men have a tendency to do on these occasions they brag about their money, physical and mental feats, women, cars, and/or horses. This usually leads to some kind of contest being set for later on with both parties wishing to hell they'd never made the bet. However, they usually stick it out because of that old infection, pride. This bet was for ten thousand dollars at 440 yards, thirty days later.

Roy Gill always left the matching of races up to Lyo. That was part of the deal between them. He was embarrassed to tell Lyo that he'd not only matched the race, but he and Tanner had already put up five thousand dollars apiece as forfeit money. The race was on.

Pelican had been turned out in a three-acre paddock with plenty of grass for sixty days, and Gill had gotten him matched with a very tough horse who *was* in training. Unlike earlier days when Lyo would get a rare bet and just pull the horse in, run him, and win easily, this would be a tough race even if Pelican had been in perfect shape. So Lyo started working him in the same manner they all did with mares, geldings, or stallions. Since *he* hadn't made the match, Lyo was worried a lot more than usual. About a week before the race, he decided to see where they were really at.

He took Pelican and Tonto Gal to the gate and really put the hammer down. The mare outran him by two lengths, and the time was only twenty-three. Lyo Lee started trying to fall dead and said, "Lord, what kind of a mess has Gill got me into this time?" Right there a ghostly thought came into Lyo's head.

He walked the stallion and breezed him a bit and ran him at Tonto Gal again. The time was 22.8, but Pelican was lapped on her. He walked him the next day and then the following morning ran him at Barbara B—a mare just a bit faster than Tonto Gal. The race went down in 22.1, with Pelican taking her by a neck. Lyo said, "Well, lookee here." In training a mare in those days all you did was walk her, breeze her slowly, walk her, and breeze her slowly, then a light blowout and you were ready to race. It worked on mares then, and it does now, to a degree. But everyone was training studs the same way. Lyo Lee learned and introduced another method right here.

At the old fairgrounds in Tucson, they ran the quarter mile against Be Seven, beating him by a lap in 22.2. They could have had a faster time but didn't want to look any better than it took to win, hoping they'd get another match.

They did. One more. A long year later though.

The hard facts are that Lyo learned you have to work a stallion. Really work him to win. The word was passed around and handed down. Nowadays it's exactly the opposite of the 1940s; the studs usually dominate the quarter horse world instead of the mares. Lyo doesn't take credit for being smart; he was just doing anything he could to win that race. He does look back with some remorse and regret at the fine stud horses he handled. He says, "I didn't have enough good sense to work hell out of 'em."

Lyo Lee had the Gill Stable in Phoenix for the races at the state fairgrounds. It had been a year since they'd been able to race Pelican. The year of his prime. They alternately turned him out to pasture and used him as a pony horse.

Suddenly a friend of Lyo's came rushing down to the track, saying excitedly, "Say, Lyo, I think I got you a horse race matched. There's a feller staying at the Santa Rita Hotel that's got a little ol' mare that outran everything in California at three-eighths."

"Whoa, whoa there," Lyo said, "does he know about Pelican?"

"Not yet, but you better get 'er down damn quick."

"Well, did you find out what this mare is?"

"Yeah, she's called Tidy Step, from a thoroughbred stallion named Tidy. I never got the name of the dam."

Lyo told his friend to go on back to the hotel and put up the forfeit money, and since he said he'd run anybody, he didn't have to tell him the name of our horse. "Just say you have a friend that'll run at him."

This is what you call "winding up the toy."

It worked, and the next day they drew up the contract stipulating that they'd use their own jockeys at an equal weight of 114 pounds, and they'd hire the state fair track starters and officials. The race was to come off a week from Saturday.

Lyo was glad that for a change he had Pelican with him ponying horses and occasionally walking him out. He'd give him a couple of good workouts, and, though that would be a short time for other horses, Pelican would be more ready to go than he'd been for 50 percent of his prior races.

Lyo called Roy Gill in Tucson and told him to get his ass and a bank full of money up here. He added, "We've found another bird's nest on the ground and it's full of golden eggs."

Now the owner of Tidy Step started talking around town and was told that he was crazy. He was informed several times that Pelican was undefeated at three-eighths and held the world record for that distance as well as a couple of others. The man began feeling that he might have overstepped a little. It was natural that he'd be nervous when everybody he talked to said he'd already lost his ten thousand dollars. The man wasn't stupid, but perhaps he was justifiably overconfident.

It turned out that the straightaway at the Phoenix track was 550 yards. So Lyo went to the man and said, "If we go the full 660 we're goin' to have to run on around the turn for another 110 yards. Whoever draws the post position has quite an advantage." The man agreed to the 550 distance.

The talk about the great qualities of Pelican never stopped, but the man also learned that Pelican was a slow starter about two times out of three. So, he came to Lyo and said, "You're a gambler, Mr. Lee, a sportsman and a good sport to boot so I wish you'd give me a chance to win part of this race at the quarter pole. That'll make the race worth twenty thousand and if I could get lucky I could break even."

Lyo took it. Then Lyo's jockey came to him bubbling out, "Hey, boss, that man came to me and bet me two thousand against two hundred that he'd be ahead at three hundred yards. I took it."

Lyo blew up, "He's trying to sucker you into crowding our horse too early so we'll lose the big end of the race." Lyo went on more colorfully from there until the jockey was in tears, and then he added, "It's your money, but I'll tell you one thing, if you don't win the race, I'm gonna kill you."

The jockey had always been a strong believer in Lyo Lee and had never failed to listen carefully when he spoke. He said, "I shoulda known better, boss. Don't worry . . . we'll take him all the way."

158

The man had drawn the post position and was kicking himself for agreeing to the 550 yards when he could by contract have held Lyo to the 660. His trip on the jockey's mind hadn't worked, either.

Licata got Pelican out of the gate first and fast. Pelican was leading the mare a half length at three hundred, one and a half lengths at the quarter pole, and his twenty-seven-and-a-half-foot stride gave him a win of two and a half at the 550 finish.

Lyo said, "So, we sent that good man back to California a little less jubilant than when he'd arrived."

That was the last quarter horse race they ever got down. Pelican stood high at twenty-six wins and two seconds, one of the latter being his loss to Piggin' String and the other time he'd been pulled at Del Rio. The word was out on Pelican all over the West now. At great expense and time, they probably could have had another pari-mutuel race or two, but there was no way it wouldn't be a losing proposition. The noble horse had won himself out of business once more.

However, there's more to the story. He would run again as a thoroughbred with astonishing results.

It came about long before the Tidy Step match that people had come to know Pelican and love him to the point that they'd drive or fly long distances just to see him run, even though they might not have a dollar down. To those who knew the horse, he was a major star. One of those was A. D. Woofter, the man who raised him.

A crowd was standing around watching and admiring Pelican as he was being walked after the Tidy Step race. Woofter accosted Lyo: "You know, everybody but me has got well off this horse. It's a dirty shame. I raised him and I deserve something more than the few hundred I got when I sold him to Marvin Ake."

This is what you call "regretting the deal" or "being pissed at the results."

Mr. Woofter went on, "Do you think this horse can run five-eighths?"

Lyo explained to him that he'd tested Pelican secretly several times at five-eighths to a mile and a quarter, and he could sure eat those distances up.

Woofter then wanted to know if there was anyplace they could run a thoroughbred at that distance. Lyo was kind of stupefied at the question for a minute and then he answered, "Yeah, there are a few places around, including Wheeling, West Virginia and Lincoln Downs at Providence, Rhode Island."

Woofter went on to relate that Pelican was a registered thorough-bred and he had the papers. Only he and his son, Paul, knew about it. He was registered under the name Silent Partner. He told Lyo that if he thought the horse could win at five-eighths, he'd give him the papers. All he wanted was to be tipped off so he could get a good bet down. Lyo figured that Woofter had some counterfeit papers that he wanted to deal off on him, and that could sure get a man in a lot of trouble. Just the same Woofter told him he was going on back home and that he'd mail the papers to him.

Well, Lyo had forgotten about the incident and was surprised about a week later when the papers arrived. If he'd been subject to fainting spells Lyo would no doubt have bounced off the hard earth. The description was a page long and practically named every hair on the horse, including the gray spot on his hip, the gray spot on his mane, and the gray spot on his belly under the cinch. The right hind leg was white up to the hock in front sloping down to the back . . . the bald face that extended over his eyes but circled around the orbs, and on and on to the tiniest detail. Pelican had to be the horse that was described on the papers.

"The horse was registered before Marvin Ake ever bought him," Lyo said. Evidently the colt looked so bad, even though he'd registered him, that Woofter thought Marvin would like a quarter horse better for ranch work, never dreaming that he'd race him or even take him off the ranch. All things considered, Woofter can hardly be blamed for his actions, though it is reasonable to believe that as the horse's fame grew he sometimes gazed over the edge of sheer cliffs sorely tempted to test out his flying ability.

Woofter owned a thoroughbred stud named Montosa James. The stud was listed on the papers as the sire, and a mare called Covollie as the dam. It had been widely believed until now that Joe Hancock, Jr., was the quarter horse sire.

Melvin Haskell of Tucson, head of the American Quarter Horse Association and a writer on the breed for several magazines, used Pelican as the prime example of how a quarter horse could always outrun a thoroughbred. So Lyo quickly reasoned that he couldn't even run a matched five-eighths anywhere in that part of the country. It was a hairy situation. That wondrous, innocent animal named Silent Partner and/or Pelican was being cut off again because someone had messed with his ancestral papers.

Lyo talked to Roy Gill and told him, "Well, if we're ever gonna race this horse again as long as he lives we're gonna have to run him as a thoroughbred."

Gill agreed. Lyo explained about Haskell and a few other things and added that they better get as far from Tucson as possible. Gill agreed again. They had mostly thoroughbred speed horses in their stable now so they'd have some early action up there in Rhode Island until they could get the right situation set up for Pelican.

First they went to Hot Springs, Arkansas, because Lincoln Downs didn't open until after the Oak Lawn meet closed.

Lyo took a string of good fresh horses that had been wintered in the fine climate of Arizona and hit the Arkansas boys who had to do a lot of their training in the snow and mud. It's called "gettin' the edge."

Lyo was using Pelican for a pony horse again. He met a man named Wills who was associated with track investigations across the country. Wills was actually an undercover agent for the FBI.

Lyo and Wills got to be pretty good friends—going out drinking, playing, and dining together quite often.

Lyo said, "He drank quite a bit . . . in fact, he consumed a little too much." One night after dinner they were drinking and talking about horses. Lyo had just won a good race with a horse called Phantom Sea. Lyo told Wills he had a pony horse out there that could outrun most of the horses at Hot Springs. He had, in fact, secretly run Pelican at Phantom Sea for seven-eighths. Pelican had walked away from the ten-time stakes winner without having trained for a single day for that distance.

Anyway, Lyo continued and correctly told Wills that he'd won a lot of quarter-horse races with him, but he'd never had a chance to run him on a thoroughbred track. This is what you call "settin' up the deal."

The FBI man replied on schedule. "No problem. You've got the papers on him so I'll come back in the morning and take a look, and see if you want to go ahead and run him."

Lyo was quietly elated, but told Wills that the horse didn't have the required tattoo because he'd never needed it.

Wills said, "That's all right."

He came down the next morning and Lyo gave him the papers and led the horse out. Wills said, "Well, there's no doubt that this is the horse described on the papers. He's sure no ringer." So Wills called in the official tattoo people and they put it under Pelican's lip. He was now legal to run on a thoroughbred track, and Lyo was protected.

Lyo had never intended to run him at Hot Springs at seven-eighths. He wanted to get the five-eighths down, then move on up to seven and, step by step, to a mile and a quarter, taking down big bets as they escalated. Gill agreed once more. Of course, by previous testing, they'd already found out that Pelican was up to the enormous step-by-step challenge. This is what you call "justified ambition."

When the Hot Springs meet was over, Lyo loaded all their horses on a railroad car and shipped them to Lincoln Downs at Providence, Rhode Island.

Now, there wasn't *any* "form" on Silent Partner. He'd never raced as a thoroughbred so he was listed as a maiden. However, Lyo skipped the maiden (never won a race) race, and put him in a handicap instead with a bunch of good horses. The distance was the required five-eighths. Lyo had his jockey hold him back so that Silent Partner was recorded as coming in sixth, with long odds of fifty to one. Of course the story was zapped around about these dumb southwestern cowboys coming up here and trying to make a pony horse compete with real race horses. Lyo had left Pelican's mane naturally long and even a little shaggy unlike the neatly pulled ones of the northeastern bluebloods. He looked pretty ragged amongst the city slickers and of course that drew extra attention to Pelican as he came in way back in the pack.

This is what you call "seeing what Lyo Lee wants you to."

Anyway Lyo always liked to run a horse over a track before making any sizable bets on him. Different horses like different tracks. He did feel that Pelican could run on any kind of track, but he wanted to be sure. Also, the horse had never run around a turn in an *official* race.

Roy Gill was talking about laying down fifty thousand dollars on the race, so Lyo was under heavy pressure to set the proper music for the orchestra of which he was the sole conductor. The only way anyone could bet big money here was with the bookmakers and hope word didn't get back to the mutuels and kill the odds.

Gill put fifty thousand dollars down, over the phone, to his favorite and trusted bookmaker, who had assured him he'd not let the word get back to the race track and ruin the payoff. Talking of bookmakers—Lyo said Gill's trust was misplaced because bookmakers are not stupid or they couldn't stay in business. If too much money is on big odds they'll call a cohort and bet them down through the machines.

The night before the race Lyo called Mr. Woofter and tipped him off about the race. Then he tried to tell Gill he didn't feel the bookies would hold the money at the same price as when the horse would come out of the gate. Gill disagreed.

Pelican né Silent Partner came out on the board at twenty-to-one odds. If the price held, Gill's bet would return a million dollars. Just after the horse left the paddock the price dropped to nine to one and by the time they were about to head for the gate they were at four and a half to one.

Lyo's and Gill's spirits dropped down into their boot tops. As radical as the price change had already been they were scared rootless the odds would wind up dead even by the time they closed the windows.

They didn't have any idea where the leak had come from—the bookies, Woofter, or from Gill's own stable. It didn't matter now anyway. The money was down. They were in line. They were off!

Pelican aka Silent Partner won easily, finishing just off a track record of fifty-eight seconds flat with a three-lap lead, *coasting*. The payoff wasn't so bad. They took down almost a quarter of a million dollars. Now they could move up through seven-eighths and a mile and sixteenths and "really tap 'em out."

"*But*, the splashy brown hit the fan in globs," Lyo said. "It created a disturbance in the racing business almost like a declaration of war. All the newspapers were full of the cowboys coming up there with a horse that looked like a wild mustang and taking them down the line. It was bad publicity for me and more so for this great horse. It was a big write-up in the *New York Times* that led to the real problem."

Bob Waldo wrote in part, *A horse that looked more like a nice cowpony than a thoroughbred was a medium of a 'killing' for the boys in the ten-gallon hats and high boots here yesterday afternoon. Mysterious money began showing up for Gill Ranch Stables. . . . The five-year-old son of little-known Montosa James and Covollie performed like the 'good thing' he was supposed to be, winning handily by three lengths. . . . He is known to be one of the fastest quarter horse performers in the West, winning innumerable races against the 'speedballs' in Texas and Arizona. In drubbing many of the horses that managed to beat him at this same track less than a week ago Silent Partner returned $8.40 to win. . . . Yesterday, however, he combined with the champion quarter horse rider, Tony Licata, to race the remaining eleven horses into the ground with his dazzling speed.*

The aforementioned Melvin Haskell, president of the American

Quarter Horse Association, who lived in Tucson, subscribed to the *New York Times* to keep up with the racing world. The paper was about four days late reaching Tucson, but there he saw the picture of Lyo and Pelican on the front page of the sporting section. Now after all his support of Pelican and honest belief in the animal as an example of the perfect running quarter horse, Haskell was understandably angry. He was also powerfully positioned and personally wealthy. He did not take kindly to this horse being headlined as a thoroughbred and making him look like an idiot.

Even though the head of the Jockey Club had told Lyo to go ahead and run Silent Partner/Pelican because they weren't interested in quarter horses, the situation instantly changed when Haskell got into it. Haskell pointed out, accurately, that the registration papers around the country had two different sires: Joe Hancock, Jr., for the quarter horse Pelican, and Montosa James for the thoroughbred Silent Partner.

Gill told Lyo that when the dust settled, he'd probably have a *choice* to run Pelican as either a short- or long-distance horse, but not as both, and in that case he was going to choose to go with him as a quarter horse. Well, Lyo knew that decision put them out of business. Even before the new and vast publicity, they were unable to get a short race matched. Now it would be impossible. So with Gill's blessings he took the horse to Cleveland, Ohio, for one last go.

He entered him in a seven-eighths with instructions for the jockey to pull him. The odds were good because nobody except Lyo Lee, Roy Gill, and the jockey Licata believed that Pelican was unusual enough to run and win at seven-eighths. They pulled the horse and came in fourth. Since this was the last go around, Lyo decided to hold him again even though the odds were at twelve to one. If the horse lost twice, the odds should be enormous on the third and *killer* race.

Well, Pelican, with his natural love for people, must have temporarily become disgusted with them. At the turn he took off and ran away from the field in 1.23, still coasting.

Lyo said, "The only way the jockey could have held him would have been to stand straight up in the saddle and rear back like he was trying to stop a team of runaway mules."

The grand adventure was over. Pelican had taken control and ended it running naturally and grandly several lengths ahead of the rest of the field.

They retired him to stud in Arizona and used him as a cowpony, just as Marvin Ake had started him out. None of his colts amounted to anything. Marvin Ake had bred a mare with Pelican before he sold him to Gill. The colt, which he named Penguin, won only one race before Marvin gelded him. Marvin used Penguin as a cowhorse until he died.

Pelican was a freak. All the gene mappers in the world couldn't figure how this running marvel came about. He was crowded only once, and even then he set an unbeaten world's record in the three-eighths. If you forget the four times he was pulled, his record was twenty-eight wins and two places. Even the great Australian horse Phar Lap and the mighty John Henry would be tested dearly to match his overall ability. He could run any distance, on any kind of track. He was sound as an anvil, better natured than a puppy, honest as Abe Lincoln, and, with reasoned consideration, probably the greatest all-around race horse that ever lived.

Lyo said, "Pelican was a horseman's dream. He was what breeders had been trying to get since horses were first tamed. When you think of the small amount of training he received, the kind of tracks he ran on and the far greater methods of training, feeding, and doctoring we have today, as well as the mathematical odds of hundreds of thousands more horses to choose from, it's doubtful if we'll ever see anything to surpass him."

Yes, he was a joyful accident in history. He was so good that he was mostly idle and untrained for lack of competition. He chewed tobacco and slept stretched out like a dog, loved people and was loved by them. Among other things he was called Red Apple, Pelican, and Silent Partner, but for sure he must be called a creature of love and true greatness. Let's toast him and be thankful he passed our way—running.

CHAPTER NINE

Super Bull

Winner of WWA Golden Spur Award for best non-fiction story of the year. Published in Southern Horseman, *November, 1983.*

THERE ARE all kinds of bulls in the world, that's for sure—Angus, Brangus, Charolais, Jerseys, but Super Bull was a Hereford—and if Jimmy Bason, cowboy and rancher, had known about this particular one, he probably wouldn't have bought the S Bar S outfit. This bull would give him more trouble than a street full of terrorists and drive him as crazy as a bee-stung bear.

The Bason's land starts just west of the historical little mining and cattle village of Hillsboro, in southwestern New Mexico, and goes all the way to the top of the Black Range Mountains. When Jimmy bought the ranch in 1962, it was the S Bar S, but his brand was F Cross and he intended for every animal on his spread to carry that marking.

He started riding and looking for strays. He soon found a bunch of wild Hereford cows and calves enjoying the springtime grass in South Percha Canyon. A few of the cows and all the calves were unbranded. This had to be changed.

Jimmy went for help to three absolutely top-notch mountain cow-boys, Joe Wiegel, and Mac and Bill Nunn. They brought with them their best rock horses. These animals could run a cow up a tree and back down a badger hole. And would they ever need them, because

South Percha Canyon ranges from seven-to-ten thousand timbered feet in altitude and is as close to straight up and down as they come and still have a rock roll instead of drop.

In three days of hard riding and skilled tracking, they'd gathered seventeen head. They all agreed that there was at least one waspy old cow and her bull calf left. Jimmy knew that these good hands had work and responsibilities of their own, so he thanked them and said they could go on about their business. It wouldn't be any problem at all for him and his grulla horse, Billy Bob, to finish up.

Well, that old S Bar S cow was a smart one. She turned back on her tracks and over. She'd run up and down the nearly sheer slopes in a zig-zag manner and then cut back

JIMMY BASON riding Billy Bob in the Blank Range. Photo by Pat Evans.

and hide like a mountain lion in thick, brushy patches. The bull calf followed right along, making the same moves as his mother.

Jimmy and Billy Bob wore down after about four days, and as embarrassing as it was, Jimmy called on Rob Cox, another hellacious cowboy from the Organ Mountains near Las Cruces, to come give him a hand.

Two running, plunging days went by. No cow. No calf. Tired cowboys. Tired horses. Rob had other ducks to race, so Jimmy was once more left alone to face the rugged wilderness.

In this rough country he had to work by sign instead of sight. He looked for freshly overturned rocks and broken brush, but mainly he trailed by tracks and by the squirts and drops of green, mostly digested grass that falls behind a running critter. The way it splashes points out the direction she's going.

This vast land of steep slopes is covered densely with pines, spruces, and all kinds of brush and rocks and is some of the roughest terrain in America. To emphasize how wild it is, the great Indian leaders, Geronimo and Chief Victorio, chose it as their last stronghold after thousands of soldiers had pursued them for years.

SUPER BULL country, home of the Warm Springs Apache. Photo by Pat Evans.

South Percha Canyon stretches along Highway 90 for six miles, and along this whole distance there were only four trails that dropped down from the road. Jimmy finally got the old cow and calf headed up one of these trails. He could tell by the freshly steaming, green droppings that he was right on 'em. Then he saw them top out and vanish on the winding highway. He topped out himself, and the green sign told him which way they'd turned. He had to get her before she reached one of the other trails. Billy Bob charged right down the pavement while Jimmy shook out his loop. He knew he could only catch one of the two, so when he pulled in roping range, he decided to take the cow. He figured the calf would hang around hunting for its mother. He threw the loop. He caught. Billy Bob set up, sliding his hind legs under and screwing his tail in the pavement. If he hadn't been a top rock horse, there would have been a hell of a wreck. The cow was jerked down hard right on the yellow line knocking enough breath out of her to turn a windmill for thirty minutes.

Jimmy bailed off with his piggin string to sideline her—that is, tie two feet together on the same side so she could move around and easily get her breath, but couldn't get away. He had slipped the loop of the piggin string on one foot when she found some lost wind and really started kicking and bawling. A tour bus full of Japanese had stopped on the highway and about fifty excited, camera-toting Orientals were circling around jabbering, scuffling, pushing, and trying to take pictures. Here it was—the wild and wooly West in action right before their shining, dark eyes.

The old cow didn't like one human being much less a whole highway full of folks making more noise than a tenth anniversary class reunion. Billy Bob was boogered by all the racket, but kept the rope tight anyway. Jimmy was being kicked, butted, and generally abused by the crazed cow. The more Jimmy yelled at the Japanese, the closer they came with the cameras, smiling, pointing, snapping pictures like they were recording the Resurrection itself. At last Jimmy got the attention of the bus driver and screamed at him to get these photographic maniacs out of his way so he could finish his job. The driver finally waved and pushed the crowd back. Jimmy tied the cow. The bus moved out with many smiling faces mashed against the windows.

Jimmy rode down to the pickup and horse trailer, then drove back to take the cow home. The maverick calf with tiny nubbin horns was off the road somewhere out of sight, but probably nearby.

The next day Jimmy rode leisurely back to the spot where he caught the cow, expecting to find the bull calf bawling for his mamma. It wasn't there. He slid his horse off down the trail, confident he'd easily find the calf. They'd cleaned the country of wild cattle so any fresh tracks were bound to be the little baby bull's. Well, he rode for several days and although he found sign, he never saw the calf. The little critter was running the same country as his mama, backtracking and pulling the same tricks she had. Jimmy was getting the first tiny inkling of the marvelous events yet to come. Well, no bother. He had fences, windmills, and other cattle to look after. He'd let Billy Bob rest awhile, then come back and get the little feller.

When Jimmy returned to the scene, he found the calf tracks and other damp sign. He saw him with his own eyes. He ran him with his own horse. The little bull would run—no, he would fall—off the mountains at least three times as fast as the best cowboy and horse possibly could.

Jimmy said, "That calf just wouldn't go where any well-thinking animal should. If I jumped him at the bottom of a canyon, he would charge up through bush so thick it would have stalled an army tank and then he'd bounce across piles of rocks so agilely that if a mountain goat had seen it he would have fallen dead from pure jealousy."

Jimmy never got a loop. He did get very tired. After three hours of these games, Billy Bob was sapped out, too. So, Jimmy decided that all his other chores had suddenly become extra urgent, and besides, if he pulled out for a couple of weeks maybe a rain would eradicate all the old tracks and he'd have a clean shot at him.

Rob Cox came back to help again. They both made runs at the calf, but neither got close enough to throw a loop. The anguish mounted. Jimmy was finding it harder and harder to go into town now. The kind and considerate populace showed its deep concern by asking him about the elusive bull every place he went. One morning, as he was walking out to saddle his horse, even Sue, his patient wife, yelled after him, "Are you gonna go play with Super Bull again today, Honey?" That's the day the maverick got his name. Jimmy humped up like he'd been shot in the butt with a sackful of rattlesnake fangs, and with a great show of willpower kept his teeth, clamped together.

Super Bull was getting bigger and stronger every day. Jimmy and Billy Bob were getting weaker. Sometimes Jimmy would spot Super Bull through field glasses way across a canyon just lying in a flat, grassy spot looking back at him. All the time Jimmy was riding down the canyon and up the mountain, the calf would be resting. He had every advantage.

A lot of people, including Jimmy, had seen Super Bull grazing along the highway where the ditches fostered lots of tender green grass and weeds. He especially liked to graze there at night. He wasn't afraid of cars or pickups—only horsebackers. So? First Great Grand Plan: Sue would drive the pickup while Jimmy rode in the back. He tied his rope to the headache bar, then they practiced driving slowly back and forth past Super Bull. At first the young bull didn't even look up from his meal. Then he started watching them as they passed by. He still grazed though. Jimmy tapped against the back window and Sue pulled the pickup over closer to the ditch so Jimmy could make his throw. He did. At the first swish of the top, Super Bull knew something was wrong. He'd heard that swishing tune before. He took off. The rope sailed out and barely caught the top of his head and one short horn enough to jerk him slightly sideways. Sue gunned the pickup after him, but Super found one of the four trails before Jimmy could get his rope ready for another throw.

Jimmy crawled back inside the cab with Sue and said, "If his horns had been an inch longer I'd uh had 'im."

Sue said, "Well I guess we'll just have to wait until you both grow up." It was teeth and jaw grinding time again.

That winter, when the sun beamed and the wind eased, Jimmy made several runs in the snow. If Billy Bob had been a world class skier, he and Jimmy might have had a chance, because Super Bull busted in and out of the drifts like a dolphin in sea water and lost them every time. Jimmy got more than a normal amount of remarks and ridicule from all his cohorts, which made for an extra long winter.

One rancher asked him, "Hey, Jimmy, you gonna call in the air force? They ought to get him easy. I hear old Super can't fly over a quarter of a mile without having to land." Just because Jimmy had been in the Strategic Air Command didn't increase his appreciation for this remark.

Then an out-of-work miner volunteered to use his dynamite expertise to close all the trails. Jimmy didn't bother to ask the miner how he would get down into the canyons to chase Super Bull if all the trails were closed. All in all, it was just more than a long-shanked cowboy could listen to without getting a skullache. Yes, it did make the winter longer and the obsession stronger. Spring came again in all its bird singing glory, but Jimmy paid no attention to their merry chirping, nor did he smell the wild flowers, or notice how the water sparkled from the melted snow.

Super Bull was a yearling now with nice little horns. Jimmy and Sue tried the pickup trick again, but couldn't get close to him. Well Jimmy would just borrow a neighbor's pickup and fool the dumb animal. He soon found out that Super had now added *all* pickups to his list of no-no's.

Then came Second Great Grand Plan. The flash of Einsteinian genius was blinding. Simple. They'd go after him in a car. He'd never expect that. They'd just wait until he was grazing by a strip of highway so steep it would be impossible for him to jump off. Jimmy would leap from the hood of the car and bulldog him. When Sue made her next remark, Jimmy began to suspect that the loyalties of his faithful companion for fifteen years might be wavering in favor of the bull. As he pulled his hat down over his ears to prepare to mount the hood of the car, she said, "Now you be careful, Honey, and don't cripple poor little Super Bull. That's getting to be an expensive, valuable animal." Jimmy doesn't remember whether he shortened his teeth or not.

Jimmy tied a rope to the undercarriage of the car, then laid it in a coil on the front seat beside Sue. Jimmy would bulldog the animal and try to sideline him with his piggin string. Sue was to jump out and hand him the secured catch rope for insurance. If Super didn't tear the bottom out of the car, Jimmy figured they should have him.

They watched and waited until Super was in perfect position. The sides of the road dropped almost straight off for a half a mile, and it was at least that distance to the next trail exit.

Sue eased the car along past him, turned around, and passed him going the other way. Super grazed on, ignoring the car. The plan was working to perfection. The young bull, who now weighed around eight hundred pounds, was about to be had.

Jimmy put the piggin string in his mouth to free up both hands. Closer. Closer. Super loomed up in the car lights like a circus pet. There! Jimmy leaped. Super leaped. Jimmy grabbed both little horns, but had landed so far back he couldn't get enough leverage to throw the bull. Super charged out ahead bellowing and scattering the thin green with Jimmy desperately trying to pull himself forward to brace his feet.

The bull, suddenly and without hesitation, bailed off the side of the impossible drop. Super was really snapping brush in his descent. Sue could hear the racket from the car. She waited. She waited some more with the car lights locked on the spot of sudden departure. Just as she was about to take a flashlight and have a look, two hands grasped the side of the highway. Then the forearms and a head appeared. Then the rest of the battered body arrived on the road. Jimmy's shirt was ripped like it had been run through a CIA paper shredder. His handsome face was peeled all down one side, and there were knots and scratches from the top of his six two frame to the bottom of it. He still had the piggin string in his mouth.

As he stumbled wearily to the car to get a dose of well deserved sympathy from his admiring wife, she said, "I see you didn't use your piggin string, so I assume Super Bull is alive and free . . . unless, of course, you broke his poor little neck."

"#*&#@@#&* . . . &&#%@$#&*@@," echoed across the land.

Just the same, Jimmy maintained his vigilant pursuit. He couldn't very well stop. His closest friends, his nearest neighbors, his pretty little wife, and even his four-year-old daughter, Stacy, kept it constantly on his mind. Only Brent, his three-year-old son, seemed to care about his predicament. He had nightmares—he'd catch the bull, but the rope would always break. Once he dreamed he caught and jerked him down tying him perfectly, but that changed and he was tied to the bull and they were sailing through a blue western sky falling swifter and swifter to jagged rocks a mile below. Oh, if he'd never heard of that critter! Oh, if only no one had!

Super Bull was a year and a half old now. He was unbranded, unmarked, and gaining in weight, condition, and brains. Super belonged only to himself. Something—anything—had to be done. Third Great Grand Plan had to produce better results.

Jimmy said, "I figured I was on my third great plan, but Super was on his sixth and probably heading for the seventh. Since it was such a dry year, I decided I could salt Super down the hill with some nice green blocks of hay."

It worked. Jimmy would drop the hay a little farther down the hill each day. Super would eat it and wait for the next batch of bait. He was moving closer and closer to the smaller hills and an open cattle guard gate. Once through that, Jimmy would shut it and capture him at last.

It was June. Jimmy and his neighbors were branding. Jimmy was having to get up at four o'clock in the morning, work all day, then deliver the hay to the bull. Super Bull didn't have a clock, so he was sleeping and fattening up while Jimmy was being worn all over like a ditch digger's hands.

Jimmy forgot about the work though, because he now had the bull taking the bait four miles down the canyon and still gaining. Glory, glory, hallelujah, and fried chicken on Sunday! Just one more block of hay and Super should be through the gate. Then it clouded up and started raining, raining, raining. The grass came up green, tender, and delicious all over. Super had no use whatsoever for a dry block of hay. To make matters unhappier, some of Jimmy's gentle cows found the open gate and wandered up the canyon into the wild bull country. It took him three days, riding across the boggy ground, to gather them. He decided, however, the mud would be an advantage. He could run the bull now as fast as he could ride and the tracks would be clear and sharp in the wet earth.

He was giving Billy Bob extra grain and doing lots of talking to him. Since Sue's unfaltering faith appeared to be wavering, he could only share his woes with his horse. Well, Jimmy and his four-legged confidante ran Super Bull with all they had for three days. Even Super was beginning to tire, so he took a trail going to the highway. Jimmy followed the muddy tracks, and with a last surge of energy they were closing in on him. It was three quarters of a mile to the next trail. Super was almost there. They had to do it now! Jimmy threw his thirty-foot rope when Super was twenty-nine feet away. It just caught one horn and the end of his nose. Billy Bob set 'er down. Super flipped over the side of the canyon and landed in the middle of a ten foot oak tree hanging upright with his four legs way above ground. Jimmy stood there and looked him right in the eye. He couldn't reach him, but he could have spit on him.

"We got 'im, Billy Bob!"

All Jimmy had to do now was sideline Super with the piggin string. The dawning. How was he going to get out there to the bull? He was wearing heavy leggings and a brush-popping coat. He couldn't risk the time to take off these cumbersome garments, but he wasn't any ballerina either. He put the piggin string in his mouth, stood on the edge of the road and jumped. He'd forgotten one little thing—a tree that's already holding up about nine hundred pounds of bull might not handle an additional two hundred pounds of cowboy and costume. It didn't.

The bull bellered, twisted, kicked, and the tree slowly began to bend down. Down. Super Bull's feet touched the ground and when he got traction, he really zoomed out of the tree and down the canyon. With the main weight gone, the relieved branch snapped up—boing! Jimmy clung to the top looking around to see if a squirrel, a pissant, or somebody had seen the event. Billy Bob was the only witness and he would never tell. Super Bull tore through the downhill brush still unbranded. Jimmy climbed out of the tree marked all over.

Jimmy didn't want to be inhumane to the bull so he decided to give Super a few days rest. During this period of recuperation he met a professional hunter-trapper who used a tranquilizer gun on mountain lions. Jimmy wanted to know if it would work on cattle. The trapper said, "Why, I seen 'em knock elephants down on TV, ain't you?"

The Greatest Grand Foolproof Plan of All.

Jimmy tried to sneak out without Sue seeing him. It didn't work. Not only did she go along, but she brought Stacy and Brent to witness the event.

They picked up the trapper, and he said they'd just need one dart if he found the muscle. Jimmy insisted on four in case he missed. Jimmy drove the car up highway 90 until they found Super following a neighbor's cow who was in heat. Super Bull was harking to his calling and like many males before him was vulnerable.

Jimmy drove slowly to within fifteen feet of him. The trapper fired. Super Bull just kicked at the dart and went on sniffing the air. The trapper said all they had to do was drive up ahead a couple of hundred yards and wait about fifteen minutes, then Jimmy could just walk over to the snoozing bull and tie him up. Easy pickin's. At last the moment of truth. D-Day. He was glad his proud family was there to witness and verify his success.

One hour later, after some discussion, they decided to shoot Super again with a stronger dose. They did. The fifteen minutes turned into another hour. They doubled the next dose with the trapper protesting that it might kill him. Super kicked at the dart with his hind leg and went on sniffing after the cow. This process was repeated, increasing the dose each time until all four darts were in him. Super maintained his pursuit of the opposite sex. He hadn't been watching TV.

Jimmy turned the radio up loud on *Louisiana Hayride* trying to drown out the unnecessary comments from the spectators.

He thought the bull must surely be groggy by now. He would make one last valiant effort. He mounted the car hood again, piggin string dangling from both sides of his mouth, and Sue drove him within jumping distance. Yipppeee, he had the thousand pound bull by both horns! He held them for about a hundred yards through the dense downhill brush. The crowd waited on the highway. Jimmy crawled back on the road into the daylight to a shattering round of applause. His piggin string was gone, but no one asked if he'd tied the bull.

The confused trapper had obviously forgotten to figure the difference in weight between a mountain lion and a bull; however, he insisted on ten dollars apiece for his lost darts. Jimmy rode back the next morning and found his piggin string and all of the brightly colored darts where Super had rubbed them out against tree trunks.

As the weeks went by, Jimmy made many more grand plans but kept them all to himself. He didn't even divulge them to his horse. It was such a rank, snowy winter he couldn't have used them anyway.

Spring came. Jimmy was driving his pickup over low rolling hills to check some loading pens that had a water tank sticking out on both sides of the corral. The pens were out in the flats not far from headquarters. He topped the hill and suddenly slammed on the brakes, leaned over the steering wheel and stared so hard his eyebrows joined his hairline. There was Super Bull ambling slowly along, bellering low in his chest, heading straight for the open gate to the corral where a bunch of cows were watering.

Jimmy eased out of the pickup thinking that every move he made sounded like a battery of cannons exploding. He crawled on his belly and crept from bush to rock like one of Geronimo's warriors. Then there was no more ground cover—just fifty yards of wide open pasture to the corral gate.

He crouched behind the last bush getting ready to take off like an Olympic dash man. It suddenly hit him that he and Billy Bob had done a hell of a lot of dashing without any results. He simply stood up and walked slowly, casually across the open ground like he was taking a course in daydreaming. The calm exterior camouflaged a heart that was pumping all the blood his plumbing could handle and lungs that were overloaded to the bursting point with that clean mountain air.

When at last he placed his hands on the swung back gate his palms were wet enough to fill a sponge. He closed the gate. Simple as that.

The three-year-old bull had already picked out his next mate and was courting her with enthusiasm. As multitudes of males before him, he'd been captured by sex. Why not? He had nothing left to prove in the Gila Forest.

The next person to accost Jimmy with a sarcastic inquiry about his bullish escapades got this answer, "Oh, you mean Super Bull? Nothin' to it . . . caught him afoot."

At first Jimmy wanted to shoot him and even worse, castrate him, but instead he branded him with the F Cross and called his special friend, Rob Cox, to come look him over. Rob liked the young bull's conformation. Jimmy was relieved. Even though he couldn't stand to have Super around, he wanted him safe and happy. It was agreed that Rob would take him back to the Organ Mountain Ranch. A lot of bulls don't like the strain of doing their duty in rough, high country. It was plain natural for Super Bull. He was turned loose at seventy-five-hundred-feet altitude to live out the rest of his days eating and breeding in paradise.

Even now when Jimmy Bason and Billy Bob ride the South Percha Canyon, they instinctively look for the wild bull's sign. They are never going to find any. They just made ONE Super Bull.

PART III

Max's Early Horse Paintings and Mixed Media Drawings

Moment of Truth.

Tail to the Wind. From the Field family collection.

Meeting by Moonlight.

The Family.

Blizzard.

Ghost Rider in a Ghost Town.

In My Valley.

Busting Drifts.

Late for Supper.

Look Out, Ma!

Valley of the Moon.

The Mare

IT WAS the most fantastic story Forest Ranger Joe Healy had ever heard. "It just can't be," he said in stunned disbelief. "Don't you realize if she's over thirty years old, that would make her almost a hundred and twenty in human terms?"

"Yeah, something like that," Randy Lindsey answered. "She does truly exist. I first spotted her tracks about three years ago, and I felt just like you until I finally saw her for real a couple of months back. Yeah, she's up there alright."

Randy was a young cowboy who worked for Jimmy Bason's F Cross ranch. Bason leased out most of the grassland on his hundred thousand acres, so he needed only his son, Brent, and one extra cowboy to help take care of his small herd. Jimmy was lucky . . . Randy was a "throw back" to the Old West. He liked living by himself in a line shack, and preferred to work with horses instead of a pickup truck. He wanted to carry on the old-time traditions.

The two men were sitting at a table in the one-bar, two-church town of Hillsboro in southwestern New Mexico. The bar also had the only restaurant available for thirty miles.

Ranger Healy knew that Randy would never lie to him about a thing like this, but he found it almost impossible to believe that a horse could have survived, totally alone, for all those years. He leaned forward across the plate of red chile burritos and the bottle of beer, saying softly, "Does anyone else know about this?"

The young cowboy said, "Only Jimmy Bason . . . and he don't want anybody to know. He says the do-gooders and the do-badders will both try to capitalize on her." He paused. "In fact, he'll probably fire me if he finds out I slipped up and told someone."

Joe laughed softly, "You don't have to worry, Randy, I won't tell anybody except my daughter. She's crazy nuts about animals, you know. That's why she's definitely decided to become a vet. And, by dogies, she'll never have another chance to see anything like this. That mare has to be some kind of miracle. My God, even gentle horses, that are pampered and cared for, don't live that long. I'd say this is about the rarest dang thing I ever heard of. It's like being first in line at the Second Coming. Yeah," Healy said as if to himself, "Pauline's got to see this horse."

Randy reluctantly agreed to describe the area the mare currently habituated. He was unaware that their conversation was being overheard by a vacationing young reporter for an El Paso, Texas, newspaper, who was sitting at the next table with his wife and two children. The young man hurriedly grabbed a pen and pad from his pocket and, with noticeable excitement, started scribbling.

• • •

Joe Healy drove the pickup, pulling a trailer containing two good saddle horses, as near as the rough terrain would allow, to the designated wilderness area. He and his fifteen-year-old daughter, Pauline, quickly set up camp. They had enough supplies to last over a month if that's what it took to find the wild mare. They had come prepared and totally dedicated.

They rode the piñon-and-cedar-covered foothills. Then made their way up to the edge of the tall pines on the mountain. They roamed for five days looking at the ground, hoping to find a sign of the horse. Even in their anticipation of the latter, they still enjoyed the markings of the other wild creatures. They actually saw twenty or thirty deer, ten elk, a coyote, many kinds of birds, and even glimpsed a black bear disappearing into a patch of heavy timber.

On the sixth day they found her hoofprints. The tracks were at least a week old, but to the Healys, they were as new as first frost. The excitement of discovery surged through all the tissues, nerves, and thoughts of their bodies, but nevertheless, on the seventh day they rested themselves and their horses.

Pauline said, "Daddy, if she's never had a colt, she's still a filly no matter what her age, right?"

"Now don't get technical on me, Pauline. As old as she is, we're gonna call her a mare."

Pauline pushed her long, blond hair back from her face, and said in a soft voice filled with wonder, "She's really out there. We've found her unshod hoofprints. Poor thing . . . all alone. Just think of all the bad weather, and the predators, and the loneliness she has endured, and now she's so old. Wonder how she's done it?" Her blue eyes widened in astonishment at the frightening images.

Joe Healy searched for a special answer for this question, but he could only come up with "It does seem impossible. She must be blessed. That's the answer, Pauline. She's blessed."

Father and daughter rode out of camp at dawn the next day. The two had spent a restless night, but now they were keyed up and tuned in to the whole world. It was midafternoon when they found some more recent tracks—these were only a couple of days old. Joe recalled Randy saying, "I was ridin' old Birdie, when I cut my first sign of her. I just knew she had to be the last of the wild ones. I never had a feelin' like it before. It was sorta like I'd just invented the first saddle." Healy was having some of the same feelings now. A sense of the primordial permeated his being. He couldn't have been more in awe if he'd just come face-to-face with a living dinosaur or the Loch Ness monster.

Pauline almost cried aloud, but instead, she let the tears rivulet silently down her cheeks. To her it was a sacred moment and she looked up to the heavens. In the distance, she saw several buzzards circling. She lifted her wide, blue eyes above the birds to a patch of sky and then on above that, she saw something that caused her to cry out, "Daddy, look! Look way up there!"

He looked in the direction of her pointing, but his vision missed what she had so briefly seen. His eyes moved, by nature and training, back down to the tracks they had been following. Pauline reined her horse in line. Now her eyes were focused on a movement nearing a huge cumulus cloud. She stared in wonder.

• • •

CHAPTER ELEVEN

The mare was born in the spring of the year the Space Age dawned. In October 1957 the Russians fired Sputnik 1 into the heavens. It circled the globe at altitudes ranging from 141 to 588 miles above Moscow and Washington, D.C. It traveled at 14,700 miles per hour. The people of the Soviet Union rejoiced and justifiably felt enormous pride. The Americans were embarrassed and scared. There was an outcry for more defense spending and the whole educational system of the free world to be altered. The emphasis was placed on science. Literature, all the arts and old-time basic schooling were greatly neglected. The Space Age and the mare had been born.

Far below on the solid rocks of the Black Range, the colt frolicked, nursed, and grew stronger daily. She did not know, or care, about this monumental change in the world. From the beginning, she was more agile and faster than the other colts in one of the dozen or so scattered bands of wild horses. Her chestnut coat glistened in the sun and her large, dark eyes were full of adventure and mischief.

Her first winter was an easy one with little snow. The horses fared well in the rolling hills between the private ranches and the national forest area, but the springtime came dry and the grass was short.

The ranchers moved their cattle into the wild horses' domain under individual leases with the government. There was competition for the shriveling grass between the wildlife, the mustangs, and the domestic cattle. The ranchers and Forest Service joined forces to get rid of the wild horses.

They built log-pole traps around waterholes in an attempt to capture them alive. They tried roping the young, the old, or the lame. This effort only delivered ten head of the wily bunch, and in the process they crippled three cowboys, one ranger, and twenty-two of their tame horses.

The ranchers and Forest Service executives argued over other means to dispose of this threat to the welfare of their cattle and consequently their families. During one of their meetings, word came of a forest fire in the area. It had been started by lightning from a small, shower cloud. The flames caused the dry trees and vegetation to snap and pop like infantry machine guns.

One small band of horses was trapped and perished. All living things ran together now, to escape the inferno. Deer, elk, and cattle raced alongside coyotes, bears, and cougars. Rabbits dashed in and out of the flames until some caught fire and fell in kicking, smoking bundles. Everything attempted to escape in a terrible panic.

Most small things like lizards, ants, grasshoppers, spiders, tree worms, squirrels, skunks, and nestlings were cooked as black as the forest floor.

The colt raced beside her mother as the dominant stallion of the band circled, squealing commands, kicking, biting, and trying to drive his harem and offspring to safety. The prevailing southwest wind joined in the chaos and whipped the flames in circles and drove them forward with destructive speed. The smoke could be seen one hundred aircraft miles away in El Paso, Texas. Fire fighters tried to organize, but their efforts were futile against the raging force.

Then the winds suddenly quit as if on command from the gods and the fire died out at the banks of the North Percha Creek. It had decimated the five-mile width from the upper Animas drainage to the creek. The existing forage would be much sparser now.

The ranchers moved their cattle back to the home ranches with great effort and much loss of weight. The decision was made—the wild horses had to be destroyed. They organized and came with camping gear, horses, and rifles. They rode for weeks driving their prey into the burned areas where they killed them.

Joe Healy's father, John, who was a ranger at the time, led the onslaught. He instructed the rangers and cowboys to try to "bark" the wild horses. That is, shoot them through the top edge of the neck knocking them unconscious so they could be saved for live capture. It didn't work. The fire, followed by the cracking of rifles, the squeals and groans of dying animals, created a madness of desperation. The stallions lost control of their bands and ran about as erratically as their broods. Over a hundred and thirty horses were slaughtered.

The area became, and looked, like a battlefield. What with the dead horses scattered about through the massive burned area and the buzzards gathering from miles around to join the coyotes, bobcats, bears, mountain lions, and other meat-eating predators to feast on the carcasses.

The rangers and ranchers agreed there were none left to scatter the seed. They were wrong by *one*.

The yearling colt had been barked from a long distance and when she regained consciousness, she raced blindly across the scorched earth through the stench of the rotting bodies and kept on going up and up until the greenness of undefiled timber surrounded her. The sweat had turned to a lather over her entire body and her lungs bellowed in and out in painful gasps.

She kept going until she was deep into the high forest and her legs began to tremble and caused her to fall over and over. Then she stopped. She could move no more. She was sore and weak for several days before she found a spring and enough feed from brush and the scant grass to live. She was totally confused about where she was or what had happened to her world.

Then the late-summer rains came and the earth was soaked, cleansed, revitalized, and so was the colt. The soreness and the gauntness disappeared. She was alone in several hundred thousand acres of wilderness. But she lived.

The rains made good feeding for the grazers, and the remains of the horses and the other burned animals gave plentiful food to the predators. This one winter, when she needed help so much, the fanged animals had no need of her flesh.

The spring grass and vegetation came again. She was feeding and nourishing her muscles and bones, and rapidly growing into a fine two-year-old equine specimen. She looked better than she felt. The flashes of fire still raced behind her eyes, and over and over she heard the death screams of her mother. Sometimes she would hold her head high, with nostrils straining wide, thinking she smelled the smoke from the scorched forest floor and the rotting flesh of her family and ancestors. After these flashbacks of horror, she would tremble and run about, trying to escape the imagined destruction. Finally, she'd calm and return to her normal watering, feeding, and exercising. The fearful images slowly grew dimmer as she grew older.

She was walking to her secret waterhole when the warning chatter of a tassel-eared squirrel become louder and more urgent. It was October the first, 1961. Roger Maris, who played baseball for the New York Yankees, had just hit his sixty-first home run of the season, breaking Babe Ruth's old record. Just as the standing ovation of the crowd drew him out of the dugout for the second tip of his cap, a heavy force hit the filly on the back.

The mountain lion had leapt from a limb above her and dug his fore claws deep into her neck. His rear claws were locked into her hips. With powerful, open jaws and long, meat ripping fangs he reached for the place where the neck bones join the skull. The instant she felt the force of the lion's weight, and the sharp pain of its claws, she bolted straight into a heavy growth of young trees. Before the lion could close his jaws on the death spot, a limb smashed into his forehead and dragged him off her back. In so doing, the claws raked through her hide and into raw flesh plowing permanent lines and eventual scars on both sides of her neck. The claw cuts were painful for a while, with the swelling and draining, but they healed. From then on, her mind was alerted to the warning sounds from other possible victims of predators.

The five-mile-wide and ten-mile-long burnt area had come back lush green. The grass and brush had fought the timber seedlings for space and won. The small surviving trees were scattered widely apart. All the new growth made, for a few years at least, lush summer grazing. For a long time she spent as much of her life here as possible. The trees were so far apart that she could watch for the death drop from above and avoid the tearing claws of the lion. The deer felt as she did, and grazed right alongside her. In the fall and early winter she and the other foraging creatures would move high up, out of the healed area, and feast on the oak brush and mountain mahogany pine, putting on fat to hold them through the sometimes hard winters.

She wasn't so lonely anymore. She had the company of wild turkeys, band-tailed pigeons, quail, squirrels and chipmunks, blue jays and mountain grouse, hawks and eagles. Some of the creatures lived at all altitudes, changing locations with the seasons and the food growth, while others were found at only certain heights in special terrain. There were many creatures here she would have to study in order to live out her allotted span of years.

Fortunately, she had found a secluded spring soon after the earlier holocaust. The timber and rocks, while completely encircling it, sat well back from the waterhole. On this special terrain she could drink peacefully, knowing that she wouldn't suffer a sudden attack. She maintained a constant alertness as far as her knowledge at this point allowed.

In late September, she went to the spring and found it frozen over. This was a new surprise . . . another type of warning she must learn to heed. There was much more danger on this mountain than the long toothed predators, and after this winter she would always remember that early ice and falling leaves, along with higher, more frigid winds, meant heavy storms soon. She didn't have that knowledge frozen into her genes at the time the great snow came.

The dark clouds moved in formation, low, caressing, over the peaks, like Alexander's legions. And underneath them the wind fought with the trees, thrashing them about in agony and sending the flying things coasting up and away on its mad currents. But below, where the wind was less, many of the four-footed animals failed to move out in time.

The snow stuck for a moment on the millions of branches and limbs before being shaken loose by the wind over and over, thousands and thousands of times. The white, frozen crystals were swept and piled into massive drifts higher than the mare's head. She was all right for a few days, pawing the snow down to the little clumps of bunchgrass and oak brush.

She rapidly consumed all edible food in the small radius she was able to control. Soon she had to struggle harder, pawing into the deeper drifts. Her exertions caused rapid weight loss. Her lungs had to pump more warm air which formed ice crystals around her nostrils and eyes, restricting her breathing and vision. She was in a white, frozen world and was quickly turning into an immobile ice sculpture.

She could only paw feebly now, and began to lose interest in making any effort at all. She was dozing. Her weakened neck allowed her head to drop down almost to knee level. She felt warm, dry, and totally without concern for food or anything else. Soon one foreleg slid out to the side. She was teetering with her whole body about to fall over, but she felt as if she was running in the summer warmth again with the gray male colt. They were jumping about, dodging and chasing each other with their short tails in the air, and heads up like the Royal British mounts. They were full, free, and safe. It was a glorious moment.

Suddenly then, she was certain that she smelled the smoke, envisioned the fire, and heard the squeals and screams again for the first time in months. The fear became so real she began actually running from it. Then she whirled and ran back toward it, craving its imagined warmth. After bursting through drift after drift, she began to feel the cold again, but kept plunging through the forest down, down, always down. Eternity returned. She now fought to reach lower ground as years before she had struggled for the high.

Her lungs pained terribly as she sucked in more and more frozen air, just as she had once breathed the hot ashes and fire-scorched winds. As before, there came a point where her afflicted lungs could not supply enough fuel to keep her body moving. She stood quivering, and made loud gasping sounds as she tried to take in the warmer air of the foothills.

When she could finally see again, she discovered that the drifts were much smaller here. There would be no problem pawing through to the grass and even some of the bushes could be reached with hardly any effort at all. She survived until spring once again. Never, not once, would she be trapped in the high country by the felonious storms.

By spring, she had gained back almost all her weight and strength when she spotted two black bear cubs climbing over and around a dead log, chasing and cuffing one another about in the purest of fun. One fell, hanging on just a moment before tumbling the short distance to the ground. The mare, feeling good after the grinding winter, eased forward in a friendly gesture to the cub. They had barely touched noses when the little bear whirled and scampered away, and the mare heard the loud "whoof." The sound was followed by a blasting slap to her side and neck. The mama bear had been plunging downhill at such speed that her swipe at the mare was slightly off. The blow to the horse's neck and ribs had not been the solid finishing strike the bear had intended. Even so, it knocked the mare stumbling to the side. Her neck and rib cage were numbed where the mighty paw of the five-hundred-pound beast had struck.

As the bear whirled back to finish the mare off with her teeth and foreclaws, she received an unpleasant surprise. The mare's adrenaline had flushed up ancient resources of genes. An old experience imparted the knowledge to her brain that her numbed body could not outrun the bear. She whirled and started kicking back toward her attacker. The bear stuck her lower jaw right into one of the mare's hooves when it was at its apex of power. The bones cracked like a bull elk stepping on a tiny dry stick. The other hoof caught her on the left eye, chipping the skull around the socket in several places and knocking the bear's remaining vision askew. In a few weeks the coyotes got the cubs and the buzzards discovered the starved body of the mother bear.

The mare's left shoulder had torn tendons that caused her great pain as she traversed the uneven ground trying to feed. Another wide scar undulated with the muscles beneath the skin from the blow of the bear. Since she hadn't fully recovered from the decimation of the winter, it would be late summer before the scar healed and the soreness left her.

By early October, she was well and sufficient winter fat was already on her bones. With this recuperation also came a feeling of longing. Something was missing—something that was a part her—something that she had every right to be sharing. The vacancy left an aching in her heart, her womb, and her animal soul.

She thought she saw a blur of her own kind, her own blood, in the bushes and trees, but no matter how hard she looked and searched, the images she ached to define would not come clear. This ineluctable feeling pervaded her all during, and past, the twenty-second of October, 1962, when the Cuban missile crisis began. President John F. Kennedy ordered the blockading of Cuba and revealed the discovery of Soviet missile bases on Cuban soil through air reconnaissance photos. The president went on television and gave media interviews in the Oval Office. The two leaders of the superpowers exchanged many accusations and threats. The hearts of the world stood still in dread.

For six days, the mighty powers threatened and blustered. US bombers, loaded with atomic bombs, flew patterns up to the edge of Soviet territory by the hour. The warships were about to pair off for battle. The Russians, vastly outnumbered in the nuclear bomb category at the time, held out six days before they gave in. Never before had the world been so close to destruction in just a few minutes of madness. It has been debated ever since whether Kennedy saved the world by calling the Russians' bluff or gave it away by not taking Cuba while it was in his grasp.

During the six days of worldwide tension, the mare grazed contentedly and enjoyed the cool nights and warm days of autumn in peace. The forest has many eyes and ears, watching, listening, always aware, and now she knew how to use them to her advantage. These animals would voice the movements of danger to her instantly. She only had to listen and act to be safe.

As the other world started breathing again, but as yet looking over their collective shoulders, the mare spent a mild winter with plenty of forage. When spring came, some tiny bit of fat was still left under her long winter hair. She would soon be slick and shiny.

• • •

After many years of gaining knowledge through painful experiences and her natural force of observation, she finally chose her favorite spot for repose. About halfway down, between the jagged peaks of the high mountains and the lower meadows, there was a mesa with Mimbres Indian ruins on top. From here she could walk around the edges of the pueblito and observe the far-spreading wilderness in every direction, just as the Indian occupants once had.

Here in her part of southern New Mexico, hundreds of these ruins existed. Some archaeologists dated them back a thousand years, but the exact time period is as much in dispute as how an entire nation of mostly peaceful Indians vanished completely. They did leave behind them, their rock houses, burial grounds, stone and bone tools, arrowheads, and traces of jewelry. However, there were very few implements of actual war. Their main gifts to history were their wonderfully constructed, and uniquely designed black on white pottery.

Here in the ancient ruins, the mare felt a comfort and peace greater than in any other spot in her domain. When the hidden blood longings and blurred visions came to her, she headed to this spot to share it with the ghosts of its former inhabitants like retreating to a Benedictine monastery. She heard drums and chants and sometimes saw incomplete images in the air, but she didn't know what they were— only that she was comforted.

After the time of the Mimbres and before the time of the satellites, there had been many battles in this part of her range. Geronimo, Chief Victorio, and Old Nana had made this area the last hideout from pursuing cavalry. Only half a mile below her, an isolated squad of buffalo soldiers from the Ninth Cavalry had encountered a small band of Apaches. It became a running battle. A black sergeant named Moses Williams, realizing two of his wounded buffalo soldiers were surrounded, charged back, catching the Apaches by surprise, and saving the soldiers' lives. Sergeant Williams was awarded the Congressional Medal of Honor

In 1963, President John F. Kennedy was assassinated by Lee Harvey Oswald in Dallas, Texas. It shocked a nation and a lot of the world into near paralysis. People will never forget where they were when they heard the news. The mare knew none of this, nor would she have cared, for hers was and had truly been another world. Much more would pass in both dimensions.

The mare was honored in the year of '67 by the weather. The forage was plentiful from the summer rains and the snow of the high country had melted early. She prospered . . . but in the cities of America the flower children came to full bloom, shouting peace and free love, while the rock music cascaded its battering and often deafening, beat across the land and cheap dope altered minds and history forever. In the Haight-Ashbury district of the lovely city of San Francisco, the children lay about the streets with minds bent and bodies so inert they could barely follow up on the prevalent misguided theory of love being free. They had presumably started out innocent and wound up tasting the refuse of the gutters, seeing visions of such complexity that for man there was nothing left but the accidental and sometimes purposeful ultimate quest—suicide.

That same fateful year ended in near tragedy for the aging mare, even more innocently than it had for the children of the streets. She wanted companionship . . . a direct communication of some kind. During one of those periods of deep loneliness, she was craving something like the image she saw reflected in the water as she drank from her favorite spring. That's when she followed and, in a friendly gesture, stuck her muzzle down to a porcupine. The animal with thirty thousand barbs swung its short tail and imbedded fourteen of them into the left side of the mare's nostrils and face.

In a couple of days one passage was swelled completely shut and the other barely open so that she gasped for breath even while standing still. She started losing weight and strength immediately. The swelling and pain grew so great that she would rub her face against trees, rocks, bushes, the earth itself, and slink her head in circles trying to dislodge the darts.

Now the coyotes witnessed this and stalked her. They were far too smart to risk her deadly hooves, if she had been well. Due to their small size, they could only down big game when it was ill or injured. By her erratic actions, the coyotes knew she was both. So they patiently circled and watched, for days. Even with all her pain, the mare watched them, too. She turned her rear to them ready to strike out hard with her hind feet.

Slowly, some of the quills worked their way out, while only a few burst open the swelled spots at her rubbing. She was forced to graze solely on bush leaves. It was slow and painful. She was weakening fast.

Finally one coyote leapt at her nostrils. While she was busy with the first, the other tried to hamstring her. The coyote did manage to get hold of her muzzle just long enough to puncture it. This helped the poison ooze out, and the swelling started down. She kicked the other one in the side and sent it rolling down an embankment with three broken ribs. The wise coyotes left her alone and chose to dine, that day, on game already dead.

She could eat better now and gradually the barbs either worked themselves all the way out or a protective gristle formed around them. She became strong again. It seemed that no matter how long she lived and how much knowledge she acquired, there was still wisdom to be gained that could come only from pain. Just the same, she knew, and had survived, most of the deadly dangers of the wilderness at least once. She had paid a highly inflated price to gain a few years of relative tranquility.

The last year of the sixties was a good one for her. Most of her scars and injuries were healed. She spotted a bobcat on a rare daylight foray. It crouched in the grass stalking a quail. That same day Armstrong and Aldrin would complete one of mankind's most sought after dreams. They landed a space ship on the moon. Scores of millions of people worldwide were tied with invisible ropes, to their television sets. The bobcat didn't know any more about this than the mare. It was hungry and the solution to that problem hid motionless in the grass some ten feet ahead.

The cat's ears twitched ever so slightly, trying to catch any sound or movement from the intended victim. The soft, furry belly was actually touching the ground at its lowest point. Its short tail switched once as the cat leaped forward. The quail raised up, took three stride, and winged into flight. About four feet off the ground the bobcat's claws hooked into the bird's belly. As they fell back to earth, she locked her jaws on the last flutterings, and crouched, holding it tightly as she looked about for any competition. As soon as the bird was dead, the cat took off toward its den in some rocks out of the mare's sight.

That same day, as the mare wandered, browsing in the brush a golden eagle dropped from the sky into an opening, hooked its powerful talons into a fat rabbit and flew up to some bluffs to dine. The forest gave sudden voice with squirrels and birds chattering, then became cautiously silent again. This was all so natural in her life that the mare took only a cursory glance at the necessary killing. This golden eagle had landed, and so had the one on the moon. One in an action as old as animal history and the other as new as birth. New worlds had surrounded the old forever.

A mother elk tried to graze while her bull calf lunched greedily at her bag with switching tail. Three forest moths played in and out of a sunbeam like happy, little angels. The mare, witnessing all of this, would have fed in contentment except the yearning for something more of her own self struck her several times a month now.

She might have felt better about one human endeavor presently occurring if she had known about it. A lady known as Wild Horse Annie from Nevada, had raised so much hell, enlisted so many supporters, and grabbed so much attention from the media that a federal law was passed protecting wild horses. Of course, it came far too late for the old mare's immediate ancestors. As her life moved in its eternal cycle of daily survival, the world around her was accelerating with a momentum that seemed to gain in speed like a great boulder rolling down a mighty mountain toward a tiny village.

In 1973, the Arabs put an embargo on oil, and while millions of Americans waited in line for hours at gas stations frustrated and unable to move, the mare browsed on luscious foliage and enjoyed an unhurried, uncluttered existence.

Oil prices escalated, and some poor nations became rich and many rich countries poorer. Wealth shifted about like the hearts of young lovers. The Watergate scandal dethroned a president and his men, changing the political attitudes and history of the free world for decades yet to come.

During these outside occurrences, the old mare had, on several occasions, seen a flash of gray in the timber and brush to the east of her Mimbres ruins lookout. She knew somehow that this was a replica of herself. She felt a kinship here at the ruins, and she had the same feeling for the glimpses of gray. She now took excursions trying to get a solid sight or smell of her illusory relation. But none came—no matter how long she wandered about on swiftly tiring legs, or stared with her dimming eyes, or sniffed with her knotted, scarred muzzle. The only place she could conjure up the flashing vision was from the same spot on the east side of the Mimbres ruins. There only. But she kept on searching, season following season. She would return to the magic spot and wait, sometimes hours, sometimes days, until forced to move away for food and water. But the gray thing began to appear more often. She felt warm and elated at each sighting, even if it was blurred and filmy.

Things had been working in her favor for several years now. A chief forester named Aldo Leopold had written an enormously influential essay entitled "The Land Epic." It led to the creation of a huge official wilderness area named after the forester. The mighty Black Range was to the west of the free area. Gerald Lyda's Ladder Ranch, one of the largest and most famous in the Southwest, touched it on many sides. The Cross Triangle joined to the north and Jimmy Bason's to the east. The old mare lived, protected, right in the middle of it all.

Now that no private vehicles could ever enter her area, she sometimes watched the backpackers walking into the Animas Creek area to camp and relish nature. She would watch them through the bushes, standing as motionless as an oft-hunted buck deer. As long as they didn't carry cracking rifles, as did those who hunted yearly in the lower country, they were nothing but a pleasant curiosity to her. Many elk had migrated across the Black Range from the Gila Wilderness to hers. She enjoyed their presence and bugling calls, but it did little to allay the growing sense of an impending personal event.

Friday, September 18, 1987, the two-hundredth anniversary of the Constitution of the United States, the mare spent looking out the canyon from the ruins, hoping her gray companion would show. It was an anxious day for others as well.

The Polish Pope John Paul II arrived in San Francisco toward the end of what would probably be his last junket to the United States, amidst about two hundred thousand picketing AIDS victims and sympathizers. The pope kept calm.

Headlines around the nation said that the United States and the Soviets had reached an accord on diminishing the number of missiles in the world. When the mare had been born into the Space Age, America had far superior numbers of arms, but now on this day, the Soviets were ahead. Not many people on either side really believed the negotiations were being held for the good of all mankind.

As patriotic parades were held all across the land on this great day, the old mare went on, patiently looking. Then she saw it. Now the gray mist had taken on a little more solidity and form. Her heart beat faster. The figure didn't disappear this time but just inside the bushes as she strained harder than ever before to see and realize what part of her it was.

• • •

The year of the celebration of the Constitution passed with many wars in effect. In Lebanon, Afghanistan, all over Africa. The Iranians and the Iraqis went on butchering one another and the ships of the world filled up the Persian Gulf supposedly to protect oil tankers for the Western world market. While the old mare looked for her compatriot there were, in fact, over forty blasting, slashing, mind-numbing wars being fought, and oddly mostly ignored by the preponderance of the world population.

The calendar moved on into the presidential election year, with the candidates made up of preachers and lawyers. The old mare's body was as ravaged as the polluted and war-torn earth. The scars on her neck, ribs, and shoulders from the attacks of the lion and the bear looked like little, erratically plowed firms. Her back was swayed, her eyes were dull and clouded over. Her once long, flowing mane and tail had been matted and stuck together with burrs and stickers of all kinds for years. The natural indentations above her eyes were sunken, creating round shadows. Her ribs looked like wagon bows sticking through thin, worn, chestnut-colored cloth. The old gunshot wound in her neck hardly mattered in comparison with all the rest. Her tattered ear bent over like one on a generations-old toy rabbit. She had spent had extended life searching for peace, hurting nothing except those who sought to destroy her breath and blood.

Unbeknownst to her, children of the cities, farms, and ranches ran around playing astronauts and aliens from outer space instead of cowboys and Indians as they had at the time of her birth, and most of their lives as well as those of their parents were hourly directed by computer buttons and little images on various screens. Her natural methods of survival had mostly remained the same through her decades here in the Aldo Leopold Wilderness. These ancient rhythms went back to the forest fire, to the Conquistadors, to Spain and Egypt, and throughout history. Since the beginning of man, her ancestors were hunted for meat or used as beasts of burden, as creatures to make war with, and at timess for racing, hunting, and even many forms of pure pleasure.

Her genes cried and tugged at her being, taking her back sixty million years to the Eocene epoch, or time of the Dawn Horse, when she would have been the size of a small fox terrier. Now as she strained ever harder to make the gray object clearer, she heard the Indian ruins and the accompanying chants become louder. The fuzzed objects were suddenly delineated. Some of the Mimbres Indians were dancing in a circle of spectators. Their brown legs and feet moved faster and faster as the drum's volume increased. Her heart beat in synchronization with them as she looked across the canyon and back to the Mimbres.

She was extremely excited, but a mellowness absorbed her at the same time. The drummer's hands, at their ultimate speed, pounded the hide drums and the moccasined feet thumped the earth with all the skill and power left in them. Intense vibrations filled the air and permeated everything. The sound and movement stopped at its peak—and for just a moment so did the universe, in total quiet and stillness.

Then four elders squatted in a rectangle. Each one took a turn standing and making a gesture with both hands in supplication to all four winds. A medicine man and a medicine woman stood before the mare now, and in contrast to the former solemnity of the ceremonies, radiated smiles of love and compassion toward her.

The medicine man reached into a doeskin pouch and gathered a handful of seeds from all the vegetation of the land. He leaped high in the air and hurled the seeds out over the mare. The seeds turned into uncountable bluebirds. They flew up, up, and dissolved the thin mists of clouds across the sky, and moved ever higher, growing into numbers so great they became a solid mass of blue. The birds moved past the sun and the bright land of the sky was reborn.

Just as the medicine man landed back on earth, the medicine woman leapt upwards in a floating jump. She, too, reached into her doeskin bag for seeds, also throwing them above the mare as her compatriot had done. These turned into multitudes of white doves fluttering skyward forming a great flat-bottomed, castle-domed cumulus cloud. She drifted back to earth standing next to the man. Both lifted their arms above their heads and yelled with all the force of their throats and lungs. Their cries were a mixture of all living things of the mountains—the lions and the insects, the bears and the bobcats, the hawks and the hares. All.

The mighty crescendo of sound moved up and became a symphony of drums and hand-carved flutes, spreading so wide it finally softened to a simple, sweet sigh. Instantly the Mimbres Indians vanished from her vision as they had so many centuries before from the earth.

And now, across the eons right to the present, she saw the grayness move out of the brush and become a circular movement. It was a great, shining, gray stallion who pranced with arched neck and high-tossed tail, back and forth directly across the canyon at about her level. Her scars were no longer felt, nor the stiff limbs, nor any of the lumps of the years. She was possessed with an inner feeling of permanent warmth and peace. Her eyes became so sharp she could see the nostrils of the stallion flare as he turned his head to nicker and squeal to her. She heard it as clearly as the bells of Notre Dame, and knew all its meaning as she always had and always would. She saw the stallion racing across the canyon, through space, toward her, mane and tail streaming. Then he sailed up and up above the grass, the brush, and the trees. She whirled agilely about, leaping down the rough terrain and then ascending sharply, racing in a soothing, golden vacuum straight toward her mate, at last.

CHAPTER ELEVEN

• • •

At the very moment Pauline Healy had yelled for her father to look
in the sky above the descending buzzards, an El Paso reporter, a photographer, and three cowboys, who were expert ropers and trackers,
were moving their pickups and gear toward the Healys' camp. If the
Ranger and his daughter had been listening into the quietness, they
would have heard the truck engines straining uphill.

From another direction came the chawp, chawp, chawp of the
helicopter as it passed over Jimmy Bason's ranch loaded with people
from the Associated Press. The Healys didn't hear the sounds below
because the discovery that lay before them blocked out all else.

The Ranger felt his horse's muscles tense beneath him and saww
three coyotes scatter away from a chestnut carcass.

He said with an infinite loss in his voice and a painful expulsion
of breath, "Ohhhh . . . nooo. We're too late! The coyotes and buzzards
have already beat us to her."

Pauline's wide, wondering eyes were locked on a movement in
the sky. She did not hear her father, or see the signs and activity on
the ground. Three tiny clouds, each one bigger than the other, raced
across the blueness to the cumulus cloud and right up on top of it.
There the girl saw a stallion, a mare, and a colt playing together in the
upper mists and lights of the massive formation of white moisture.
They were silhouetted proudly against the sky. Forever. Anyone could
see them who knew how to look.

With an imponderable smile on her suddenly beatific face, the girl
said softer than the whisper of a saint, "There will never be another
her. Never."

CHAPTER TWELVE

The Ghost Horses of Tulsa

DOES A trip from Taos to Tulsa to find twenty thousand dollars in buried gold coins with a great guy like Woody Crumbo the Elder, seem like a worthwhile trip? Well . . . yes, it does. And, it was.

But I must start at the beginning.

I had left the heart of the Hi-Lo country to live in Taos hoping to become a professional artist and had been fortunate enough to be accepted by the great pioneer Potawatomi Indian artist, Woody Crumbo, as his sole pupil. During his lifetime he placed over five hundred paintings in museums around the world including the Corcoran, the Metropolitan and The Gilcrease in Tulsa. His work was also collected by hundreds of accomplished individuals like Wort Phillips of Phillips Petroleum—the founder of the famed Philmont Boy Scout ranch at Cimarron, New Mexico—Winston Churchill, Queen Elizabeth II and many other notables.

. . . And he was my mentor. So when he told me of his knowledge and interest in the location of this coined yellow metal I accepted his words as if he had simply said, "The sun is hot." Anyway, this trip would be a welcome relief from covering canvas with images for awhile.

To attempt an understanding of the equine adventure to come, a few earlier actualities about Woody must be revealed. He was orphaned at the age of seven and ran wild for a time along the Arkansas River, surviving on small game and fish.

The summer he was ten-years-old, a Creek/Muskogee outlaw,

George Island, talked him into staying a couple months with him in the woods at his cabin near Sapulpa, Oklahoma, mainly to do chores during the two and a half months left before school started.

It was a time of revelatory horror for the great artist-to-be. The child was in fear for his life every second because George Island was a robber, a killer, and just plain-born-as-mean as a stepped on rattlesnake. Not only that, he was crude, unkempt, and missed the coffee can three out of four times when he spit tobacco juice.

The one thing Woody gained from this stay was that ol' George had him ride out a couple of broncs. In spite of being thrown over and over in the beginning, his fear of the murderer made his natural trepidation of gentling the bucking horses as negligible as being forced to eat a candy bar. When the horses were finally working, reining, and stopping right, the outlaw took the saddle away from him saying he needed to learn to ride Indian style which to George Island was bareback.

Crumbo continued riding until he entered college. Much later in Taos, he was a fine horseman and I rode with him many times.

Woody retold the story that Ol' George kept telling him—that he should ride west of Tulsa a piece (designating a location) where all this yellow coin was buried. An outlawed friend of George's had robbed a bank just north of Tulsa and mounted on a fine gray gelding had outrun a posse and buried the money near this sandstone bluff west of the city. With a spur he had chipped a fish hook sign on the rock face about ten inches tall. The money was buried fourteen steps south of the sign. As George related: the friend had been waiting for a safe return to get the money when some unknown enemy had waylaid him outside Tulsa and put a .45 bullet through the back side of his heart. George claimed he was too stiff and sore to ever retrieve the wasted treasure. He gave no other reason. All he asked of Woody was to bring it back to him just to enjoy the sight—then . . . young Woody could do with it as he pleased. After George's insistence that he tame spoiled horses at the age of ten, Woody had one of those feelings often referred to as "sneaky." He was dead certain that somehow Ol' George would make him dead as well, and take the money for whatever uses natural-born murderers feel necessary.

George Island became famous during those days for escaping being hanged after three different murders, three times by the infamous and implacable Hanging Judge Parker. The first two misses have never been fully explained except both his tribal members medicine men and women gathered and made medicine and danced dances to save him. One can't help wondering why and what for. Maybe to make a horseman out of Crumbo will have to suffice.

The third time is a horse of many different colors. George Island was in a cell with the notorious Cherokee Bill—both scheduled to be hanged a day apart—Bill first.

Someone had smuggled a pistol and shells to Bill. He told George that there was no way he could make it out because the guards were too numerous. He gave George a plan. George took it. Bill started shooting out the food slot, up and down the walkway of the jail, screaming obscenities.

As instructed George took the gun away from him and was pistol whipping the wadding out of Bill when a horde of armed guards opened the door.

The unbelievable actually came to pass. Multiple robber/murderer, George Island, was pardoned for his valiant efforts to prevent Cherokee Bill's escape. It would seem that frontier justice was confused—for George, in truth, was meaner than Bill, and that was *mean*.

One can easily understand why young Woody sneaked off to school a day or so early. In a few years he went on a scholarship to the main Indian college in America, Bacone at Muskogee, capital of the Creek Nation, to study art. He was so good, the day after he graduated, he was made head of the art department. Only a short while later he won the right to do the large murals in the new Department of Interior building in Washington, D.C. His accomplishments after that would take a book all its own to list.

Woody was the main buyer for Thomas Gilcrease and his great art museum. He acquired artwork from all the Taos Founders, and of Remington, Russell, and most of the leading Indian artists of the day. More than eighty-five of those in the museum collections were painted by the hand of Woody Crumbo. Gilcrease purchased everything Woody painted including six of his nocturnals in oil.

So it is totally understandable why I instantly agreed to go with him to Tulsa on his long-delayed search for the buried, golden treasure, and it also should be easy to understand why we were slightly taken aback, when we arrived at Tulsa and discovered that this land that held the gold was owned by Mr. Gilcrease himself. This very fact would necessitate that our search would be in the darkness of night.

Woody was sure he had found the gate west of town that led up a wooded draw toward our spot. We drove my station wagon as far as it seemed feasible. With a metal and glass coal oil lantern, a pick and shovel, and nervously growling insides, we made our way back toward Tulsa up the draw.

I whispered to Woody, "Why didn't we come on the full moon?"

"Because gold is not a thinking man's metal," he stated matter-of-factly.

It was at the very least a small miracle that we found the fish hook chipping in less than half an hour. But it was there! Woody stared speechlessly at the revelation mouthed to him so long ago by Ol' George the multiple murderer who was so mean his own son-in-law had killed him out of fear. But one thing for sure, George Island was not a liar. There it was.

Our amazement subsided and we stepped off the fourteen steps and started digging. I with the pick and my artistic/spiritual mentor shoveling by the light of a lantern.

Suddenly a crack of lightning hitting the ground a quarter mile or so away jarred us into reality. We were amazed again as the fiery shafts from the heaven's arc lighted. We expected the woods to be afire. Instead huge drops of rain fell. We had earlier seen, by the lantern light, a shelf of rocks sticking out slightly up the bluff. We clambered up, almost at the top of the rim-rock, and took shelter in the cavelike space beneath the ledge. Woody extinguished the lantern to save fuel. It became as dark as the insides of a vein of coal.

The lightning quit as suddenly as it had fired, and the cloud that created it moved silently on. Our eyes adjusted. We could see the universe of stars out beyond the earth that we were pin-pricking, looking for a few pieces of gold, as humankind, it seems, had always done.

The silence was so profound it became noise. It was impossible— one would think, but we sure as all angels did think—that we heard chains rattling, clanking, and moving up the erratic slope toward us. The noises would go away, making muffled sounds as they left. Then they would come almost to us again, then retreat again. I was truly paralyzed, except for the shaking the cold chills created.

Woody began chanting a Kiowa prayer song. He had been adopted first by the Creek, then the Kiowa, as well as by the Sioux Nations, but it was a Kiowa medicine man, Opetone, who was his spiritual guide in more than one dimension and now he sang from his gift. Opetone (Wooden Lance) had broken out of imprisonment at Ft. Sill and led the

very last Indian raid on Texas. Opetone had given Woody the wherewithal to cause the retreat of the chains of evil. The chains moved on
down and away from us into the great silence.

Woody struck a match, lit the lantern, and said, "Let's get this job
done, Max."

I agreed. My fear had dissipated—just like the strange little storm
and the terrifying sounds on the side of the small mesa. I swung
the pick franticly. Woody shoveled furiously. After a short time, we
stopped to catch a little more air in our overpumped lungs. We sat on
the dirt pile and looked into the hole. It was about two feet deep, three
feet wide, and four feet long, I would have guessed.

We foolishly smoked in those days, so we lit up. Soon it was my
turn to say, "Let's get the gold."

"We should be about there," Woody figured.

"Yeah," I said swinging the pick hard at the earth. It struck far
quicker than I had judged and with a loud clang. My hands, my arms,
my whole body was jarred so hard I dropped the pick. In pain I leaned
over, picked up the lantern and held it directly above our diggings.
Instead of being hollowed out, the hole bulged up in the shape of a
human and a liquid slowly oozed out of it in a slow stream. My first
thought was of blood, but it was darker. I looked up intending to query
my mentor, but the lamp light showed his downward staring eyes of
such intensity that I grabbed the pick with my still slightly numb
hands and scrambled out of the hole without looking down again.

Woody had already begun shoveling the dirt pile back into the
hole without let up. He finished. He walked back and forth on it, then
using the shovel, tamped it down with some ferocity.

He said, "Mother Earth is not ready to give us this gold . . . yet."

There is no use going into detail here. We got out of there. We
almost ran back to the station wagon and rapidly headed it toward
the safety of a highway. We drove until we found a small motel on the
way back to Taos.

All I can remember about the conversation later that night was
when I asked him, "What in hell was that?"

"A person," he answered.

"A rock person? How could that be?" I asked. "My pick hit something as solid as rock."

"I don't know right now."

We had dug where the miracle of the fish hook sign was found
under George Island's instructions from years back. It had been

delivered there on horseback, but our real equine adventures were still ahead of us as we both went on with the various phases of our art careers. We occasionally had a few discussions about the happenings at the wooded bluff west of Tulsa, but we always arrived at the decision Mother Earth had made for us.

We slowly regained confidence and the feeling we were being tested, that night, to see if we deserved the unearthing of the precious metal. We sacrificed some funds and bought a rather expensive metal detector. Testing it around old adobe Spanish ruins, we discovered it found—to perfection—ancient horseshoes, rusted cans, pans, buckets, and nails. This boosted our already high expectations in pursuing our treasure hunting.

Both of us being born optimists, we soon decided the time was nearing when the great Mother Earth would release the booty to us.

Many changes would be made in our plans before the next trip took place.

First, we decided to take the horse trailer and our two horses and ride them to the treasure site. Woody's horse, Felix, was a horse that came to him by an Idaho cowboy who simply pulled up at his place southwest of Taos, unloaded the horse from his trailer, visited awhile about Idaho, then said in terms of absolute certainty, "I'm supposed to go to Arizona. Felix is yours, Woody, no matter what. But . . . I'd like to sell you the horse trailer so I can eat and gas up to be sure I'll make it to where I've got to go."

Woody bought the trailer and inherited a magic horse. He was almost all black except for an odd white streak that wrapped across his face and down part of his left side. He had the glassy, light blue eyes of a full blown pinto. The horse could cut, stop, work cattle, pleasure ride, and I'm sure could add and subtract into the fifth dimension.

I had Powderface, the first combined top roping and riding horse of my life. This roan was later renamed Roanie by my cousin, David Evans. He had been a professional roper until he tore up his knee. Now he only did matched ropings. Much later I gave him the roan and while training him for a big match roping, Powderface—while in a dead run—just fell dead. I think he did it because I gave him away. He got even.

It is no strain to understand why Woody and I actually made plans and were preparing to take the best horses of our lives—or so we felt at the time—to a place where the gold had been delivered on a horse, and the man delivering it, had later been ridden down by men on good horses and shot dead as last-year's-dream. It made sense, both common and spiritual. I was all for our new plan.

We were having after-lunch coffee at Foster's Cafe when Woody's brother-in-law, Tom Tune, walked in and joined us. Of course there was no way we could possibly know this would be a fateful meeting. Tom was a mechanic, a durn good one. He saw the world as held together by tools, tightening nuts and bolts, and the careful adjustment of various timed motors. He had part of it right.

People who are involved in many other dimensions often forget that some other people may not see things the way they do. Tom was one of those people. So, as Woody and I were discussing the elusive gold coins underground near Tulsa, Oklahoma, Tom sat down within hearing distance of us and ignored such talk as fanciful and foolish—anyway, as far as he was concerned. However, when we started discussing the wondrous merits of our new metal detector, his attention span increased immeasurably. If he had been a fox his ears would have been standing above his head like the pointed radar disks of today.

Before the coffee session was ended, Tom agreed to accompany us and handle the metal detector with long-trained precision. It was decided that he would test the metal detector over and over until he felt a part of it—even in darkness.

After another cup of coffee and a piece of pie, the return to Tulsa had been settled—with some changes. We let Tom Tune's ability with machinery influence us into a different vision. A well worn path that didn't fit.

We would take disbelieving Tom with us. We would *not* take our horses. We changed the date for the Oklahoma trip so we would arrive at the Tulsa site on the full moon.

We both watched Tom as he left for work. When he had disappeared from sight, Woody said, "He's going to use that machine to prove us wrong—and stupid."

"He is unable to see past his eyes," I added.

"Maybe this trip will give him a different line of sight. Maybe." Woody was seeing many things as he uttered these words that have remained indelible even amid my complicated memory cells.

He said, in an aside to me, "We will find it this time."

The blue moonlight was electric when we arrived in Tulsa. The wondrously soft breezes were inhaling our growing expectations like the lungs of a mastodon . . . I could feel the earth beneath me pulsating, breathing, waiting with massive ease for our beginning.

We parted a little brush so Tom could see the fish hook indention in the sandstone bluff. He showed no emotion, but whispered to Woody, "Step off the fourteen steps and stand there." It was an order. Tom had mistakenly thought he was in charge of the precious blue night.

Woody obeyed and stepped it off. He stood on the spot, upright as a flagpole, his big chest stuck out like a rooster's and he waited with great patience.

Tom picked up a stick and scraped a big square with Woody in the center. Then with the precision of an army parade sergeant he turned on the metal finder and plugged in the sound phones and mathematically, mechanically walked across the square north to south until he had covered the square. He stopped behind Woody about four feet to south and we could hear the machine buzzing with greatly increased volume. My heart reached the same tempo notifying my entire chest of discovery. Gold fever!

Then to our dismay he did the same calculated parade from east to west finally arriving at the same place with the same shattering sound in the quietness of a night that was beyond painting, photography, or recording in any other way but the part of your soul that savors beauty. Contrasts.

Tom stood up like Charles de Gaulle and scratched an X in the ground, saying as if he had taken a swallow from a bad cup of coffee, "It's probably some old rusty horseshoes or a slop jar."

We ignored him and dug as before, only faster. Hadn't the high-tech world given us a certainty of rare collector's gold coins? Ah, the red brown Oklahoma soil was picked and shoveled by two dumb artists faster than a badger or a backhoe, except of course, when Tom intruded to insert the knowledge of the machine with his own in a superior movement. The deeper we dug the louder the buzz and the faster the needle whammed and held against the peg.

As we reached about three feet and the same test held up, I had a combination of high anticipation and doubt. First because we had the treasured coins almost trickling through our fingers and at the same time I tried not to reason that the bank robber had buried the wealth intending to retrieve it later. So, why go deeper than his trove?

I sat down on the abundant pile of disturbed earth and pulled out a pack of cigarettes and passed them to Woody and Tom. You've heard the old saying "Three on a match" . . . ? Well, I didn't let it happen. I lit Woody's and Tom had to dig out his perfectly performing metal lighter.

As Woody and I deteriorated our lungs and breathed in the pure blue air to counteract it, we were all three looking up at the ledge. The moon had moved over to light part of the cave where the dark entities had come to put us in chains. It all seemed so far away now. So unimportant.

Woody broke our triple reveries with, "The next shovel will get it."

Tom said, in a quiet but superior rebuttal, "Probably a vein of iron."

We were all silent. The only sounds in the night were the low buzz of a few unknown insects and the haunting cry of some night bird in the midst of the woods. The world was big. The sky that held the stars, dimmed by the moonlight, was bigger. The backwards and forward and sideways and up and down movement of time stopped. All motion ceased.

Then it came from the distance above the rim rock. A thunder of four mighty hooves. We all stared into the sound. Invisible sound. It was coming above but straight at us and then it leaped. We all three fell over south off the dirt pile waiting to be smashed by the mighty hooves, but there was only a sound I'd never really heard before. That of a horse displacing air as it hurtled through space, right over us.

The human mind will always offer up many surprises. I wondered if this horse was blue like the great oil painting of the dappled blue spirit horses Woody had invented and so many others emulated later. Or maybe it was his painting of the rainbow horse that delivered souls through the cosmos, avoiding wayward angels, to safely deliver its chosen spirit rider safely to the next dimension. All of this, and more, plunged through me as the horse pierced the sky above us. Then we heard it land in a great clattering of rocks and race on and vanish in silence far, far faster than it had come. Instantly.

We all three sat slowly up staring south now away from the rim rock, but full on our faces and even glinting in our eyes was the light of the blue, blue moon. Oh, what a silence it was. All the more profound when it was replaced by a far distant unmistakable sound of horses coming toward the rim rock at full speed. Close as before, but much louder. We could feel the skin of the earth quivering under the terrible pounding of all the racing hooves. I knew, and I looked at Woody, and knew that he knew as well. The posse of horses pounded to the edge and in ones, twos, and threes, they leapt into space above us.

Tom had jerked his head back to the rim rock, but Woody and I looked on south waiting for the horses to land. To our surprise it was so far away it was only a few soft thuds and a softer sound of exiting into another time—another place. All the horses had evanesced into the place from which they had come.

The silent moon stared down one-eyed at the three of us who were unmoving, and I do believe until now unthinking for a time without calculation.

Tom broke the multi-dimensional spell by standing up abruptly, stiffly bending down to gather up the pick and shovel then walking with his Lincolnesque stride—long and swift—toward our vehicle.

Woody said, picking up the metal detector that Tom had seemed to worship only a while back and had now abandoned, "We better go before he drives off and leaves us."

He might have done it, too, because the motor was just catching the first sparks of fire to gasoline when we arrived. Tom drove all the way home, the entire distance back to Taos, only stopping for gasoline. No talking, no coffee, no good-just-getting-the-heck-out-of-Oklahoma.

Woody and I slept some, but we didn't talk either. What we would have to say could only be to each other. Tom never said a single word ever again about our journey. I often thought that he denied to himself it ever happened—any of it—and it couldn't be fixed with even the finest amalgamated steel wrench ever made.

Late the next day Woody and I met at the Sagebrush Inn and after many beginnings with no ends, decided we had been blessed with the ghost horses of the gold robber and the posse that ran him down. We believed this was true and I added with a laugh that the coins had probably turned to ghosts as well and we would never have been able to feel them or spend them or even have the pleasure of giving them away.

In later years, we grew to accept that a billion dollars in rare coins could never replace the oh so rare golden moments gifted us and shared with human ghosts as well as with the ghost horses of Tulsa.

CHAPTER THIRTEEN

The Horse Who Wrote Stories

YEAH, that is right, it was a horse that started it all—the stories, the books, the movies, the paintings, and he came close to ending it for me, as well.

I was back home at my little ranch in northeastern Union County, New Mexico, after recently spending six and a half months of straight infantry combat from Normandy's Omaha Beach, to the Brest campaign in Brittany, to the Ardennes Forest in Belgium and Germany.

Before leaving for the dogface days of World War II, I'd sold all my horses and cows at auction. Upon returning, I wanted to acquire *one* good horse to start over. Since I was a lousy bronc rider to begin with, I wanted a gentle, well-trained horse.

I had "broken out"—or rather as the PC'ers insist—I had *trained,* a string of rough broncs for Pete and Ben Jones, neighboring ranchers, just before leaving my wife, daughter, and the land I loved more than tequila gold or homemade ice cream to get shot at by SS men. Not much of a swap off when I think about it right now.

I had chosen the village of Des Moines, New Mexico, as my new headquarters. George Larkin had a grocery store in town and a big cow ranch southeast of town. In his store he sold on credit—especially to the small ranchers whose land adjoined his. With the ranchers' unpaid grocery bills, he obtained considerably more land and livestock. So, when I inquired about getting a fine horse, he obliged me.

Mr. Larkin had a foreman I was later to fictionalize as "Les" in *The Hi-Lo Country* novel and film. Les was a fine horse trainer. George took me, and my gear, down to his ranch. He had called Les ahead on the party phone line, and the foreman had a horse waiting in the round corral. I didn't even have to rope him. He walked toward me as I stood in the middle of the corral with the bridle over my shoulders.

Now, in the novel, I made him a sorrel, but in actuality he was as shiny black as newly mined coal. I named him Blackie right there. He took the bit like it was a handful of sugar. I hand brushed him down and saddled him up. I led him up three steps, gathered the reins in his mane with one hand and the saddle horn with the other and mounted.

Les had put a fine rein on him. All I had to do was touch his neck with one rein and push my leg a little against the shoulder on the same side, and he turned like a cutting horse. I spurred him slightly and he took off in a run, and I set back on him before we hit the corral. Talk about a stop! He slid those hind legs underneath him with his front legs forward, and it was all I could do to stay on him. Three years away and a rider can lose his seat; of course, it usually comes back in a little while. I rode him out in the horse pasture and tried everything I would need him to do for starters. He was a hell of a good horse, coming five-years-old, and just right.

Now my wife and I had quite a bit of personal business to attend to—furniture to acquire, repairs on the house, and corrals for the home place, before I even thought about going in debt again for some cattle. So I paid Larkin the seventy-five dollars he asked, and it was agreed I'd get the horse in a month. I was thrilled. So was George Larkin.

Even though my small ranch was about fourteen miles south of his, it was spring-fed and Larkin knew he could trade it to anybody—if I defaulted on any bills, because he also knew that by the time I got the place in shape and went in debt to stock it, I'd probably be buying groceries on credit. That was slick planning, except I traded with the only other grocer in town, Toby Smith.

There was a car dealer in Morton, Texas, who owed my dad some favors, and he sold me the very first new Dodge pickup delivered to his postwar dealership. I had the only new pickup in Union County. It was black and shiny, like my horse. When my wife drove me down in our new Dodge pickup to claim my horse, I was feeling pretty damn sassy.

I decided instead of loading him in the pickup, I would ride Blackie home. I was hand brushing him before saddling, when I felt some new scars on his neck that had mostly healed over. Might as well get to it. Les really liked this horse and didn't want to give him up, so, he had spurred scars in his shoulder to spoil him. I knew how he felt about giving up an animal. When I was younger, working for Ed Young on Glorieta Mesa, I'd been certain I'd owned a horse named Flax—but I didn't. Flax was Ed Young's horse by title, and now, this horse was mine by bill-of-sale.

Despite my fears of what had taken place, I proudly rode him to my ranch. His smooth running walk kept the tender skin on my tail and inner legs from peeling. I was sore, but pleased with Blackie even though I'd already figured that Les had done his best to spoil him for me without letting his boss Larkin know. Oh, what suckers we *trusters* can turn out to be.

I was enjoying the moment—thankful to just be alive—as I rode over my *malpais*-mesa-surrounded outfit checking fences, watching for coyote and bobcat tracks, trying to figure how many blue quail there were to draw from for part of our sustenance. I'd forgotten all about the new scars in Blackie's neck, even though, when I had saddled him, he humped up enough to make the back skirts of the saddle stand up a couple of inches, but not enough to figure he'd buck. Anyway, he had such a smooth gait, I was lured into a little laxness.

I rode up to the big spring half a mile downhill from the main house. Blackie walked out into the mud to water. I just reared back in the saddle enjoying the plentiful water and the gramma and buffalo grass growing across my pastures as lush as a Bel Air carpet. Blackie pulled his muzzle up from the cool water and turned to move on. When he raised the first hind foot out of the muck, the suction caused it to make a popping noise. That was the excuse he'd been waiting for. I'm still here to tell you that horse could buck. I lost one stirrup, then two, and all I could see was his black mane flying. He'd sure swallowed his head.

Blackie was hitting the ground hard and kicking backwards before he turned in midair. It felt like my spine had been replaced by peanut butter. I tried to fall off but he bucked right under me for about three more jumps—each one felt like he'd ripped me in half, right up between my legs and out the top of my head, which was the appurtenance I failed to drive into the ground when I finally bucked off. At last the world slowed its spinning and I was able to sit up and look for my hat. It took awhile, but I finally discovered it was mashed flat on top of my numb scalp.

I spotted Blackie who was already up the hill past the house and heading for a barbed wire gate—a *shut* gate. The stirrups were flopping up above the level of the saddle seat when he slammed on the brakes. He turned and just stood there looking back down the hill for Ol' Max.

I cursed him with all the epithets I could get breath enough to yell. Then I decided to check out how many of my bones had been broken. I did that by standing up. To my amazement, I could move every one of my limbs. So the next chore was pulling my smashed hat from my head, putting it back on, and walking uphill over a half-mile past the house to congratulate my noble steed.

As I went past the house, my wife yelled from the porch, "What happened?"

I didn't even look her way, but I said, "Walking and falling zig-zag across France and half of Belgium/Germany just wasn't enough exercise for me." And I'm sure, neither one of us knew what I meant.

Blackie was not smiling over his triumph. Nor was I. One rein was broken in half where he had somehow stepped on it in his one-horse race up the hill. I took out my pocketknife and cut the bridle off the bit. Then I took the end of the other leather rein and tied it in its place, and pulled it over his head and neck. It was too short, but it was all I had.

I was ready for him this time. I mounted, squeezing the saddle horn till it yelled "ouch," and rode to the gate of the round corral. I managed to open it without dismounting. Then I rode him around and around inside those poles spurring him faster and faster. Hell, he seemed to enjoy it, so I gave up, fed him some hay and oats and stumbled for the house.

The next time he got me was when I dismounted to open a gate into one of the big east pastures of the adjoining A. D. Weatherly outfit. I was cutting across to the Jones' boys place to help them build some fence, when I saw where a really big old coyote had gone right through the wires of the gate without leaving a particle of fur. I was amazed almost every day of my cowboying and ranching life enjoying and observing the multiple, often magical, talents of these creatures. That's where my mind was as I led Blackie through the gate at the

Joneses. I shut it, mounted, and tapped him lightly with my spurs as he headed downhill to a long draw, headed north.

I think I must explain that Blackie could read minds, and when a simple mind like mine went blank or wandered into some foreign subject, such as the brilliance of coyotes, he knew it.

The next thing I became aware of was the fact that he had jumped up into the realm of eagles and when he came jarringly down, I myself learned to fly. My new skill was short-lived. I hit the ground so hard I saw heavenly bodies sparkling all around my prone one. This time, however, I stayed with my Glorieta Mesa training and held the reins. Ol' Blackie was bending down and his dark, soft muzzle touched me in false sympathy. When I finally retrieved my breath well enough to mount him again, I decided to contest him all the way, so I would know if it was ever going to be possible for me to ride this wonderfully gaited, reined animal that so resented my presence on his back.

In spite of what Les had done to him, I pulled my hat way down, took as deep a seat as the saddle and Blackie's backbone would allow, choked the moisture out of the saddle horn and spurred him right in the healed over scars ol' Les had given him. He answered by turning twice to the left and whipping back to the right as he left the ground. I somehow stayed with him until he came down trying to tear holes, big holes, in the skin of Mother Earth. Then I departed again, trying to hold on to at least one rein. However, after doing the impossible, by staying up in the fresh mountain air for a magic spell, gravity finally moved the entire world up to wham me in the butt and the back side of my body with such force that my fingers flew apart and the reins went downhill with the runaway horse.

It took me longer than I wanted to discover my breath this time. I was also very slow getting up, as I was busy praying my bones were still in my body and connected. I was also pleading to the Great Mystery in the Sky to arrange for Blackie to dive off a bluff into oblivion when he got to the bottom of the slope where there was a little rock-strewn creek and some steep sandstone bluffs.

I had been thrown without mercy at the earth's gravitational center, and then left to die, and the powers I so beseeched for favors had either ignored me or were busy with more important things.

Blackie raised his head from the creek water as it dripped from the bits. The reins were intact, and I'll be a one-eyed goat if he didn't snicker a welcome at me.

Now there is not a lot of benefit that I can see in revealing how Blackie was smarter and meaner than I was. The outwitting and unloading continued at times of his choosing. He had dislocated a knee, an elbow, and a shoulder twice—mine. Several times I thought my neck was broken and my head caved in as well. I was wrong about the last, I think, but he had forever reshaped my hat. There were uncountable minor things such as bruising, torn tendons, pulled muscles, and other extreme inconveniences; but flip the pancake over, and that sucker could work the outside circle from sun to sun on a roundup, and take me to cattle like a professional roping horse when I had to educate a bunch-quitter or doctor a bovine critter for fixable ailments. Above all he was a hellacious heeling horse at a branding. He seemed to enjoy dragging calves to the fire, and it was a pure pleasure for the both of us because that had been all that got me by in those kid days on and around Glorieta Mesa.

I did put a ride on him one time. Once. I was taking my two best wolfhounds over to loan to my hunting partner, Uncle Tom Creswell. I rode along scanning for coyotes. Each of the hounds wore a ring on its collar, which I ran a rope through. I held both loose ends in my free hand. All I had to do was drop one end of the rope and it would slide slickly through the rings as the dogs took off after a coyote. Today, I didn't spot one and got to Tom's without a problem from Blackie. Tom knew I had some day labor coming up on neighboring ranches and wanted to get in some fun hunting with our hounds before I went back to slaving for a living.

When I got there, Tom and his wife had gone to town or were visiting somewhere. Since our dogs were well acquainted from previous hunts, I put my hounds in the pen with his, tied the gate shut, and started the eight-mile ride back home.

I could tell by Blackie's ears trying to see me backward—yeah, ask any working cowboy—most good horses have eyes in their ears. He was waiting for me to doze off or let my mind wander before he fired. And sure enough, he caught me off-guard an inch or two when a covey of blue quail ran across the road ahead, but it wasn't a total disaster this time. Right there the barbed wire lane narrowed for about a half a mile. He went up and out and the third jump came mighty close to the flesh-ripping fence. However, he was like a mule about barbed wire—he understood its danger and avoided it even when his mind was set on driving me into the ground like a five-foot eleven-inch nail.

The fourth or fifth jump, my head was snapping back hard and I'd lost a stirrup. Miraculously I got it back and this gave me a spurt of confidence. If I could head him west with the lane and keep from pulling the saddle horn loose, I had a chance.

That's when I learned something new. It was easier to whop the ground *once* with my body than to have him jar me in the saddle a *dozen* times or more. Just as I was straining to straighten up and pull myself back into the saddle at every jump, and my entire body had been turned into a well-shaken martini, the black sucker just quit and took up his running walk as if nothing had happened. It had, though. Blackie's sides were heaving and there was heavy sweat on his flanks and shoulders. I was so weak I nearly fell off. But my ego would not allow that. It was my one great victory, and I looked all around hoping somebody had seen this mighty deed. There wasn't a pair of human eyes to be found. I might as well have made the ride on top of Mount Everest or in the middle of the Sahara.

If I'd had a gun, a coin would have been flipped to see which one I shot—him or me. I understood at last that I couldn't handle this horse. He knew I had lucked out on this single ride and I knew it even better.

No matter how things are planned, they are destined to change.

It was shipping time. Farrel Smith, whose big ranch headquarters were only five or so miles northeast of me, had gotten rich during the rainy war years running Corriente steers imported from Mexico. This year he was experimenting with fifteen hundred head of Black Angus steers. He sent a hand over to get me to help them with the roundup and the fourteen-mile trail drive into Grenville to the shipping pens there. I wasn't feeling too well from an inner ear problem and I said "no" with regrets.

Well now, Ol' Farrel hadn't gotten rich because of the inability to think, so he sent Bill Caperton, an old-time cowboy—who I really liked—over to ask me again. I thought Bill was still foreman as he had been when I left for the war. Naturally, this time I said yes.

At this time, there was a shortage of any regular crews in that part of the country, so, a bunch of old *worn-outs* and *reluctants* like me spent three days on the roundup. I used Farrel's horses on the roundup and saved Blackie for the drive to Grenville.

Fortunately, I'd never met the big old overbearing foreman now in charge. He knew horses and cattle pretty well, but a sparrow splatter would have smothered his knowledge of human beings. I resented his taking old Bill's well-earned place, I suppose.

We started on the big drive so early in the morning that we left by the light of the moon. For about seven or eight miles we had barbed wire fence lanes. We could use a pickup's headlight beams rolling past the point rider. Blackie and I along with Bill and another hand named Max something-or-other were put on the drag. It didn't matter. I'd used up my dizzy medicine the day before and wondered if I'd make it anyway.

We were halfway there before noon and nobody I knew ever served a noonday meal while working cattle in those days except at a neighborhood branding where all the women brought food and a visiting picnic was made out of the work.

Farrel had prepared ahead as usual and several old semi-retired, broken-up hands that lived in Grenville were waiting down at the shipping pens to help us. We were slowed awhile because for three or four miles there was a stretch of open country and the herd was harder to keep gathered and moving. Soon, though we got another lane and shoved the last steer into the pens at around midafternoon. The bawling, the dust, the yelling, the cattle prods, and all, made a hell of a mess as cattle car after cattle car was loaded to transport the stock to buyers in Kansas for feeding, fattening, and then steak dinners around the world.

Suddenly that cockeyed inner ear problem hit me and I snuck off hoping nobody would see me heaving up an unfed stomach. Then I sat down on some boards along an already emptied pen trying to ride the whirling world. I must have dozed off as my battered brain went back momentarily to the irony that a five-hundred-pound railroad shell had created this problem a short while back at St. Vire, France. Here I was trying to work cattle at another railroad thousands of miles from the site of the exploding shell.

I heard words. I don't remember them exactly, but they were harsh. As I fully awakened I saw the big foreman looming above me like a movie monster. I instantly felt the board I sat on and it had been split. So I stood up probably trembling and lifted the smallest part of the board at the same time. It was far too long, but I examined it like I was going to use it to strike a baseball. To my relief the monster stomped away, still cursing with words I do not care to remember.

I felt cold. It was. An early north wind was gathering force and seemed to me as if it was straight out of the arctic. I ambled over and saw that all the cattle were loaded. A couple of pickups and a car were pulling out and a bobtail truck followed carrying all the horses but one—Blackie. The foreman had ordered that I be left behind to ride the eleven miles north from the Grenville shipping pens to my front gate.

I had somehow forgotten that every few years an October storm whams the Hi-Lo country. If I'd had any sense at all I would have stayed in Grenville. Anyway, a determined storm was gathering in me to make the ride home.

About three or four miles out of Grenville, the wind picked up in velocity. I could see a huge bank of clouds coming our way blanking the setting sun. There was a little hotel and restaurant still open in Grenville during those days, but I can't recall having the slightest sensible thought of turning back. I had foolishly made the drive without a bandana. I took out a handkerchief and tied it around my face.

Blackie's tail and mane were whipping around like they might be blown out by the roots. He had his neck and head down as low as he could and still walk straight into the growing wind. First it started to sleet. Then the small snowflakes came and before you could say "stop" the flakes became huge and ground covering even in the breath stealing wind.

I kept looking for the graded road, but soon it was night and I couldn't see it at all. It wouldn't have made any difference if it had been straight up noon, the clouds were down on the ground, it seemed, and made up of one great solid snowflake. We were blind and I was helpless. I'm sure I must have prayed out loud, but I doubted any higher powers could see or hear in the weird moaning of the storm that had swallowed Blackie and me like a burial shroud.

The only way one can understand the lost blindness, the nonbeing where there are no compass points—not even up or down—is being there. I do not recommend the experience of suddenly being nowhere at all in a pulsating, white darkness.

I held onto the saddle horn as a newborn does its mother's breast. That was all that kept me anchored, as long as my hands didn't get so numb I couldn't feel it. Luckily, I had brought a pair of cloth lined leather gloves in my chaps pocket. These kept my hands from getting so numb I'd lose the reins or the saddle horn. There was nothing left but to try to stay atop Blackie.

I know it seems extreme to say that, eternities later; I sort of gathered my senses and realized we weren't moving. Nevertheless when time ceases to exist for you, what else is there to feel?

Gradually I realized that we weren't moving. I reached down and touched Blackie's neck. He was holding his head up not far from the ground. Sure enough, we were in front of my home gate. I was so stiff that I just sort of fell off him, and did in fact, fall down in about a three-foot drift, but the elation of the possible continuation of life gave me a charge of energy. It was a mile uphill from the gate to the ranch house where my wife and four-year-old daughter must be envisioning me well fed, warm, and content in the Grenville Hotel.

If Blackie had brought me this far in total blindness, one more mile in a suddenly softening wind should be a cinch. It was.

Now, before we reached the house, the adrenaline had not only caused me to move, but also to think for a change. I've heard many different stories about this mythical ability of horses that I don't think we humans are meant to know. I believe we lost the ability to understand this seeming phenomenon eons ago. This was the second time already in my young life that a horse had unbelievably delivered me home in a blind blizzard: Ol' Snip, up on Glorieta Mesa, and now Blackie in the Hi-Lo country.

Even though the storm had been vicious, and in places created drifts several feet deep, it soon dissolved or melted away before real winter came. I don't remember hearing about any livestock losses.

I have to give Farrel Smith credit; when he found out about the monster foreman leaving me behind to face the threatening storm, he instantly fired him, and the critter quit the country. I had not told anyone, but I was sincerely relieved since I dreaded the chore of eventually being forced to use him for batting practice.

I'd forgotten that I'd put the word out that I wanted to sell Blackie. Then one day I was having a cup of coffee at the kitchen table when I heard a yell outside. I got up to check it out. There were two horseback riders dismounting as they saw me coming toward them.

It was Wiley "Big Boy" Hittson and his younger brother Tiny. I later called Tiny "Little Boy" in the *Hi-Lo Country* novel and movie. We shook hands, had a few "how you doin's" and Big Boy got to it. He looked out in the corral at Blackie and said, "I hear you want to sell that ol' pony."

A lot of surprising emotions shot through me, as if I'd been plugged into a high-voltage light plug. The horse had saved my life. He had also entertained me quite often by bucking me off in cactus beds, rock piles, plain old hard ground, and twice in clumps of spear like yucca bunches. Being a fallible human being with faster-than-light-itself thinking ability, I reasoned that Blackie had saved me so he could enjoy finishing me off at a time of his own choice.

"Yeah," I said.

"How much you want?"

"Just what I gave for him. Seventy-five bucks."

"Tiny, take your catch rope and go get him."

He wrote me a check. It was good.

Tiny led Blackie up. Big Boy unsaddled his sorrel and threw his rig on Blackie and rode off leading his horse with Tiny riding even with him. It may sound strange, but unexpected tears welled up in my eyes as I just stood there and watched the three horses and two men become smaller and smaller on their nine-mile ride back to the Hittson place.

I sensed something for sure. Buying the horse from George Larkin, and his foreman getting jealous and spoiling him for me, got the beginning going. Many unusual events were launched at the moment I said "Yeah" to the horse sale. It would all grow and grow. First: into a killing, then a great doomed romance, then a novel, and new acquaintances with some of the world's wildest and most noted people, a motion picture actually shot in the country where the horse deal started. The movie would include Woody Harrelson, Patricia Arquette, Billy Crudup, Sam Elliott, James Gammon, and Penelope Cruz's American debut and thirty million dollars brought into the poor state of New Mexico that didn't somehow come from even poorer taxpayers' pockets. But those stories have been told in hundreds of other places over the long, long years and are still going on. This is Blackie's story.

From what I gathered, Blackie only tried unloading Big Boy twice, and then with no choice given he settled down and made Wiley an outstanding cow horse. Blackie was quartered up and fast enough that Big Boy could easily have made a calf roping horse out of him, sold him, and even way back in the late forties tripled his money. Big Boy was a good amateur bareback bronc, bull rider, and "dogger," steer wrestler, but the nearest he ever moved ol' Blackie to a rodeo arena was once when he decided to get all duded up in old-timers' real garb and ride him in the Des Moines (Hi-Lo) rodeo parade (See photo on page 226).

Whenever Big Boy was working for Hoover, or Farrel Smith, or The T.O. or other big outfits, I'd sometimes help with roundups and branding. He generously let me use Blackie to heel and drag calves to the branding fire. It was a great pleasure just to sit on him as he moved with a fluidity only the best athletes have. Besides, I knew he wouldn't dare toss me over a low-flying bird in front of Big Boy. Despite all of our early misadventures, I still felt a kinship to him and of course I always will.

I sold my ranch, my family left for Texas, and I went to Taos to become an artist. Big Boy helped move my belongings and me in his old Chevy pickup. The Larkins' cowboy—the one who had deliberately spoiled Blackie—had a lovely wife, but she was leaving him. So it only seemed right that Big Boy give her his respect and his companionship. When he left me there in Taos to head back to the heart of the Hi-Lo country, I said, "Tell Mona (fictional name) and ol' Blackie hello and give them my love."

His face showed one of his rare grins, and he said, "You betcha."

Later Wiley was at the home place. His mother, Tiny, and two even-younger brothers were branding. Big Boy and Tiny got in an argument over the way the home place was being kept up. Tiny knew he didn't have a chance fist fighting Big Boy, so he shot my best friend to death.

Pat and I drove over the Rocky Mountain range from Taos to Des Moines. We were late because we had been informed late. The doors to the church were opened for the pallbearers to carry him out. The Marine Hymn floated out across the little town and the vast lands around it, which he had represented and become part of and would now be covered by.

We drove up to the graveyard on the hill behind Hi-Lo. Folks broke off in small groups. Strange. I only heard the droning of the preacher, not his words. My mind was on the good times we'd shared and one of those was a horse named Blackie.

Afterward, only a few of us were invited out to Mrs. Hittson's. It was hard for me to be nice to Tiny, but I think I was. I owed it to the family and Mrs. Hittson had enough to face holding the place together without any added trouble.

We got ready to go back to Taos and continue in our world of art, horses, and a million other things that wouldn't have existed except for the cowboy ex-Marine just placed six-feet-under the top of the first hill north of the little town . . . and . . . the black horse in a corral behind the Hittson place.

Mrs. Hittson wanted me to have Big Boy's .30–30 rifle. I took it. She handed me the big hat he'd been wearing when he was killed. I was honored to have it. Then she offered me Blackie.

BIG BOY MATTSON (Wiley Hittson) lead character of the book and movie *The Hi-Lo Country*, mounted on Blackie, the horse who wrote the stories. Author's collection.

I said, "No, thank you, ma'am. He belongs here in the country where he and Big Boy worked. Besides, a smart horse like Blackie will still remember that I'm not much of a bronc rider."

Decades later, the fine actor, James Gammon, who played Hoover— the old-time rancher that Big Boy respected so much—wore Big Boy's hat in *The Hi-Lo Country* film.

He said, sincerely, "I'm much honored."

I know I was, as well, and wherever the spirit of ol' Blackie was, I feel sure he bucked about ten feet straight up in full agreement. He could buck all over horse heaven if he wished. He had sure earned the right. After all, Blackie was the horse who wrote all those stories.

The End.